The Poetry of Shell Shock

This book is for my dear friend Barry Price
To complement his library and the search he has undertaken
for understanding and the recognition of truth.

John Maton
2009

The Poetry of Shell Shock

*Wartime Trauma and Healing
in Wilfred Owen, Ivor Gurney
and Siegfried Sassoon*

by DANIEL HIPP

McFarland & Company, Inc., Publishers
Jefferson, North Carolina, and London

LIBRARY OF CONGRESS CATALOGUING-IN-PUBLICATION DATA

Hipp, Daniel W.
   The poetry of shell shock : wartime trauma and healing
in Wilfred Owen, Ivor Gurney and Siegfried Sassoon / by
Daniel Hipp.
       p.   cm.
   Includes bibliographical references and index.

   ISBN 0-7864-2174-6 (softcover : 50# alkaline paper)

   1. English poetry — 20th century — History and criticism.
   2. World War, 1914–1918 — Great Britain — Literature and the war.
   3. Owen, Wilfred, 1893–1918 — Criticism and interpretation.
   4. Gurney, Ivor, 1890–1937 — Criticism and interpretation.
   5. Sassoon, Siegfried, 1886–1967 — Criticism and interpretation.
   6. War neuroses — Great Britain — History — 20th century.
   7. Soldiers' writings, English — History and criticism.
   8. War poetry, English — History and criticism.
   9. Psychic trauma in literature.
   I. Title.
   PR605.W65H57 2005
   821'.91209358 — dc22   2005012773

British Library cataloguing data are available

On the cover: *top* ©2005 Brand X Pictures; *bottom* ©2005 Clipart.com

Manufactured in the United States of America

McFarland & Company, Inc., Publishers
   Box 611, Jefferson, North Carolina 28640
   www.mcfarlandpub.com

Contents

To Henry

Preface

This study of British poetry of World War I, seen in the context of shell shock and the psychiatric approaches to treating this condition, originated in 1992, when I began my graduate studies at Villanova University and took a course from Dr. Vincent Sherry, a scholar of Joyce, Pound, and other modernists, titled "The Art, Literature, and History of World War I." Coming into this course, more or less directly from my undergraduate studies, I had absorbed the understanding of the Great War in the simplified sense common to undergraduate literary survey courses. In courses with titles such as "British Literature II: Milton to the Present" or some other such ambitious and unrealistic descriptor, the most a student can hope to take in about the relationship between World War I and the modernist period is that both occurred early in the twentieth century and that the war, like one of the dominant tonal strains in the literature, was a bleak, self-destructive, hopeless affair.

Studying the period with greater depth, however, led to my discovery of poets writing concurrently with the pillars of British and American modernism, men and women who wrote directly about the war as they experienced it in the trenches or from the home front. And while a specific focus upon the artists of war enabled me to see the extent to which its horrors could be represented directly, it also raised the question of how preexisting traditions of art and poetry could be relied upon or needed to be modified to find a form fitting for the trench experience. And when I saw war poetry in the larger context of early twentieth century modernism, a central question began to formulate itself: Should literary historians regard the Great

War as a symptom of the modern condition — the explosive end of Victorian optimism and industrialism, the tangible proof that doubt and skepticism in both the goodness of humankind and something higher than us was a philosophically legitimate position? Or should those seeking to place the war in this intellectual context regard the war as more of a cause of the modernist frame of mind? That is, since the war introduced levels of destruction and horror hitherto unimagined, art created in its aftermath that chose to confront and represent it, even obliquely, needed the new modernist vocabulary that we see arise in the mature works of Joyce, Eliot, or even Wilfred Owen.

Including Owen in the previous sentence introduces an additional question that this study hopes to address: How does a reader describe the relationship between the soldiers in the war, who wrote about their experience, and the civilian artists, who experienced the war as a part of the European consciousness but remained on its sidelines? All criticism of First World War literature is in some way indebted to Paul Fussell's *The Great War and Modern Memory*, and this study is no exception. Fussell explores in depth the notion of the "two fronts" of the war: the Western Front in Europe and the seemingly oblivious and ignorant civilian "front" confronted at home by the soldier, who — no doubt like the survivors of all wars — struggled to find an understanding audience, who thought of the war in decidedly different terms. This division between those who were there and those who were not contributes to many of the different approaches of the war poets in addressing their audiences — to protest, to educate, to elicit sympathy, and certainly at moments to horrify in ways that war poetry had never attempted previously.

I seek in this study to investigate a further purpose that such art served these soldier-poets: namely, to speak to themselves. World War I introduced the medical and psychological phenomenon of shell shock (which was given several names before this collective descriptor was decided upon), a response to trauma that manifested itself upon the soldier's body and psyche in various ways. One frequent symptom of the condition was mutism, an inability to speak. Poetry of war becomes the means by which the war experience can be confronted and spoken of; poetry of war, I argue, becomes an avenue for healing to occur.

Interestingly, of the three poets discussed in depth, Wilfred Owen is the only one who was unambiguously shell-shocked. Ivor Gurney's diagnosis of "deferred shell shock" seems, with the benefit of hindsight, to be a misunderstanding of his psychological state — an uncertainty that has persisted to this day in the continued debate over just how to diagnose his mental illness, to which this study hopes to contribute. The shell shock of Siegfried

Sassoon likewise has been the subject of dispute and protest; scholars and biographers dispute the diagnosis. By grouping together these cases of two officers and an enlisted man, I seek to provide a broad understanding of the role that shell shock played at this historical moment — artistically, in providing the impetus for the poetry; politically, in making manifest the suffering and trauma of soldiers fighting a war of attrition; medically, as the psychiatric community struggled to understand and to treat it.

I owe a great deal of thanks to the advisor of my doctoral dissertation out of which this work has emerged, Professor Vereen Bell of Vanderbilt University. His graduate course in modern British and American poets (Yeats, Eliot, Frost, and Stevens) provided me with one of the more useful shorthand definitions of modernist poetry among the many circulated in scholarship of the period, i.e., that the modernist sensibility is characterized by the ability to believe in two contrary ideas at the same time. Confronted with the evidence and knowledge that the modern world is chaotic, disordered, fragmentary, the human mind (and particularly that of the artist) creates form, structures, and wholes in response — "momentary stays against confusion," as Robert Frost puts it. This study argues that that idea of the poetic mind as the organizer of an irrational and confused reality forges the link between the poets of the Great War and those more conventionally understood to be the modernists writing before, during, after, but not within it.

Finally, I would like to thank several individuals for contributions that assisted the development of this study. Thanks to the other members of my dissertation committee, Professors Mark Jarman, John Halperin, Paul Elledge, and Michael Rose. Thanks as well to Vanderbilt colleagues Roger Moore, Craig Watson, David Macey, Kurt Koenigsberger, Eliza McGraw, and Gary Richards. I'd also like to thank several Aurora University colleagues, Richard Westphal, Hanni Taylor, Kathleen Carroll, Sara Elliott, Jay Thomas, Lora de Lacey, and Andrew Manion, for the institutional and intellectual support that assisted the publication of this work. Thanks also go to my wife, Julie, for the encouragement she provided in both the completion of my doctoral dissertation and the subsequent revisions to it. I am grateful to the estates of Wilfred Owen, Ivor Gurney, and Siegfried Sassoon for permission to quote from the poems and letters. And a very special thanks to Pamela Blevins, whose work on Ivor Gurney allowed me to expand and improve my initial thoughts about his life and poetry.

Daniel Hipp
Aurora, Illinois

Introduction

The years following the Armistice in November 1918 began Britain's period of reckoning over what had been gained and lost through the four years of fighting. The year 1922 marked the appearance of two vastly different approaches to assessing the state of the Western world as it attempted to recover from the devastation of the war. One was T. S. Eliot's *The Waste Land*; the other was British Army's *Report of the War Office Committee Enquiry into "Shell-Shock,"* commissioned by His Royal Highness King George V and presented to Parliament. These texts seem to make an odd pairing — an official government document alongside an epic and experimental work of creative genius. And one need not see *The Waste Land* as a poem confined to the postwar context out of which it emerged; Eliot crafts the entire work into an allusive web that suggests a timelessness and universality of its message. Eliot, however, injects a contemporary quality into the poem which situates it in 1922, in the aftermath of the World War the world still struggled to comprehend. And apart from being a vortex into which rush many of the canonical and non-canonical texts of Western and non–Western literature, the poem and its composition suggest that *The Waste Land* served a personal function for the poet, a function which offers a point of connection between the poem and the War Office report.

Eliot had been brought to the edge of nervous collapse by 1921 because of strains in his marriage and stresses from his work, and his biographer Peter Ackroyd attributes the breakdown as well to his inability to provide a structure by which to organize the disparate elements of a long poem conceived in fits and starts for the better part of 1921.[1] He revised the manuscripts and created the poem's final section, "What the Thunder Said," while hospitalized in a sanitarium in Switzerland when the combination of stresses upon his life became too great to endure. The poem's interest in recording the fragmented nature of postwar European life would seem to speak to the poet's sense of his own fragmented consciousness. The chaos that is the poem emerged from Eliot's perceptions of disorder in the world around him, perceptions which were brought on at least in part by the unrest within his own mind.

Ackroyd discusses Eliot's description of his emotional anguish: "he was not afflicted by 'nerves,' as his original doctor had thought, but rather from '*aboulie*,' ... a withdrawal into negative coldness, with an attendant loss of mental vigour and physical energy.... He was the passive sufferer, the Tiresias who could not act."[2] His psychological torment had reduced the normally active, industrious, and controlled poet to a state of emotional paralysis, where his voice as an artist had been effectively rendered mute. At the hospital in Laussane, Eliot was undergoing experimental methods of psychotherapy administered by Dr. Roger Vittoz. According to Ackroyd:

> His method of treatment was an unusual one in which the emphasis was on (in lay speech) taking the patient "out of himself." His patients were required to perform simple tasks over and over again, and were asked to solve puzzles. Vittoz also believed in a contemporary version of the "laying on of hands" in which he would by physical contact and suggestion draw off the weight of nervousness of self-absorption which incapacitated or paralysed those like Eliot who came to see him.[3]

Though his methods were unorthodox, Vittoz' therapy seems to have operated upon a sound premise — that the key to the patient's healing would come through a shifting of his mental energy from an incapacitating perspective that could look only inward to a stance that brought the patient into contact once again with the world by means of active endeavors. Acquiring the confidence at succeeding at certain tasks and observing that one's mental acumen might be used to yield practical results reminded Eliot of the benefit of creation and production. Vittoz' therapy turned the victim of paralyzing emotional torment once again into an active creative agent whose creations contributed to his emotional stability.

One might say that Eliot, in fact, wrote his stability back into existence. What emerged from this psychological reconditioning were the final lines of *The Waste Land* where the poet puts forth a formula for the spiritual rebirth and redemption of the world, a formula which shared certain qualities with the process he had recently undergone. This prescription of sorts would restore order and wholeness out of the chaos and destruction that modern life has become, of which the war and Eliot's own life have been symptomatic. *The Waste Land* concludes in the voice of one of the poem's many changing speakers:

> I sat upon the shore
> Fishing, with the arid plain behind me
> Shall I at least set my lands in order?
> London Bridge is falling down falling down falling down
> *Poi s'ascose nel foco che gli affina*[4]
> *Quando fiam uti chelidon*[5] — O swallow swallow
> *Le Prince d'Aquitaine a la tour abolie*[6]
> These fragments I have shored against my ruins
> Why then Ile fit you. Hieronymo's mad againe[7]
> Datta. Dayadhvam. Damyata.[8]
> Shantih shantih shantih[9]

Within these closing lines, Eliot offers clues to what he believes are the means by which the world, and perhaps the poet, can heal themselves; the ruined tower, "*la tour abolie,*" of the Prince of Aquitaine seems to speak to Eliot's own "*aboulie.*" In his allusion to Dante's *Purgatorio*, Eliot suggests that "hiding himself in the fire" is the means of "refining." That is, to immerse oneself in the flames of purgatory and to suffer leads to salvation. This suffering, like Hieronymo's, is of a psychological kind. When the speaker claims, "These fragments I have shored against my ruins," Eliot is suggesting that human consciousness possesses the capacity to erect structures of stability out of the destroyed landscape, to forge meaning out of disorder through imaginative processes. The value that emerges out of such redemptive action is solidified through connections established between individuals by means of the *Upanishads'* edict of "Give. Sympathize. Control." Eliot argues that the solidification of selfhood, found through the control of the self, has the potential of leading humanity to a utopic state of harmony and sympathy for one another, to the "Peace which passeth understanding."

But fragments do not necessarily make for the sturdiest of emotional structures, and the flames of Purgatory suggest there is much psychological and spiritual suffering to endure before that peace is reached. This suffering and search for peace is chronicled by the *Army Report of the War Office Enquiry into "Shell Shock"* which discussed the 28,533 official cases, occurring within the British Armed Forces from 1914 until the close of 1917, of an ailment that had become one of the most visible signs that though the Armistice had been reached, the war was far from over for many of its participants.[10] Babington believes the War Office's figure is far too low and estimates the number of shell shock victims at eighty thousand.[11] Despite the essential distance between Eliot's perspective upon the war and the experi-

ence of these participants, his recipe for human salvation offered at the end
of *The Waste Land* has much in common with the methods enacted by cer-
tain soldiers of the Great War to reconstitute a sense of coherence or whole-
ness out of the ruin the war left in its wake. The fact that Eliot completed
the poem while recovering from his own psychological breakdown offers a
connection in terms of psychological suffering between his means of per-
sonal healing and that experienced by soldiers in the war grappling to make
sense out of their own experience.

But how does the perspective of one of the founders of High mod-
ernism, one of the literary elite, relate to the experience of those who actu-
ally participated in the war? Paul Fussell in *The Great War and Modern
Memory* evokes the unbridgeable distance between those who fought in the
war and those who could glean only a fraction of its horrors from their sit-
uation of safety in England. The ignorance of the civilian populace, not
altogether unlike the perspective of man like Eliot who studied Philosophy
at Oxford while the war raged across the channel, became an enemy more
loathed than the Germans to many soldiers in the trenches.[12] Maurice Bowra,
a survivor of the war, states in its aftermath, "Whatever you hear about the
war, remember it was far, far worse: ... Nobody who wasn't there can ever
say what it was like."[13] Eliot's approach, taught through his therapist, is to
move "out of himself," a desire which perhaps leads to the multiple narra-
tors of *The Waste Land* and the structure of myth and of the epic that is the
scaffolding upon which the narrative of rebirth is affixed. The result is a
poem that appears to stress Eliot's personal detachment and objectivity
despite the personal experience that has gone into its composition. But the
effect of the therapy, reflected in the message of the poem, is to lead the
sufferer from a state of passivity, metaphorically blind like Tieresias, to a state
of action connection to and involvement with the world. The poetry of the
First World War's soldiers, even when the work of Wilfred Owen or Siegfried
Sassoon is described as achieving a state of objectivity or emotional detach-
ment from the war, depends upon the perspective of the individual who has
taken an active part in a war which had rendered him a passive victim. To
these men, the war was something that could not be removed from their con-
ception of who they were. The identities of these "war poets" were inextri-
cable from the events in which they participated, and the poetry that emerged
depended, for the poets' psychological survival, upon the imaginative recon-
struction of these events into poetic vehicles through which they would forge
a new sense of wholeness.

Eric Leed, in *No Man's Land: Combat and Identity in World War I*, takes
as the subject of his investigation the ways in which the war "mobilized,
articulated, and modified the resources of signification available to the indi-

viduals who entered its bewildering and terrifying reality."[14] His focus is upon the actual participants of the war and the manner in which they were changed irrevocably by what they endured, the ways in which existing identities brought into the experience were altered and broken down. This investigation will be concerned with the aftermath of this process of breaking down, the methods available to the psychologically crippled to put themselves back together again. The problem for survivors of the war came in efforts to communicate the war's full impact, to forge an authentic voice that could give expression to what was perceived during the conflict as to some degree inexpressible. Rather than to remain in states of psychological isolation, soldiers attempting to reconnect with the world and to construct a coherent sense of self out of the fragments of identity the war had left behind were forced to create a new means of giving linguistic shape to what they had seen and participated within. This study will investigate the role that poetry played within such efforts to reconstitute individual identities out of the raw material of a war that had dismantled the pre-existing identities of its participants, often rendering them quite literally without a voice with which to articulate the experience.

Like Eliot writing *The Waste Land* from the sanitarium in Switzerland, the British poets Wilfred Owen, Ivor Gurney, and Siegfried Sassoon each found themselves, in different degrees and for different specific reasons, psychologically altered by what they had experienced. Owen was hospitalized in April 1917 for "shell shock" in Scotland, where he met Siegfried Sassoon in June of that year, hospitalized for the same affliction, though political issues were involved in his committal. Ivor Gurney found the war, ironically, to have been a place of relative stability within an otherwise tormented life, but wounded during the war's final year, his doctors observed signs of mental illness which evolved into incapacitating psychosis by 1922. For each of these men, poets before the war, poetry served as the way in which they could inscribe continuity into their lives to retaliate against the war's propensity to render the lives of the participants discontinuous. Poetry functioned as the means by which they returned to the war through memory and imagination, and poetry enabled the men to bring themselves back from psychological breakdown to a state of stability, based upon an imagined but real relationship to the war which poetry about war enabled them to create and discover. These three poets also reveal, within their poetic efforts at healing, their anxieties about the roles as soldiers which questions of class, rank, and duty asked each to play, anxieties which are in part responsible for the character of their specific psychological and traumatic response to the war. It is hoped that through an investigation of the specific therapeutic possibilities which poetry offered the men, each "shell shocked" in his own unique way, to imagine and create a new and stable poetic identity out of their reconstruction of the experience of war in verse, that further light might be shed upon the psychological impact that war has upon its often forgotten victims.

When Wilfred Owen (1893–1918) enlisted in the British army in October of 1915, he was unprepared for what he would eventually find at the front. His letters from 1914 show that to Owen the war was an abstraction from his perspective of safety as a tutor to adolescent boys in rural towns of France, far away from the fighting. But the pull of war intensified: he enlisted and was given a commission as a Second Lieutenant. His attitude toward the war would soon change. While his letters through most of his period of officer training 1916 show a man able to block the potential dangers of war out of his mind, the life he was forced to endure in the trenches, entering the lines as the Somme offensive drew to a close, made the physical and psychological reality of suffering central to his experience. On the last day of 1916, he arrived at the front lines in France and was given command over a platoon of infantrymen. He fought, experiencing the same movement from the front to support to rear trenches as did all soldiers, from January to May of 1917, until his weakening sense of control over his environment and over himself evaporated entirely. Readers today are fortunate to have the narrative of Owen's experience at the front intact because of the meticulous care his mother Susan expended to be sure that almost all of his letters home survived. By means of his descriptions of the front, not subject to censors since he, as an officer, was the censor, one can understand the factors precipitating the onset of his shell shock.

In April 1917, a heavy barrage of German artillery fire forced Owen to lead his men into an underground dug-out where they huddled in waist-deep rain water for fifty hours of continuous shelling. Owen watched men he commanded die before his eyes, but he and most of his men were able to escape alive. Soon thereafter, Owen was blown up by a shell and was rendered semi-conscious by the force of the blast. Days later, dazed and unresponsive but safe behind the lines, Owen was declared unfit for service and soon arrived at Craiglockhart Military Hospital in Edinburgh, classified as suffering from shell shock. He remained at Craiglockhart for five months, where his stammer and nightmares about his experiences were slowly alleviated by means of the therapy administered by his doctor, Arthur Brock, by the friendship he formed with Siegfried Sassoon, hospitalized by a different set of circumstances, and by the new type of poetry about the war Owen developed during this period of recuperation. The discussion of Owen's shell shock will investigate the methods of reconstructing the experience of war and the formation of a new voice and poetic identity in the last year of his life. Owen's late poems mark the development of a personal poetic idiom which captures both the complexities of that experience and Owen's personal feelings of guilt for others' suffering, while forging a public voice which speaks out against war and for those whom war has rendered incapable of speaking for themselves. Owen's poetry during his final year contributed to his healing from shell shock and enabled his return to the trenches during the final months of war. In one of the war's final bitter ironies, Owen's healing caused his death. On November 4, 1918, when the terms of Armistice had already been established, Owen led his men on a mission to construct a makeshift bridge over a canal heavily fortified by the Germans and was killed by machine gun fire. His mother learned of his death seven days later when the bells rang to signal the end of the fighting.

Ivor Gurney was born in 1890 to a mercantile family who lived in the county of Gloucester in relative comfort. The failing health of Ivor's father, David Gurney, in the 1920s, however, and Ivor's gradual lapse into mental illness during the decade following the war made their middle class lifestyle tenuous, and after the war, the social system that decreed that Ivor would serve as a private within the trenches also forced the struggling poet and musician to survive on a meager pension. The role of mental illness in the life of Gurney, both before, during, and after the war is so central to our understanding of his response to the role he played within the fighting, that this dimension of the poet's biography will be discussed with greater depth in the chapter which focuses upon him. At all stages of his life, however, Gurney regarded himself as an artist and saw his creative capacity as the power which could redeem any of life's hardships. He was a student at the Royal College of Music when war was declared in August 1914, applied for service in October, was rejected for poor eyesight (rather than mental instability that would prove to be his actual disability), and was accepted after reapplying in February 1915. He served with the First Gloucester Battalion fighting in the north, near Ypres, for most of 1916. His battalion moved south, toward the Somme River, near the end of that campaign as 1916 drew to a close. In and out of the hospital for minor wounds, Gurney was able to keep his mental instability, always a source of concern to family and friends prior to the war, in check during his service, but wounded late in the conflict and recovering in hospital as Armistice was declared, he began to demonstrate symptoms that were diagnosed as "Deferred Shell Shock" and would later degenerate into patterns of psychosis from which he would never recover. He remained in an asylum in London from 1922 until his death in 1937, writing poetry and music of wildly varying quality, believing that he was imprisoned unjustly and that he was controlled by electrical impulses emanating from the floors of his room. The discussion of Gurney will investigate the ways in which the poet, primarily in the war's aftermath, utilized poetry that returned through memory to reshape the experience of war to create beauty and order out of this "private" experience and to attempt to resist the psychological processes that brought him to his eventual state of mental incapacitation.

Siegfried Sassoon (1886–1967) was born to a landed family in the county of Kent where he grew up in a world of wealth and privilege, spending his adolescence fox hunting and reading and writing poetry. His family instilled heroic ideals into the youth since birth, naming him Siegfried after Wagner's hero, so it is no surprise that Sassoon enlisted in the British Cavalry on August 3, 1914, the day before war was declared. When the fighting evolved into trench warfare and horsemen were rendered obsolete, Sassoon served as Second Lieutenant in the First and Second Battalions of the Royal Welsh Fusiliers, "which were to distinguish themselves as elite fighting units, known for their active and aggressive trench tours."[15] Perhaps because of his able and brave leadership of his men, a command which earned him the nickname "Mad Jack" and earned him the Military Cross and other citations for bravery, Sassoon spent a considerable amount of time in England during these years, hospitalized for trench fever in August 1916, for a shoulder wound in April 1917, for shell shock in July 1917, and for a head wound in July 1918 where he remained until the Armistice was declared in November. These years of active duty throughout the war's duration, however, became only a fraction of Sassoon's psychological involvement with the war years. His volumes of poetry, *The Old Huntsman and Other Poems* (1916) and *Counter-Attack and Other Poems* (1917) were published during the war, but he returned to his combat experiences and memories in poems of later volumes, such as *Picture Show* (1919), *Satirical Poems* (1926), *The Heart's Journey* (1927), and *Vigils* (1934). As his poetic career progressed and the First World War receded into the past (soon replaced by a Second World War), Sassoon became a writer of increasingly meditative and spiritual verse. But despite his attempts to lay the war to rest in his poetry, it continued to resurface. Sassoon's prose writings show an even greater obsession with this period of his life. His autobiographical trilogy, *Memoirs of a Fox Hunting Man* (1928), *Memoirs of an Infantry Officer* (1930), and *Sherston's Progress* (1936), provided Sassoon with the forum to revisit and reshape the war years into novelistic forms, as he cloaked the events of his own life into those of his protagonist George Sherston. *Siegfried's Journey: 1916–1920* (1945) removed the veil that Sherston provided and served as the author's final statement about the most pivotal period of his life.

Metaphorically speaking, one might say that Sassoon remained mildly "shell-shocked" for much of his literary life, unable or unwilling to release himself completely from the war's impact upon his self-conception. His attitude toward the war saw changes throughout his four years of service; as late as December 1915, Sassoon writes in his diary, "But I am happy, happy; I've escaped and found peace unbelievable in this extraordinary existence which I thought I should loathe."[16] But, like many other enlisted men and officers serving alongside him, the Battle of the Somme from July to November of the subsequent year marked a change of the poet's heart, and Sassoon soon became one of the war's most vocal opponents. Though never psychologically crippled by the war, even when hospitalized for shell-shock in 1917, he never achieved freedom from it either. This continuing connection to the events of 1914–1918 seems to have been an integral part of Sassoon's conception of personal identity throughout his life, as he struggled, time after time, to "get it right" in poems and prose about selfhood and warfare. As the title of his poem from 1962 suggests, "The rank stench of those bodies haunts me still," he continued to be plagued by what he had seen and participated within in France almost fifty years earlier.[17] The discussion of Sassoon will seek not to investigate this entire span of time during which the war lived on in memory; rather, the focus will be upon Sassoon's enigmatic case of "shell shock" occurring in 1917. Though his hospitalization was entangled in a political attempt by British authorities to minimize the impact of the protest that Sassoon had lodged against the war, this period of his war life will demonstrate that the protest was itself a means of resisting the onset of psychological incapacitation and displayed the same conflict between selfhood and service which lies at the heart of shell shock. The poems of *Counter-Attack*, many written during this period of hospitalization, exhibit Sassoon's development of a new idiom that enables him to eliminate the emotional distance between himself and the men he leads, to cure himself (with the help of his doctor, W. H. R. Rivers) by resolving his psychological conflict toward the war, and to return to fight once again.

Neither Owen nor Sassoon ever reached the state of complete psychological ruin and isolation they witnessed around them at Craiglockhart Hospital in Edinburgh where both recuperated. And five years would pass after the end of the war before Gurney's mental illness would make his functioning, however oddly, in the world impossible, during which time he was an extremely prolific writer. The psychological affliction which each displayed while writing their verse most involved in the process of psychological healing was not as debilitating as it might have been. As readers attempting to understand the illness through their verse and reminiscences, we are both brought into the horrifying psychological world of shell shock and shut out from it. That is, neither Owen nor Sassoon never resembled the victims Owen describes in "Mental Cases" or Sassoon recalls in "Survivors," and thus their poetry reflects at times their distance from the torment raging within those as close as the next hospital bed. But the men seen in these poems were incapable of finding any language for their suffering, and the poets sought to speak for them as best they could. The voices that these poets created to speak for their own versions of the illness and to display their own struggles towards reconciliation with the war that contributed to their suffering show the inner workings of the mind which government documents or psychological and sociological studies could approach only from a distance. No case of shell shock is completely representative, but through the voices of these three very different poets, we can hear a version of the tens of thousands of men who suffered similar fates.

CHAPTER ONE

Shell Shock in World War I

Modern Warfare and Timeless Conflicts

Before investigating the ways in which poetry of war functioned as a means of expressing the inexpressible or of extracting value out of the experience of war, we must first explore what caused the men to break down in the first place and the form which such breakdowns assumed. "Shell shock" as a clinical diagnosis was a term introduced by Doctor Charles Myers of the Royal Army Medical Corps into the military lexicon during the First World War, specifically in September 1914 when the first cases of men suffering from what was thought to be an odd type of physical, rather than psychological, trauma began to arrive at casualty clearing stations. The men — dazed, uncommunicative, mute, deaf, blind, amnesiac, paralyzed, trembling, or subject to hallucinations, but displaying no visible injury to their nervous system to account for these symptoms — were thought to have suffered brain damage caused by the force of nearby exploding shells.[1] Later in the war, when cases with similar symptoms arose, cases which could not be ascribed to specific instances of shelling, the term came to be thought misleading. In *Shell Shock and Its Lessons* (1918), the British doctors G. Elliot Smith and T. H. Pear employ the term because it "has come to possess a more or less definite significance in official documents and in current conversation," rather than to use the more precise "war strain."[2]

The researchers who compiled the *Army Report of the War Office Committee of Enquiry into "Shell Shock"* unanimously agreed that "'shell-shock' has been a gross and costly misnomer, and that the term should be eliminated from our nomenclature."[3] The term, they argued, is misleading in its presumption that a single event precipitated the manifestations of trauma, rather than prolonged exposure to the war which wore the soldier down gradually. Other terms that came to denote more or less the same set of phenomena were "battle fatigue," "war shock," "war neuroses," "hysterical disorders of warfare," and so forth, each of which stressed the notion that exposure to the violence of war took its toll upon the psychological constitution of its participants. MacCurdy warns of any sort of label, despite the obvious need to categorize such sufferings: "the clinical types [of symptoms] covered by this blanket diagnostic term are too various to be safely gathered under one heading."[4] And no two cases of shell shock were identical, each displaying a different combination of manifestations upon the body, depending upon the details of the traumatic experiences the soldier had witnessed, the sensory organs most affected by the exposure, the length of time the soldier had been involved in the conflict, and the role that the individual had been asked to play within the war. Myers articulates the need for casting such a wide net through the use of the single term to designate the phenomena: "Indeed, the sole function which the term 'shell shock' appears to serve is to embrace under one name these disorders, of such diverse nature, arising from the emotional stress of warfare."[5] "Shell shock" does suggest a dramatic quality of the malady which it did display in its most severe instances. For the purposes of this discussion, "shell shock," despite its inexact nature, will function as the term to organize a series of complex conditions brought about by the individual soldier's heightened state of anxiety during warfare and by his participation, observation, and complicity within the horrors of the trenches and the battlefield.

To provide a unique as well as representative example of what the Army's psychiatric staff was forced to confront, the following case study will serve as well as any other. What were the psychological factors that brought about the "shell shock" of this soldier?

> A private 20 (always rather tenderhearted, disliking to see animals killed; rather self-conscious; a bit seclusive; "rather more virtuous than his companions"; shy with girls; sore throat a year or more before the war, with inability to sing or talk; always a lisper) enlisted in May 1916, spent five advantageous months in training and became increasingly sociable. However, on going to the front in October 1916, he was frightened by the first shell fire and horrorstricken by the sight of wounds and death. He grew accustomed to the horrors and five months later was sent to Armentieres, where he had to fight for three days without sleep. He grew very tired and began to hope that he would receive wounds that might incapacitate him at least temporarily for service.

He was suddenly buried by a shell, did not lose consciousness, but on being dug out was found to be deaf and dumb. On the way to the field dressing station he had a fear of shells. The deaf-mutism persisted unchanged for a month and then was completely and permanently cured in less than five minutes. He was made to face a mirror and observe the start he gave when hands were clapped behind him. He was assured that this start was an evidence of hearing; that his hearing was not lost, nor was his speech. He had no relapses during two months.[6]

As the five hundred and eighty-nine examples in E.E. Southard's volume suggest, each case presented its own set of circumstances — in terms of the patient's pre-war history, his battle experiences, and his particular manifestations of shell shock — all of which the physician attempted to take into account when assessing and remedying the particular victim. Does the patient's lisp, or his self-consciousness, or his tenderhearted-ness, or his difficulties with women, or his "virtue," or his disliking of seeing animals killed somehow make him prone to shell shock? Does his rank of private factor into his specific psychological situation? Why does the patient display deaf-mutism, rather than other common symptoms such as paralysis or a stammer? Was his burial alive the cause of his condition, or simply the final precipitating event? How was the man able to "convince" himself that he could not speak or hear, when in "reality" there was no physiological reason that such a reaction should occur? Was he faking his condition? Was he a coward? Why would the mind play these sorts of tricks on an individual?

The case of this private is typical as well as unique, and the questions that such a manifestation of trauma raises defy easy answers. The War Office report, illustrating how vast were the conditions which the term seeks to cover, breaks cases of shell shock down into three classes:

> (1) Genuine concussion without visible wound as a result of shell explosion. All witnesses were agreed that the cases in this class were relatively few.
> (2) Emotional shock, either acute in men with a neuropathic predisposition, or developing slowly as a result of prolonged strain and terrifying experience, the final breakdown being sometimes brought about by some relatively trivial cause.
> (3) Nervous and mental exhaustion, the result of prolonged strain and hardship.[7]

The War Office report called the first of these classes "commotional" shock, where the brain suffered detectable, though not visible, impact from a shell explosion, and classified the second and third types "emotional," similar in

that each was a psychological reaction to the experience of war, different in
that one could be linked to a single event while the other, more prevalent
variety (comprising eighty percent of shell shock cases) resulted from the
gradual wearing down of the soldier.[8] Another significant fact about the phe-
nomena of shell shock, observed by all who studied it, is that the condition
presented the psychiatric community with no new afflictions. All of its symp-
toms — mutism, blindness, paralyses, recurring nightmares, all owing to one's
psychological reaction to traumatic experience — had been observed before
in the civilian populace of England, Germany, and France, and America.
Before the war, such observations were classified as "hysteria," most com-
monly diagnosed, rightly or wrongly, among women. The war suddenly pro-
vided a new crop of cases resembling the hysterical, in numbers heretofore
never seen and in a population of young men that were considered fit to
defend the nation during this struggle.

Within the cases of shell shock, two distinct types of symptoms could
be observed: the "conversion-hysteria" disorders and the "anxiety-hysteria"
states.[9] Soldiers would, more often than not, display symptoms from both
clusters, but they provide a helpful way to assess the depth of the trauma
and the likelihood of a soldier's recovery. The symptoms of the "conversion"
type were often more troubling to the observer because of the toll they took
on the functioning of the victim's body, but the "anxiety" states were more
difficult to endure for the victim himself and spoke to a much more deeply
seated conflict with his role in the war, with which the soldier was grappling
in his mind. Common symptoms of the "conversion" disorders were difficul-
ties with speech, hearing, sight, or gait; paralysis or rigidity in the limbs;
and contractures of posture. In other words, the trauma within the mind
played itself out in a conversion of the specific part of the body's function-
ing. Often, but not always, these breakdowns in bodily function could be
directly linked to a single event in the trenches. According to Salmon, "a
soldier who bayonets an enemy in the face develops an hysterical tic of his
own facial muscles; abdominal contractures occur in men who have bayo-
neted enemies in the abdomen; hysterical blindness follows particularly hor-
rible sights...."[10] However, other conversion symptoms might not have a
single incident in the trenches that precipitated their appearance, or at least
not one that could be extracted from the patient's consciousness.

The anxiety states produced an equally wide range of symptoms. Most
common were fatigue (combined however with restlessness), depression, irri-
tability, jumpiness when hearing loud sounds, and guardedness in express-
ing any of these feelings of anxiety. The sufferers of anxiety states also
displayed symptoms of a much more subjective nature, particularly when
their conscious resistance to expressing the anxieties was lessened during

sleep. Early on in a patient's hospitalization, according to MacCurdy, the dreams cause the soldier to experience little benefit from his sleeping hours, but the dreams are not yet incapacitating: "When sleep does come, it is often troubled by repeated dreams of the occupational type where the soldier is trying to do whatever was his task during the day, and is having constant difficulty and meeting with no success in accomplishment."[11] The soldiers also reported having nighttime visions which were often specific to the experiences that the individual had suffered through. In some cases, the content of the dream life spilled over to the waking hours, and the patient had hallucinatory visions of the thoughts of the battlefield that haunt him. Dreams soon intensify to nightmares of an extremely violent quality which come on moments after the individual falls asleep. In these nightmares, the patient is often in precisely the same situation as he had been in while in France, without any of the distortion that is common in dreams. He must witness, every time he closes his eyes, the sight of a friend blown to pieces feet from him, or he must hear the endless barrage of shell fire which arbitrarily spared him while taking the lives of those huddled in the same dug-out. MacCurdy states, "Nothing is distorted except that he is powerless to retaliate, and his fear is infinitely greater than it ever is while he is awake in a situation at all similar."[12] According to Kardiner, the most intense and potentially debilitating nightmares are those in which the patient dreams of the horrifying experience from the trenches where its chaotic quality, which had characterized it in reality, is replaced with a clearer impression that the patient has caused the horrible event himself, either through his witnessing the death of an enemy he killed, or his witnessing the loss of a companion which the dream makes clear he should have prevented.[13] Simmel speculates that the nightmares are the attempts of the patient at self-therapy. The waking hours are spent repressing the disturbing content to avoid the immediate pain they elicit, but in so doing the patient brings about greater suffering as the content of the memory, under the weight of conscious repression, takes increasingly violent forms when it is finally given room for expression at night time. Simmel believes that the intensification of the nightmares results so that the patient will be forced to confront the memory he is working so hard to avoid.[14] The horrifying nightmares threaten to become systematic, tending towards psychosis because of the lack of necessary sleep that accompanies them. If unaddressed, the patient becomes unfit for any sort of life, let alone a return to combat.

Another form of psychological disturbance that appears to have resulted, at least in part, from participation in the war are the psychotic illnesses. During the First World War, cases which in prior wars had been thought to be psychoses were reinterpreted as having been neurotic in nature — shell

shock — before the diagnosis had come into being. But the war would yield
genuine cases of psychoses in addition to neuroses. For some soldiers pre-
disposed to the illness we now call schizophrenia, the war contributed to the
onset of conditions from which there would be no recovery. According to
Leed:

> [A]mong veterans psychoses actually increased in absolute terms
> throughout the 1920s.... Except for organic heart disease this was the
> only category of war-caused illness that rose steeply throughout the
> decade.... While the war was going on it appeared that the large
> numbers of neuroses had a great deal to do with the surprisingly few
> psychoses of combat. In peacetime this ratio was reversed. The en-
> counter with the home might collapse the last, saving reality. There
> are numerous examples of men coming home either "normal" or
> with a slight hysteria to end up, four years later, as schizophrenics.[15]

Hamilton Marr discusses these conditions under the terms, "Chronic Delu-
sional Insanity" and "Dementia Praecox," precursors for our contemporary
diagnosis of schizophrenia. The symptoms Marr observes within his case
studies seem as though they have been pulled from Ivor Gurney's own biog-
raphy: "In the army, changes of conduct and efficiency are noticeable; care-
lessness, indifference and apathy become marked; work is performed in a
slovenly and imperfect manner." The patients are characterized by "prolific
letter-writing" and "the habit of taking voluminous notes of what transpires
during their waking moments.... The subject may imagine himself to be
operated on by electricity or by wireless...."[16]

Science today has established that schizophrenia is in part determined
by genetic inheritance, and detectable changes in brain chemistry identify
the disease as a physiological condition of the brain which displays radical
and devastating effects upon psychological functioning. Many of the men
would have developed schizophrenia with or without their involvement in
the war. But the effect of the war cannot be ignored. The War Office report
concludes that "most witnesses were of the opinion that the stress of war rarely
produced insanity in the stable man, but that it acted, as is commonly
observed with other forms of stress, as a factor upon those who by predis-
position were liable to breakdown."[17] Little could be done for these men
beyond custodial care and supervision so that they would not harm them-
selves or others. They resemble the "Mental Cases" that Owen observes, cut
off from any connection with the rational world: "Surely we have perished
/ And walk hell; but who these hellish?"[18]

Even though none of the symptoms displayed were new to the medical
literature of nervous disorders, never had physicians seen such a concentra-

tion of suffering among its population — civilian or military. Upwards of eighty thousand actual cases occurred during the four years of war, many of which were misdiagnosed earlier in the war before the condition was fully understood.[19] By 1922, over sixty-five thousand British veterans were drawing disability pensions or were hospitalized for some version of shell shock.[20] In conflicts preceding the First World War, such as the Boer War and the Spanish-American War, "insanity" rates were significantly higher than recorded in documents of earlier conflicts, and the rate of recovery from insanity, according to Salmon, was "remarkable," statistics that support the notion that these soldiers too suffered from the strains of war, as yet unnamed as shell shock, rather than psychoses.[21] But the British medical authorities were not equipped for the insurgence of cases that came about as a result of the protracted "war of attrition" of 1914–1918, a war which introduced a new type of warfare, in part responsible for the increased concentration of psychological disturbances.

Smith and Pear argue that emotional responses normally associated with battle were thwarted or fundamentally altered by the prolonged exposure in the trenches; they differentiate between "natural fighting" and the current situation:

> In natural fighting, face to face with his antagonist, and armed only with his hands or with some primitive weapon for close fighting, the uppermost instinct in a healthy man would naturally be that of pugnacity, with its accompanying emotion of anger. The effect of every blow would be visible, and the intense excitement aroused in the relatively short contest would tend to obliterate the action of other instincts such as that of flight, with its emotion of fear.[22]

When the Western front settled into a landscape of trenches straddling the disputed terrain of No Man's Land between them, the soldiers found themselves in situations for which neither these sorts of instincts nor their training had prepared them. The chance of hand to hand combat was slim; casualties came about through sniper fire and shelling, from an origin across No Man's Land that the passive victims could not locate upon any single person responsible for their suffering. The enemy was detested for having been a source of the danger, but the Germans, as people, were not always regarded as the enemy, and were often seen as men in situations similar to their own. The famous Christmas Eve truce of 1914, in which Allied and German soldiers walked across the wires in No Man's Land and exchanged chocolate and cigarettes, suggests that in the mind of the British, French, or German soldier the enemy became the war itself in a dehumanized form, rather than those men in the other trenches fighting for their nation's cause.

Nevertheless, soldiers watched men dying all around them, and necessities of trench warfare denied their desires to exact any revenge for their losses. In addition to the fact that he could not attribute the loss to a single human enemy, the soldier could not mount an attack to satisfy the urge that some sense of moral order be restored by killing as his companion had been killed. The wholesale slaughters of the Somme offensive, in which twenty thousand British men died on July 1, 1916, and one million men were lost on both sides during the four months of the campaign, or of Third Ypres, Passchendaele, when attempts at progress toward the German held territory in Belgium was thwarted by mud and machine gun-fire, display that "offensive" action was often incongruous with the four years of warring on the continent. MacCurdy argues that despite the increase in cases resembling shell shock in other recent conflicts such as the American Civil War or the Boer conflict, the First World War marked a turning point for the insurgence of war neuroses that can be attributed to the added demands placed upon soldiers in this "modern" war. He states, "In previous wars the soldiers, it is true, were called upon to suffer fatigue and expose themselves to great danger. In return, however they were compensated by the excitement of more active operations ... where they might feel the joy of personal prowess."[23] MacCurdy believes that any soldier in any war must devote considerable mental energy to convert from a peacetime mentality, embracing values of sympathy and compassion for other people, to a wartime mindset where he is trained to exhibit his aggressive and brutal capacity.[24] The First World War denied the soldier's acting in accordance with either a peace or war mentality — he could be neither compassionate nor aggressive toward the enemy. Instead, the instinct for survival became foremost in the soldier's mind.

As the war dragged on, this necessary passivity intensified even as the body count continued to rise. The soldier was forced into a prolonged state of waiting, unable to act in any manner other than a defensive posture. Often, he escaped enemy shellfire through retreats underground into dugouts. At all times, he kept his head lowered beneath ground level to avoid anonymous sniper fire from the enemy trench. This uncertainty and passive expectation of possible death or maiming led to an intensification of anxiety that could have no effective outlet. And at no time did the entire ordeal seem to promise an end. Smith and Pear state, "It must be remembered that one of the greatest sources of break-down under such circumstances is intense and frequently repeated emotion."[25] Babington cites the *Official History of the British Medical Services During the First World War* which explained why the Somme battles created "ideal conditions" for shell shock:

The "artillery preparation" of the attacking force called for an "artillery reply" from the opposing side. This duel frequently lasted for several hours or days, and during this period of waiting the nerves of all were kept on edge. Then, after the attack came the reckoning of losses amongst comrades; and it was not unlikely that, owing to the call for troops, the whole acute process might soon be repeated. Little by little men became worn down by such experience, and despite their best efforts that the time would come when it was impossible to keep their thoughts from preying on the ordeals and sights of the battlefield.[26]

Because of the range from which modern weaponry could be fired, soldiers were continually anticipating the bullet or mortar fire that would spell their doom. According to Kern, "The large-bore, muzzle-loading musket of the Napoleonic era had an effective lethal range of between one and two hundred yards. The small-bore, break-loading rifle of the First World War shot a small-calibre bullet that was lethal at up to 2,000 yards and that traveled in a low trajectory and so could kill over a greater portion of its path."[27] The Great War introduced machine guns, Howitzer shells, tanks, airplane bombings, and gas, all of which rendered armies immobile, underground in the trenches, waiting for the unknown. Henri Barbusse in *Under Fire* (1916), the war memoir which was highly influential to both Sassoon and Owen, writes, "In a state of war, one is always waiting. We have become waiting-machines. For the moment it is the food we are waiting for. Then it will be the post. But each in its turn. When we have done with dinner we will think about the letters. After that, we shall set ourselves to wait for something else."[28] British forces geared up for the Somme battle for the first half of 1916, growing demoralized as the waiting continued. One Lieutenant, Geoffrey Fildes, felt reborn when finally given the command to go "over the top" in September 1916: "With a sort of gasp I became a man again. As soon as I began to move I felt my horrible mid-day nightmare slipping from my mind."[29] Leed observes that when the war became a mobilized conflict with the German offensives in 1918, "the incidence of war neurosis dropped dramatically."[30] The need for directed action to redeem the waiting contributed to the emergence of shell shock, and with so many British soldiers waiting in the trenches from 1916 onward, the cases multiplied.

Various theories emerged, beyond observing the conditions of modern warfare which made shell shock so prevalent, to explain the psychological mechanism that brought about the condition's range of manifestations. The simplest explanation offered is that the condition resulted from an extreme sort of sensory overload. Smith and Pear observe, "We must remember that a neurosis often (perhaps always) occurs as a result of the patient's inability to adjust his instinctive demands to the opportunities of his environment."[31] The environment buffeted the soldier with sights, sounds, smells, and all manner of sensations for which no amount of training could have prepared him. The continual explosion of shells, the impossibility of maintaining personal hygiene, the prolonged exposure to heat, cold, rain, and snow, the inadequate nutrition, the lack of sleep, the disease, the pestilence, and the sights and smells of decaying bodies presented the soldier with stimuli that he could not effectively assimilate. The human body can withstand only so much abuse before collapsing. Beyond the physical difficulties, the individual soldier was denied by the necessities of trench life from experiencing the emotions in any degree of normalcy which governed his peacetime existence. Grief and fear are parts of everyone's experience during life, but the trenches offered the soldier neither the time to grieve adequately before experiencing another loss to be mourned, nor the abatement of the heightened anxiety insisted upon if he hoped to survive. Smith and Pear connect the emotional experience to the bodily breakdown: "While no sign of fear can yet be detected in the face, the body, limbs or voice, these disturbances of the respiratory, circulatory, digestive and excretory systems may be present in a very unpleasant degree, probably even intensified because the nervous energy is denied other channels of outlet."[32] In other words, the emotions of fear, when not allowed to relax, turn inward upon the body, and thus this fear takes bodily form in the symptoms of shell shock.

The explanation of shell shock as a war of attrition on the body, as an erosion of its faculties, begins to explain the phenomena, but not entirely. If all men fighting in the same area were exposed to more or less the same physical conditions, why did some develop symptoms of shell shock and others not? Fenton devotes much of his study to investigating what factors of personality, heredity, and background contribute to a breakdown, compiling data on alcoholism rates, occupations before the war, age, time spent at the front, and medical history.[33] He concludes that the greatest contributory factors were the patient's history of neurotic illness and the rate of illness in his family, but that there was little else to predict who would succumb beyond this group since all men had an equal chance of encountering horrific sights or experiences, which were often at the root of shell shock. Some men, it seemed, had a greater capacity to resist the breakdown; some succumbed quite quickly. It is logical to assume that every man would have collapsed at some point, had the war not ended, or had he not suffered some other wound or been killed. The soldiers too were rotated through the trench system from the front, to reserves, and to base camps removed from the fighting to minimize the wear and tear on body and mind.

But because some men broke down after a few weeks in the trenches, some after prolonged exposure, and some not at all, psychologists set out to investigate the nature of the "crisis point." Because the manifestations of shell shock were more dramatic than fatigue, medical authorities suspected that more was at stake than mere physical or emotional exhaustion. Sigmund Freud's theories of psychoanalysis were gaining currency in Europe during the first decade of the twentieth century but were also met with great skepticism in certain quarters.[34] Having studied and theorized about neuroses in peacetime, Freud and his supporters, as well as his detractors, now had ample opportunities to apply his theories to see whether they were capable of explaining the phenomena. According to Leed, the war did enable Freud's ideas to penetrate into the theoretical positioning of many within psychiatric circles who had been resistant to them prior to the war:

> The consensus among medical officers after the war justified Freud's satisfaction that the war had, if nothing else, supplied abundant confirmation of the psychoanalytic view of neurosis. War neurosis, like neurosis in peacetime, was a flight from an intolerable, destructive reality through illness.[35]

Abraham agrees: "The war neuroses are essentially interposed guarantees, the object of which is to protect the soldier against a psychosis."[36] Even though the patient has lost control of certain faculties in shell shock, he has not lost his mind. He is, in fact, preserving his mind by removing himself from the psychological strains and is keeping himself alive by making himself incapable of performing the physical demands of trench life.

It is not surprising that early cases of shell shock were deemed cowardice, but the psychologists soon realized that the symptoms were not subject to the soldier's conscious control. The unconscious manifestations of the condition, according to MacCurdy, "were specifically directed at the man's capacity to fight."[37] One can observe the symptoms as not simply chance occurrences but as unconscious expressions on the part of the individual seeking to avoid the war. A patient may be sincere in claiming to have no idea why he is blind, or dragging his foot when he walks, but when viewed as an unconscious desire to escape his situation, one can see that blindness renders the soldier useless in military terms, that a dragging foot means the soldier cannot march back to the lines. Ferenczi sees the war neurosis as part of Freud's system of wish fulfillments in the cases of patients "who are prevented from going forward through the most violent attacks of shaking, but can carry out the much more difficult task of going backwards without trembling.... [T]he movement backwards, which removes the patient from the dangerous goal of the forward movement — and finally from the front line — does not need to be disturbed by any contrary wish."[38] Ferenczi notes also that men in states of shock will move themselves to safety, and only when they arrive at the dressing station or a fortified dugout will the debilitating symptoms come on.[39] Such was the case with both Owen and Sassoon. Owen, blown up by a shell, arrived at the clearing station dazed, and only after a period of observation did he begin to exhibit the telltale signs of tremors and stammering. For Sassoon, as well, the symptoms of his psychological crisis arrived not under heavy bombardment but while recuperating from a bullet wound in the hospital.

Freud himself in *Psycho-Analysis and the War Neuroses* articulates the notion that shell shock is a conflict waged between the competing roles available for the individual to play within the wartime environment:

> The war neurosis ... has been rendered possible or promoted
> through an ego-conflict.... The conflict takes place between the
> old ego of peace time and the new war-ego of the soldier, and it
> becomes acute as soon as the peace-ego is faced with the danger
> of being killed through the risky undertakings of his newly formed
> parasitical double. Or one might put it, the old ego protects itself
> from the danger to life by flight into the traumatic neurosis in
> defending itself against the new ego which it recognises as threaten-
> ing its life.[40]

The conflict, then, hinges upon the question of identity. The personality which comprises the soldier's peacetime identity must shift to one embracing the different set of values of warfare, while repressing the responses that someone operating under the values governing peacetime behavior would normally exhibit. Freud argues that though such a shift is a dramatic one, it is still a process that the individual can undergo successfully. The conflict arises when the dangers that one encounters prove to be so acute that following the course predicted by one's wartime ego spells certain doom. The threat of annihilation causes the peacetime ego to reassert itself through the signs of shell shock that remove the individual from danger. Certain soldiers, however, before succumbing to breakdown, embrace the role that war asks them to play with such reckless enthusiasm that death seems almost a certainty. MacCurdy explains this seeming death wish:

> There are three practicable avenues of escape; the man may receive
> an incapacitating wound, he may be taken prisoner, or he may be
> killed. One who manifests an anxiety state is always one with high
> ideals of his duty. We find, therefore, that none of them entertain the
> hope of disabling wounds. Nor do they consciously seek surrender,
> but it is interesting that they not infrequently dream of it at this
> stage. The third possibility [death] is the most alluring, as it offers

complete release and is quite compatible with all standards of duty. It is not unnatural, therefore, that many of these unfortunates who are constantly obsessed with fear perform most reckless acts.[41]

Siegfried Sassoon, before his hospitalization, revealed a possible death wish, taking risks in the lines which earned him the nickname "Mad Jack" from his men as well as a bullet in the shoulder. Significantly, Sassoon's near suicide missions in No Man's Land immediately preceded the onset of his symptoms of shell shock. The ego conflict between preserving oneself and embracing the values of warfare, which characterize such risk-taking as courageous, produced in his case another avenue for escape. Not killed, not captured, not physically wounded to the degree that would keep him from the war completely, Sassoon instead unconsciously exhibited symptoms that would render him psychologically incapable of serving.

Implicit within MacCurdy's analysis lies the fact that part of the wartime ego, which Freud observed as at odds with the ego of peacetime, contained a soldier's sense of duty and honor. Assuming a wartime identity might cause the individual to behave with aggression and hostility that he would not display without the war, but this wartime identity instilled within the soldier that courage was to be upheld at all costs. Death in battle, according to this mentality, was an honorable way out of the conflict, but every other means of escape led to feelings of cowardice. The conflict that manifests itself as shell shock, then, becomes not only a battle between instincts of self-preservation and instincts of aggression, but also between the socially constructed code of honor and the very real feelings of fear. It follows, then, that the depth of the psychological trauma which the soldier endured had to do not simply with how terrified he felt about the prospect of going back, but with the degree to which he felt that his duty denied that such fear was a legitimate response to the war. When the war finally ended, not only was the fear of death alleviated for the shell shock sufferer, but also his shame for having fallen victim to these fears at the expense of one's responsibility. Fenton states, "There were many men, especially the anxiety cases, who said at the time of the Armistice that 'a great weight had been lifted from their shoulders'; that they were 'new men.' Also the cures of many neurotic symptoms were noticeably easier after the Armistice."[42]

Statistics of shell shock victims compiled during the war display an interesting trend. The affliction, which could be roughly split into the hysterical disorders versus the anxiety states, also fell out along class lines. According to Rivers, "It is a striking fact that officers are especially prone to the occurrence of anxiety states, while privates are the chief victims of hysterical manifestations."[43] The occurrence of shell shock would appear at first glance to be fairly evenly divided amongst the troops, but since the lower ranks far outnumbered officers, the actual figures bear out that "Officers are affected in the proportion of five to one as compared to privates and non-commissioned officers."[44] Fenton's interpretation of the data is even more compelling: "The ratio of officers to men at the front is approximately 1:30. Among the wounded it is 1:24. *Among the patients admitted to the special hospitals for war neuroses in England during the year ending April 30, 1917, it was 1:6.*"[45] This disparity is striking since both groups of men lived in more or less the same physical conditions. If anything, the conditions for officers were slightly more comfortable than those of the men beneath them, and one might suspect that the officers could withstand the exposure more effectively.

MacCurdy argues that, in effect, the psychological constitution of officers allows the experience of war to affect them more deeply on a number of levels. Officers suffer from anxiety states, whereas soldiers suffer from conversion disorders because, according to the thinking of the time, officers were more intelligent. In peacetime, conversion states affected the lower classes more than they did the upper classes because "the modern educated man knows enough of neurology to realize, even if it be in a vague way, that paralysis comes from injury to a nerve or the central nervous system at some distance from the paralysis."[46] Thus, according to this logic, the less intelligent enlisted man who received a wound in the arm displayed a paralysis of the arm because his defense mechanism of shell shock that sought, like the officer's, to avoid a return to the war was less informed as to the ways which the nervous system functions and masked the psychological conflict by exhibiting "nerve damage" not consistent with the wound received. This explanation seems unsatisfactory and based upon some unflattering presumptions of ignorance of those beneath the upper crust of society who comprised the majority of commissioned officers in the war. The fact that conversion disorders, for all their disturbing appearances, were easier to cure than anxiety states suggests that the anxiety state was the more severe reaction to the stresses of war. A presumed higher intelligence and definite advantages of education do not explain why officers would react more deeply to the same experiences of loss, horror, and fear for survival than would those beneath them in rank.

MacCurdy speculates, "That one is a leader and another a follower is equally the result of a difference in ideals and emotional attitude. The private's ambition is not to think for himself but to follow orders implicitly and to sink his own personality so far as that may be possible."[47] For a private, forced into a role of subservience which denied any self-sovereignty, silently desiring a way out of that role, a hysterical disorder employed his condition of powerlessness as a means of psychological escape. Leed argues:

> Mutism and speech disorders were the most common symptoms of war neurosis, and ... this was so because the soldier was required to be silent, to accept the often suicidal edicts of authority and to hold back or severely edit any expression of hostility toward those who kept him in a condition of mortal peril. Rather than cursing, striking, or shooting his superior officer, he distorted his speech or completely denied himself that faculty.[48]

The mutism, paralysis, or any other conversion disorder for the private functions as would a "Blighty," a wound which incapacitates him and removes him from harm's way. He has not deserted or shirked his duty, nor is he physically capable of fighting. If we accept the assumption that duty played a larger role in the consciousness of the officer than of the private, we see the toll upholding such duty must take upon him:

> The fear which the patient feels must be repressed. He is ashamed of showing any evidence of cowardice before either his men or his brother officers. He is therefore the subject of a conflict which he must fight alone. He knows that he has at least a tendency to be afraid, but he also knows that he can maintain the respect of his men and officer friends so long as he keeps that fear to himself. He is constantly repressing this most natural reaction and there is accumulated, naturally enough, a stronger and stronger tendency for active exhibitions of fear.[49]

The officer must keep any feelings of dread or anxiety repressed because of the necessity that he appear to the men beneath him as sure of purpose and direction, lest the men he would send over the top lose morale and commitment to the pursuits of battle.

The effect of bottling up anxieties turned the energies spent in repression inward upon the officer. He was subject to a degree of self-inspection that persisted long after the breakdown. Even when visible symptoms of depression, irritability, or shakiness began to abate, the officer continued to feel guilt for losses he had not prevented, shame for having broken down and having abandoned duty, while simultaneously feeling terror at the prospect of going back. The War Office report identifies the added responsibility of leadership as the primary cause for such a disparity:

> To those [officers] suited to exercise it, responsibility, according to some, gave additional stimulus to the preservation of self-control, but to those ill-adapted, to men elevated to a rank beyond their capacity, it acted as a cause of mental unrest and contributed in no small degree to nervous breakdown.... [R]esponsibility while it lasted lessened the tendency to emotional neurosis, but when it ceased liability to neurosis was increased.[50]

Implicit within this assessment is the notion that some people, privates and officers alike, entered the war more susceptible than others to break down. No one could have prepared himself for the sort of conditions all were asked to endure, nor for the experiences against which one's service to country asked the individual to put forth a "stiff upper lip." But some soldiers, due to strengths within their disposition brought to the trenches, or unwavering conviction to the cause which made the unpleasant experiences palatable, had greater defenses at their disposal by which to resist the processes of war experience that wore away at such protective measures and led to shell shock, the final measure of self-protection. The poets within this study provide evidence of the role responsibility played in bringing about shell shock. Gurney, a private, feels none of the burdens of responsibility, displays little concern for the national purpose, and often appears alienated from the experience altogether, calling himself in one letter not a soldier but "a dirty civilian."[51] He is thus able to construct a vision of the war in its aftermath that puts forth his "private" methods of survival. His private vision of the war becomes, as his own sanity begins to slip away because of a psychological constitution that made him unfit to serve in the first place, his means of returning to the war experience as an emotional anchor. Owen and Sassoon, both Lieutenants, display within their records of nightmares and obsessive waking thoughts their feelings of having abandoned the men whom duty demanded they protect and lead. Owen and Sassoon both brought if not fervent patriotism then at least strongly held codes of honor and duty with them into the trenches which would not go quietly, especially when they found themselves subject to intense psychological conflict about their own role in the war. The poetry written by each while recuperating displays the methods by which these officers worked through their feelings of guilt for having left their men because of their breakdowns and by which they forged a new imaginative relationship with those beneath them that allowed for each to return to the fighting.

Therapies for Shell Shock

Understanding the causes and mechanisms of shell shock was one thing; treating the condition was altogether another. The goal of all forms of psychotherapy was the soldier's return to active combat. But as Salmon shows, this goal was not always practical if the trauma suffered were too severe. In his study to advise American military preparing to enter the war for the cases of shell shock they could expect, Salmon analyzed a sample of patients at Magull Hospital in England and observed that effective and lasting relief from shell shock took too long to recommend return to the line as a reasonable goal. Though the rate of cure was high, the likelihood that these men could be effective soldiers was not. He concluded, "It is evident that the outcome in the war neuroses is good from a medical point of view and poor from a military point of view."[52] Salmon advised the Americans that their resources were better spent on the care of men at the front, to detect incidences of shell shock before they became debilitating. Gurney, once his illness set in, would never be released from the asylum. Owen and Sassoon, however, are atypical in this respect. The responsibility and sympathy that both grew to feel for their men in France during the course of treatment outweighed the odds that suggested their return to fighting was unlikely.

The unlikelihood that many soldiers could return to fighting is illustrated by one case which confronted Dr. W. H. R. Rivers, one of the pioneers of analytic therapies for shell shock sufferers and the physician responsible for Siegfried Sassoon. He describes in *Instinct and the Unconscious* (1922) the difficulties of guaranteeing one soldier that he could even live a functional civilian life after the trauma he experienced:

> ... a young officer ... was flung down by the explosion of a shell so that his face struck the distended abdomen of a German several days dead, the impact of his fall rupturing the swollen corpse. Before he lost consciousness the patient had clearly realised his situation, and knew that the substance which filled his mouth and produced the most horrible sensations of taste and smell was derived from the decomposed entrails of an enemy. When he came to himself he vomited profusely, and was much shaken, but "carried on" for several days, vomiting frequently, and haunted by persistent images of taste and smell.[53]

A return to the front, the ideal for which the Army strove in its treatment of shell shock cases, was not even an option for this man; his trauma was so severe that the most pressing challenge was to enable the officer to hold down food before starving. Almost as shocking as this horrific, traumatizing experience itself is the officer's immediate response to the event by attempting to carry on in accordance with the sense of duty with which he had been indoctrinated. Symptoms of shell shock provided one challenge for the therapist; the trauma, and its relationship to the patient's attitude toward the war, provided another. This officer was discharged from the army after Rivers' attempts and failures to construct a means, through therapy, by which the soldier could reconcile himself to what he had endured. The officer was advised to attempt to control his surroundings as a civilian so that the memory would not overwhelm his waking life, even though the nightmares would in all likelihood never disappear.

Perhaps to a post–Freudian mentality, the idea that the cure to shell shock lay in either the traumatic experience or the conflicted response of the individual toward the war does not seem controversial. To the medical authorities at the onset of the war in 1914, such a notion was summarily dismissed. Many, ignorant of the realities which the soldiers like Rivers' patient were forced to endure, regarded shell shock as the soldiers' attempts to shirk their duties. One method of addressing the problem, in hopes of preventing further cases, was execution on the grounds of cowardice. Babington describes a soldier who was absent from his battalion during a battle near Ypres in March 1915. When he was found months later, he was arrested and court martialled: "In his defence the private said that he did not know why he had left the trench. They were being heavily bombarded at the time and he had lost his memory. He was sentenced to death and shot without undergoing any medical examination."[54] On November 7, 1918, three days after Wilfred Owen would die after having been healed from shell shock in order to return to the fighting, the last British soldier of the war was shot for desertion. He claimed that he had suffered from mental troubles, as had his parents, but the court did not find it "desirable to hear medical evidence before imposing a death sentence on him."[55] So, throughout the course of the war, shell shock was not recognized as a legitimate condition by all courts, doctors, or commanders, but its rapid increase, particularly in the latter half of the war after the Somme battles, forced authorities to decide upon courses of treatment.

One of the most notorious and, if one were to believe its practitioner, most effective treatments was the use of electrical shock or "faradism," alongside stern suggestion to eliminate the offending symptoms of shell shock. Dr. Lewis Yealland, Resident Medical Officer at the National Hospital in London, chronicled his sessions with patients in his volume *The Hysterical Disorders of Warfare* (1918). Yealland did not believe that the men were malingerers and did recognize shell shock as a legitimate medical condition which prevented soldiers from continuing to serve. But he had little patience for hearing about any suffering that brought on the condition and took it upon himself to develop therapy that could return them to the trenches as quickly as possible. Most of the patients whom he thought likely to respond to his methods were those who displayed specific somatic symptoms. Discussions of soldiers' nightmares or anxieties had no place in his "therapy," and he would tell them as much when he took them into darkly lit rooms where his faradic battery and electrodes awaited. To one man who expressed a fear that his true feelings toward the war would never be understood, Yealland responded, "I am not zealous to understand your condition.... I do not want to know anything about it, but I do know you have a stammer which is most unpleasant."[56] Yealland placed the electrode upon the part of the body which refused to behave normally — the leg in a case of paralysis; the throat for mutism or stammers — and applied a sequence of intensifying shocks while explaining to the patient that he would not leave the room until the symptom had disappeared, from anywhere between ten minutes to several hours. In one instance, attempting to eradicate a spasm in a soldier's leg, Yealland describes chasing the spasm around the patient's body until it disappeared — applying the electrode to one leg, to the other, to an arm, to the other arm, and back finally to the original limb before it was completely gone.[57]

In addition to the shocks themselves, which were questionable practices enough, Yealland employed techniques of "suggestion" to persuade the soldiers that the proper thing for them to do, in fact what they themselves wanted to do, was to be rid of the symptoms of shell shock so that they could return to fighting and duty. One soldier, unable to walk, soon began to take hesitating steps under Yealland's "guidance." Pleased with his progress, the soldier "began to quote poems of his own composition." Yealland describes his therapeutic approach:

> "Your reason for coming here was to be cured and not to quote poetry.... Emotional demonstrations are entirely out of order in cases such as yours, and I do not appreciate them, and neither will you when you consider that the result obtained is what should be expected." He then became less demonstrative and more practical, and with the change in the emotional state he lost all trace of a disordered gait.[58]

For Yealland, emotional expression ran counter to moral integrity, and to be a poet seems to be a particularly grievous indication of weakness. He did not doubt that the symptoms of shell shock were beyond the soldier's conscious control; he instead felt that the soldier was failing to display the degree of courage or respect for duty which would combat the sublimated urge for his own incapacitation. He advised one patient struggling to keep a tremor in check to "give your lazy brain some work to do."[59] In another case, Yealland observed a patient attempting to sleep who was plagued by nightmares. According to the doctor, "There was a profuse perspiration over his body, and the bed sheets were almost soaked.... So I said, 'I realise that you are tired of your disturbing dreams, and it is not pleasant to be kept in isolation. You will be out of isolation tomorrow, because you will be cured.'"[60] In effect, Yealland was replacing one nightmare with another for these victims of shell shock. If their symptoms were caused by the unconscious desire to escape from the terrors and dangers of warfare, the faradism inflicted upon them as therapy worked to "cure" the shell shock by substituting the torment experienced in the trenches with torture at the hands of a man whose duty it was to make them better. Freud, testifying in the trial of Wagner-Jauregg, the Austrian therapist who practiced electro-shock therapy as well, reported that in German hospitals, the electricity was increased to unbearable levels, and the fact of deaths and suicides because of the shock "has never been contradicted."[61]

Yealland's techniques of suggestion played upon the soldier's insecurities that his incapacitation was due to some moral weakness, laziness, or effeminacy, and without the physical means to resist the treatment, the soldier was forced into a position of choosing between two alternatives, both undesirable — healing and return to fighting and duty, or extensive and repeated electric shocks. If the patient persisted, the voltage was increased. Seeking to remove himself from the source of immediate trauma, in this instance Yealland's therapy, the patient responded by repressing the symptom that brought him to the hands of Yealland. The suppression of the manifestation of shell shock occurs through much the same process as had brought on the condition in the first place. The shortcomings of Yealland's therapy are clear. He changed the behavior of the patient but did nothing to address the causes of that behavior. And he administered the treatment in a manner that was at best manipulative, preying upon the vulnerabilities of the patient, if not utterly inhumane. If anything, Yealland's treatments would seem to heighten the anxieties at the root of shell shock. The front would become that much more terrifying to the soldier when he now realized that, once "cured" and shell shock no longer an option for escape, the only ways out of the war were through death, a "Blighty" wound, or the end to the fighting.

Rates of relapse of his patients, not surprisingly, are not recorded within his case studies. He congratulates himself often about the short amount of time required to cure a patient who had been crippled for months, so that he could move onto the next one, but he does not mention whether the same men would return to his hospital with a relapse of shell shock after another tour in the trenches replaced fear of Yealland's therapy with fear of death in battle. Yealland does include the following admission after one successful session with a soldier, however: "Two days later he returned with a stammer which came on after some annoyance with a taxi driver. This, however, was very quickly removed. His mental condition improved."[62] Rates of relapse for the army as a whole are hard to come by. Men who broke down again at the front after having been cured would likely be sent to other hospitals where other sorts of treatments would ensue, and the medical histories of such cases were hard to monitor. Or men, near the point of collapsing again, might be killed before being rehospitalized. Therapies such as Yealland's, however, were likely to offer temporary relief at best to the symptoms of shell shock. Babington writes, "Once he returned to the Front and found himself again under fire, his fear of the electric current receded, just as during the treatment his fear of active service had faded. Inevitably, his neurotic symptoms returned and he relapsed into a neurotic condition."[63] Smith and Pear articulate the problem with addressing the patient's symptoms, rather than the source of the shell shock: "The root of the trouble is mental conflict, the complete details of which can seldom be found on the surface of the complex of symptoms. To palliate them one by one is often to provoke new ones."[64] The cure was also predicated upon the notion that the patient himself played a minimal role in his own improvement, which was better left in the control of such experts.

This issue of the locus of control over the therapy raised questions as well about hypnosis, one of the most common therapeutic approaches for shell shock sufferers during the war, the practice of which Eder's statistics would seem to justify: "The treatment par excellence is hypnotic suggestion. 91.5 per cent of cases of war shock were cured by this method and 8.5 per cent improved.... The majority of war-shock patients so cured can return to the Front in three to six months."[65] The specific details of the therapy vary from doctor to doctor. Some put the patient into a hypnotic state and through suggestive techniques, informed him that his symptoms had no physical cause and that it was within the patient's power to rid himself of the incapacitating affliction. Like Yealland's faradism, these suggestive techniques could eliminate the problem, at least on the surface, but when the therapy ended with the offending symptom's eradication, the trauma itself remained intact, and a return to the front might prompt a relapse as it had in Yealland's electroshock approach. Other hypnotic therapies, utilized especially for those suffering from amnesia, recognized that a traumatic event may be the root cause of the symptoms, and sought to return the patient to the moment which he had repressed. The therapist led the hypnotized patient back to the time in the war which he could not recall and brought the memory back to his consciousness.

Presumably, Eder did achieve his remarkable percentages, but he gives no figures of relapse rates to indicate whether having eradicated the symptom, which hypnotic suggestion could achieve, had addressed the cause of the trauma so that the symptom would not resurface. Those who took analytical approaches to the source of the trauma and conflict were skeptical that hypnosis could offer any lasting relief. Kardiner reluctantly acknowledges some value in the approach in the treatment of hysterical disorders, but does not endorse it for the more serious anxiety states: "No permanent benefits from hypnosis can, however, be expected in any but the sensory-

motor disturbances."[66] Smith and Pear suggest that the problem with hyp-
nosis is that, although it may make visible symptoms of shell shock disap-
pear, it does not go far enough:

> Hypnotism has been proved to be a valuable therapeutic agent in
> the early stages of shell-shock. As a cure for certain patients who
> have passed the acute stages of shell-shock or other forms of war-
> strain, its use requires great discrimination in the selection of suitable
> cases and extreme care in its practice. It is very probably, too, that
> hypnotic suggestion by itself should never be regarded as sufficient
> treatment....[67]

Elliot-Smith suggests that the problem with hypnosis is that traumatizing
events might be brought to consciousness but the therapist does nothing to
educate the soldier as to what to do with those thoughts. He is confronted
with only the sheer terror that had been repressed. The most beneficial use
of hypnosis, according to Leed, is that which combines hypnosis with ana-
lytic discussions of the memories that have been excavated and which enables
the patient "to frame and represent the motives conflicting in the symp-
tom."[68] The therapist educates the patient on ways to address the memory,
brought out of repression, so that it can be understood in the context of the
war and in relation to the patient's behavior within the episode. Although
hypnotic suggestion depends in part on the patient's willingness to surren-
der a degree of control to the doctor (and shell shock victims were a highly
suggestible group of people), the most lasting results of hypnotic therapy
occurred when the soldier learned means of controlling his response to his
own experiences.

   Another frequently employed method of shifting the locus of control
away from the therapist and into the hands of the patient, to make him feel
responsible for his own recuperation, occurred through work and occupa-
tion while in the hospital. Rates of success for "work cures" were quite good,
and after a few months the visible signs of shell shock had disappeared and
many patients felt strong enough to return to the fighting. Patients arrived
in the hospital helpless to perform even the simplest tasks, and doctors saw
that obstacles preventing their return to mental health were the accompa-
nying feelings of incompetence and worthlessness. Systems of occupational
therapy were initiated to give the soldier confidence in his own ability to
function. MacCurdy states, "A game of cards may be all the man can stand
at first, perhaps it will be only a very small amount of light reading. He can
progress from this to the less violent out-of-door games, and as his strength
increases, be given something more productive"[69] Marr recommends basket-
weaving and necklace-making early on, and later farming and gardening

when the patient begins to improve.[70] Salmon suggests in his recommendation to the Americans preparing to enter the war that hospitals be equipped with metal and wood shops, as well as having access to arable farmland nearby.[71] But these therapists warn that doctors should not envision such as work as a guarantee of health. The work should be a stage in a progressive re-education of the patient which at first keeps the patient from "dwelling upon his subjective troubles by occupying his mind with other things," but which at every stage enables the patient to see that he is doing something useful and is contributing to the institution that is housing him, rather than being a burden to his country.[72] Dr. Arthur Brock, Wilfred Owen's therapist at Craiglockhart, employed a radical version of the work cure which he called "ergotherapy" that will be discussed in the subsequent chapter; "ergotherapy" shared with all work cures the expectation that the soldier achieve the degree of command over his own body and mind that he would allow him to return to the front to command or be commanded once again.

The danger with work cures, as with hypnotism or even faradism, lay in the presumption that these practical means of eliminating visible signs of shell shock secured an end to the malady. Doctors agreed, with the notable exception of Yealland, that for any therapy to be successful at addressing the traumatic cause of the symptoms, some form of analytic therapy must accompany these measures. Analytic techniques took as their goal the re-education of the patient to the cause of his condition, according to Myers, "so as to restore his self-knowledge, self-confidence, and self-control. For these a judicious admixture of explanation, persuasion, and sometimes scolding, is required, as in the education of children...."[73] As the scolding would suggest, however, to Myers and to many therapists skeptical of psycho-analysis (which was, after all, the invention of Britain's enemies in the war), prolonged sessions in which the therapist attempted to ascertain the patients' feelings toward his condition were the equivalent of pampering. These therapists considered too much analysis as validation of the soldier's perspective of helplessness and favored introducing discipline back into the soldier's life which would be essential if he were to return. Some thought analytic therapy, whether specifically psycho-analytic or not, simply impractical. Eder says, "To use [psycho-analysis] here is to employ a Nasmyth hammer to crack a nut."[74]

But others recognized that the months required for the "talking cure" were worth the trouble. If the therapy resulted in the patient's understanding of his situation — both the source of his trauma and his reaction to it through shell shock — then the cure, it was hoped, could be permanent, rather than a temporary relief of the symptoms, and the broken man could become a soldier again. Not surprisingly, military authorities were more

willing to invest the time of analysis into the recovery of their officers,
suffering mainly from anxiety states, than for the more expendable enlisted
men, and analysis was an approach more suited to address the specific ques-
tions of responsibility, guilt, and honor that lay at the root of the anxiety
disorders. The therapist could use specific psychoanalytic techniques in an
effort to bring to the surface the ego conflict, or as was more often the case,
he could initiate a regimen of discussions where he sought to establish a
relaxed atmosphere in order to encourage the patient to reveal the experi-
ences from his warfare that were causing the conflict. Leed discusses why the
therapy could be so successful:

> The central proposition of analytical therapy in war, as in peace,
> removed the symptom from the moral arena. The neurosis was
> not the result of a conscious decision made by the patient. On the
> contrary, the neurotic soldier was one who could make no decision,
> who could repudiate neither his desire for survival nor the ideals
> and moral imperatives that kept him at the front.... The neurotic was
> the man in the middle, the everyman. Where disciplinary therapists
> assumed the weakness of the neurotic's allegiance to duty, analysts
> tended to emphasize the strength of this commitment and the inten-
> sity of the conflict that it imposed upon those who wished to survive
> the war.[75]

In addition to enabling the patient to see that his behavior in battle had not
been suspect and that deaths he may have witnessed were beyond his con-
trol, analytic therapy sought to educate the soldier that his response of shell
shock was not morally dubious either. His powerlessness in battle had led
to his passive incapacitation in the hospital. Through this new awareness,
the soldier could use the processes of introspection to bring about an active,
self-directed healing.

Two analysts, Sigmund Freud and W. H. R. Rivers, from opposing sides
of the war, have come to be seen today as their nations' leading theorists of
shell shock, even though the approaches of neither man came to be their
nations' preferred therapeutic approach during the war. But the ideas of
these two men are the most relevant when considering the role that the artis-
tic representation of war could play as therapy for those traumatized by the
experience. These men regarded the nightmares of the shell shock victim as
offering the key to both the trauma and the recovery. Freud, who treated no
sufferers of shell shock during the war, translated his theories about neu-
roses in peace to those of war in his introduction to *Psycho-Analysis and the
War Neuroses* (1921). He approaches the war neuroses from a different angle
in *Beyond the Pleasure Principle* (1920). If, as he has postulated, innate within
human consciousness lies the instinct to seek pleasure, why does one find as

a common trait among sufferers of traumatic neuroses the tendency to repeat the painful experience through fixations of memory or in nightmares? He states, "We are therefore left in doubt as to whether the impulse to work over in the mind some overpowering experience so as to make oneself master of it can find expression as a primary event, and independently of the pleasure principle."[76] How is this tendency to dwell upon the unpleasant experience part of the drive that seeks pleasure? Freud has argued elsewhere that dreams are an expression of repressed wishes. Do the terrifying nightmares common to shell shock victims fall under the rubric of desires for wish fulfillment as well? Freud says that such impulses to repeat provide evidence of a more fundamental drive than that of the pleasure principle:

> These dreams are endeavouring to master the stimulus retrospectively, by developing the anxiety whose omission was the cause of the traumatic neurosis.... But it is impossible to classify as wish-fulfilments the dreams we have been discussing which occur in traumatic neuroses.... They arise, rather, in obedience to the compulsion to repeat.[77]

Freud argues for a model that sees the repetitive nightmares revealing a more primitive instinct than the individual's search for pleasure that would predict that the nightmares not be experienced at all. One might, however, modify Freud's model slightly to see the urge for repetition revealed by the nightmares not as separate from the pleasure principle but as part of a more difficult search for pleasure, or relief from the anxiety, as a goal at the end of the struggle. Repetition of the nightmares leads to "mastery" of the material of the dream only if the individual is able to confront the horrifying images to be found in sleep.

Marr follows up on this notion of mastering the traumatic experience in locating the responsibility for healing upon the patient, rather than upon the doctor who helps bring the trauma to the surface of consciousness:

> The real value of psychotherapy only ends when the confidence that the patient reposes in the physician, passes from the doctor back to the patient himself, so that he acquires confidence in himself. In this sense only is psycho-therapy of value, when the patient recovers the mastery of himself and no longer requires the services of the physician.[78]

The role of the analyst is to draw the patient's attention to the patterns of his thought that are in need of his mastery. Rivers' therapy, outlined more fully in the chapter on Sassoon because of the close relationship that formed between them, noted the tendency for his patients to become fixated upon

events in therapy and observed the repetitive quality of their nightmares as
offering the means for envisioning a new relationship between the soldier
and his traumatic memory. "Mastery" over the experience is not to be found
by enduring the nightmares time and time again. This sort of repetition led
only to the soldier's terror at the prospect of falling asleep. Rivers educated
his patients in methods of altering the memory in order to make its horri-
fying content palatable, advising them in methods of searching for a new
way of seeing either their own behavior during an experience which now
plagued the soldier with feelings of guilt, or their perceived responsibility
for the death of a friend that they were in reality powerless to prevent. Rivers
tells the story of one officer hospitalized for anxiety which was seen to stem
from his perspective upon the traumatizing event:

> He then collapsed after a very trying experience in which he had
> gone out to seek a fellow officer and had found his body blown into
> pieces with head and limbs lying separated from the trunk. From
> that time he had been haunted at night by the vision of his dead and
> mutilated friend.... The problem before me in this case was to find
> some aspect of the painful experience which would allow the patient
> to dwell upon it in such a way as to relieve its horrible and terrifying
> character. The aspect to which I drew his attention was that the
> mangled state of the body of his friend was conclusive evidence that
> the had been killed outright, and had been spared the prolonged
> suffering which is too often fate of those who sustain mortal
> wounds.[79]

Rivers writes that the patient brightened after this novel approach, and as
he set his mind to focus upon this merciful dimension of his friend's death,
his nightmares abated, and he soon had a dream in which he confronted his
friend's body in No Man's Land, removed the items of value, and awoke and
cried out of grief, rather than terror. On a subsequent night, the patient
recalled a dream in which he met the ghost of the dismembered friend, now
whole in body, and conversed with him, telling him of the horror he felt
when discovering his remains.

Re-envisioning one's relationship to the experience does not change the
facts of what has happened, of course, but in the case of this officer, the psy-
chological adjustment Rivers suggested enabled the patient to resume a course
of grieving as part of the resolution of the trauma. The imaginative quality
that characterizes his dreams after the period of adjustment suggests the role
that the creative capacity, both of the doctor who suggested such methods
and the patient who could put them to action, could play in the process of
healing. Marr provides an instance of a patient's relief from nightmares which
results through the process of writing:

> He was asked to narrate exactly what happened to him when he went
> to bed, and commit it to paper. He did so, and the dream no longer
> troubled him.... The explanation of the phenomena of the disappear-
> ance of recurring dreams by ... embodying them in writing, is some-
> what difficult.[80]

Marr claims not to understand the mechanism by which writing could pro-
vide relief and likens the narration of the dream to the reassurance felt from
jotting an important appointment down in a date book, but his analogy has
some merit. This authorial act extends the principle of Rivers' therapeutic
aim of enabling the soldier's revised relationship to the war experience by
making this relationship one of the patient's authoritative control over it.
Both the dream and now the narrative of the event have been the psycho-
logical creations of the soldier, but only the written record is subject to the
patient's conscious manipulations of the events. Marr tells of the "self-ther-
apy" initiated by another officer who took it upon himself to represent his
nightmares artistically:

> Night after night the subject was troubled by the face of a German
> soldier he had killed. He painted the face which appeared in his
> dream, so vividly was it imprinted on his mind on waking. This
> painting he had framed and hung on the wall of his bedroom, and
> from this time the vision ceased to trouble him.[81]

The patient succeeds in healing himself in the same manner as had the officer
who wrote the narrative of his experience — through his own creative capac-
ity which takes the horrors of nightmares, over which he could exert no con-
trol while he slept, and brings the image into the arena of his waking life.
The therapeutic quality of the act of painting comes not simply in repre-
senting the nightmare, but in the patient's "framing" of the horrible expe-
rience into a structure that he can confront during his waking, conscious,
hours, rather than during sleep when consciousness yields to the workings
of the unconscious.

Rivers, in *Conflict and Dream* (1922), makes the point more specifically
about the role of creativity as part of a therapeutic path to wholeness:

> It is possible to take the images of the manifest content of a poem
> and discover more or less exactly how each has been suggested by
> the experience, new or old, of the poet. It is also possible, at any
> rate in many cases, to show how these images are symbolic expres-
> sions of some conflict which is raging in the mind of the poet, and
> that the real underlying meaning or latent content of the poem is
> very different from that which the outward imagery would suggest....
> There is also a striking resemblance with [dreams] in that the poem

may come in a state closely resembling a dissociation from the expe-
rience of ordinary life.[82]

Rivers qualifies his argument of the similar functioning of dreams and poetry
by acknowledging that the poem "is very rarely the immediate product of
the poetic activity, but has been the subject of a lengthy process of a criti-
cal kind, comparable with that which Freud has called the secondary elab-
oration of the dream."[83] But because experiences of the Western Front were
so often so chaotic and horrible, poetry's quality of "dissociation from the
experience of ordinary life" (or in the case of war experience, extraordinary
life) provided a means by which the poet could create structuring devices
that function as critical self-commentary upon the raw material of the war
experience. All of the poets in this study — Owen, Gurney, and Sassoon —
display their own peculiar obsessions about their experience in battle which
surface in their dreams or memories to which they return in poetry. Poems
for each of these men function as the method by which the experience is not
only repeated but re-interpreted so that they can envision new relationships
to the events of war in an effort to achieve psychological stability. Sassoon,
an officer, returns to the theme of abandonment and emotional distance
within his battle nightmares and memories, distance which is at the heart
of his version of shell shock, and he imagines a progression within his poetry
to a state of sympathy and union with his men. For Gurney, returning over
and over again, in letters and poems, to the pleasant memories to found
within the landscape of war provides him with a variety of imaginative
anchors of stability as his mental state deteriorated in the war's wake. For
Wilfred Owen, the image of obsession was that of the ghastly face, a con-
glomeration of the dying faces of soldiers whom Owen commanded as a first
Lieutenant, not unlike the face of the German that the officer painted in
Marr's case study. By the end of Owen's healing from shell shock, his poetic
career, and his life, he will forge a new imaginative relationship to the war
and the participants within it, living and dead.

Owen had a bad stammer upon his arrival at Craiglockhart, which
quickly disappeared as his therapy and his development as a poet began. The
prevalence of disorders of voice suggests that putting the experience into
words forms one of the central difficulties with the soldier's comprehension
or control over the war experience. One of the struggles that the poets within
this study will exhibit in their attempts at psychological healing is their striv-
ing for a poetic idiom which will capture their experiences in warfare in a
manner that enables their controlling and reenvisioning the war linguisti-
cally. All were aware of traditions of English poetry (Owen emulated Keats
in his earliest verse; one hears the rhythms of Hopkins within Gurney) and
of England's most recent war poetry (Sassoon's earliest efforts at recording

the experience echo the idealism of Brooke). But each found that this modern war demanded a new way of speaking than that which they had inherited. To attempt to heal, private Gurney needed to speak only for himself, and at times seems to shut out an audience because of this quality of privacy. But Lieutenants Owen and Sassoon perceived part of their responsibility to their men (responsibility which contributed to their hospitalization) as the creation of public voices to speak for these privates who could not speak for themselves. It is through this public voice that we can understand the reality of life in the trenches of the Great War, but it is through their processes of developing these voices that we can understand the personal, psychological struggle of the war's often silenced participants.

CHAPTER TWO

"By degrees / Regained cool peaceful air in wonder": Wilfred Owen, Shell Shock, and Poetic Identity

Shell Shock and Ergotherapy

Wilfred Owen (1893–1918) displayed his entire process of wounding and healing from shell shock during his final year and a half of life. He spent the first half of the war in France as a civilian, moving from post to post as a tutor for young boys. His letters of 1914 show a young man aware of the global and political significance of the war at its onset but also reflect his reluctance to involve himself in the fighting. On August 8, 1914, he describes the deserted streets of Bagneres-de-Bigorre, France, after all its young men had enlisted. Wilfred, however, was not swept up into the patriotic fervor of these early days; his concern was for being mistaken as a German: "I never wear my spectacles now, as the Legers [the family for whom he worked] say they look foreign."[1] He sums up his attitude to the war to his mother:

> The war affects me less than it ought. But I can do no service to anybody by agitating for news or making dole over the slaughter.... I feel my own life all the more precious and more dear in the presence of this deflowering of Europe. While it is true that the guns will effect a little useful weeding, I am furious with chagrin to think that

the Minds which were to have excelled the civilization of ten thousand years, are being annihilated ... [*Letters* 282].

When the war is an abstraction, as it is at this point, Owen is able to think of it in grand terms of human progress. But this conception reveals Owen's attitudes about class which would be tested in the close quarters of the French trenches. With a callousness in stark contrast to the pity his late poems will display, Owen depicts European civilization as a garden which grows by means of the faculties of its greatest "Minds." The lesser minds exist within the garden as weeds which choke the health of the collective body. He displays a belief that the war will have a purifying function in effecting "a little useful weeding" of some of Europe's less desirable inhabitants, but he regrets that this destruction will extend to those who do not deserve such fates. Such elitist views toward his fellow countrymen emerged from his privileged upbringing, not from any exposure to the rabble whom he considered beneath him. The war would effect a great deal of "weeding," and not much of it useful, to men of all nations and all classes, and in this respect, the trenches were the great levelers of the European class systems. And although Owen would be forced into contact with the lower classes by leading the men of the Lower Ranks, the division of class separating him emotionally from his men will characterize his experience of war and his poetry which seeks to recapture and reinterpret this experience for therapeutic aims when shell shock introduces a psychological obstacle.

In September of 1914, Owen accompanied a doctor friend to a hospital in France where the wounded were treated. Owen registers amazement at the fact that Germans were operated on "without the slightest distinction from the French" (*Letters* 285). Now, closer to the brutal reality of what soldiers endured, Owen forgoes abstraction in favor of immediate and graphic detail:

> One poor devil had his shin-bone crushed by a gun-carriage-wheel, and the doctor had to twist it about and push it like a piston to get out the pus. Another had a hole right through the knee; and the doctor passed a bandage thus.... Another had a head into which a ball had entered and come out again.... I deliberately tell you all this to educate you to the actualities of the war [*Letters* 285].

As if the pus and holes in the head were not enough, Owen includes crude drawings of these wounds in this letter to his brother. This desire to capture the war experience through language and photographic reconstruction foreshadows the technique of realism that would mark Owen's initial war poems before giving way to more complicated representations of battle. These sights made an obvious impact on Owen, and he displays here the same self-consciousness about his role as communicator which characterizes his later feelings about his position as a war poet. But Owen did not see any other such sights for at least two more years. The impact of his hospital visit in 1914, though vivid, was short lived, and he returned to his civilian lifestyle with little discussion of the war through 1915. The contrasting responses to the war in these letters reveal the two "fronts" that Owen would occupy through the war years. As a civilian, it was possible if not to ignore the war, then surely to misunderstand and misrepresent it in terms of the values it seemed to represent when it began, such as patriotism, heroism, and the embodiment of class distinctions. As a soldier, however, Owen came to see, as did most other soldiers, the emptiness of these values and the impracticality and inaccuracy of his inherited Victorian elitism. As a poet who would soon find himself recovering from shell shock, he sought to replace these values with a construction of his understanding of an alternative and personal purpose for the fighting.

Unable to ignore the war any longer, Owen enlisted in October of 1915. While his letters through most of 1916 as he trained to be an officer show a man able to block the war out of his mind, the life he was forced to endure in the trenches, beginning in late December 1916, made the physical and psychological reality of suffering central to his experience. On the last day of 1916, he arrived at the front lines in France and was given command over a platoon of infantrymen participating in the final days of the Battle of the Somme. He fought, experiencing the same movement from the front to support to rear trenches as did all soldiers, from January to May of 1917. Though the letters from the front, mainly written to his mother, reveal Owen to be in control of his faculties, the war was taking its toll during these months of exposure. To understand both the specific nature of his shell shock that incapacitated him after these few months of fighting and to demonstrate the way that poetry of war could assist Owen in psychological recovery, even after his prescribed therapy at Craiglockhart would end in November 1917, one can look first at "The Sentry," one of Owen's last poems he would complete before his death in November 1918.

"The Sentry" grounds itself in the concrete fact of physical battle to unite Owen's most defining war experience into a coherent narrative and to reshape the experience into a form indicative of his psychological growth. The raw material of the poem comes from an experience during Owen's first stint in the trenches in mid January 1917, two weeks after he arrived, but the completion of the poem occurs over a year and a half later in France after Owen has suffered through his shell shock, recovered, and returned to the lines. The span of time Owen spent in shaping the poem through a series of drafts overlaps almost exactly the period of his recovery — from

Craiglockhart in August of 1917 to France, back at the front lines, in September of 1918. Owen could not resolve his difficulties in revising the poem into a satisfactory form until he had returned to the front and was once again experiencing the sort of combat that provided the poem's subject matter. He writes to Sassoon from France on September 22, 1918, "You said it would be a good thing for my poetry if I went back. That is my consolation for feeling a fool. This is what shells scream at me every time: Haven't you got the wits to keep out of this?" (*Letters* 578). In fact, it was not only a good thing for his poetry that he return, but it was a necessary thing for the poet's own mental condition because the completion of the return enabled Owen to face up to the trauma that had forced his removal from the lines and to represent the confrontation through the poem. In "The Sentry," Owen confronts more directly than anywhere else the "facts" of his combat experiences, as recorded in his letters. In a letter from January 16, 1917, Owen describes to his mother (whom he never spared from the truth of combat) the most vivid and terrifying war experience that he would ever endure:

> I can see no excuse for deceiving you about these last 4 days. I have suffered seventh hell.
> I have not been at the front.
> I have been in front of it.
> I held an advanced post, that is, a dug-out in the middle of No Man's Land.
> Three quarters dead, I mean each of us 3/4 dead, we reached the dug-out and relieved the wretches therein. I then had to go forth and find another dug-out for a still more advanced post where I left 18 bombers. I was responsible for other posts on the left but there was a junior officer in charge.
> My dug-out held 25 men tightly packed. Water filled it to a depth of 1 or 2 feet, leaving say 4 feet of air.
> The Germans knew we were staying there and decided we shouldn't.
> Those fifty hours were the agony of my happy life.
> Every ten minutes on Sunday afternoon seemed an hour.
> I nearly broke down and let myself drown in the water that was now slowly rising over my knees....
> In the Platoon on my left the sentries over the dug-out were blown to nothing. One of these poor fellows was my first servant whom I rejected. If I had kept him he would have lived, for servants don't do Sentry Duty. I kept my own sentries halfway down the stairs during the more terrific bombardment. In spite of this one lad was blown down and, I am afraid, blinded [*Letters* 427–28].

This letter shows the source of Owen's feelings of guilt that will contribute to the shell-shock to which he will succumb three months later. One of the sentries to die was once his servant whom he "rejected." The word choice connotes his prior judgment of the man as undesirable for serving him, and in Owen's mind, the capability to judge others granted to officers has caused this man's death. This sentry, at the time of the shelling, was under the command of the junior officer in charge of "the Platoon on [his] left," a man whom Owen likewise commanded. By rejecting the sentry, Owen has lost the ability to oversee his subordinate's safety but still maintains ultimate charge over him. So in short, Owen finds himself both responsible for and powerless to prevent his death. The other casualty within the poem compounds his feelings of guilt more vividly and immediately. Although Owen "kept his own sentries half way down the stairs," one of these men was wounded and blinded by the attack. Here Owen acts to protect the men he is required to lead, but his commands to stay out of fire are ineffectual in the face of the "terrific bombardment." He has the authority and power to act, but the violence of the war renders all actions futile. Hibberd comments, "in the dugout, he had to act as a father, ordering, encouraging, consoling — carrying responsibility and guilt."[2] Owen finds himself trapped within a situation that holds him culpable but offers no means of preventing the result, precisely the conflict that manifests itself as shell shock.

In the poem, Owen conflates the wounded and killed soldiers into the single figure of the blinded, dying sentry as a way of bringing the chaotic experience into a condensed and manageable form which, although retelling events out of his control, is subject to his creative control. "The Sentry" establishes a battle scene whose participants are united in their common terror from the bombardment:

> We'd found an old Boche dug-out, and he knew,
> And gave us hell; for shell on frantic shell
> Lit full on top, but never quite burst through.
> Rain, guttering down in waterfalls of slime,
> Kept slush waist-high and rising hour by hour,
> And choked the steps too thick with clay to climb.
> What murk of air remained stank old, and sour
> With fumes from whizz-bangs, and the smell of men
> Who'd lived there years, and left their curse in the den,
> If not their corpses....[3]

The time all men spend in the dug-out is characterized as a bombardment of all their senses, forcing them into the state of passivity that psychologists saw as contributing to the onset of shell shock as a response to such intolerable conditions. Not only do the shells present a continuous threat, but elements of nature — the rain and mud — work to enclose the Platoon within a constricted space so that the men are even more aware of their collective misery. The confinement is so pervasive that it manifests itself through smells which seem to have been there for years. The moment of crisis — the wounding — establishes the degrees of difference between the wounded man, the speaker, and the rest of the platoon. The shell that finds their door at last introduces a new rhythm to the poem:

> Buffeting eyes and breath, snuffing the candles,
> And thud! flump! thud! down the steep steps came thumping
> And sploshing in the flood, deluging muck,
> The sentry's body; then his rifle, handles
> Of old Boche bombs, and mud in ruck on ruck.
> We dredged it up, for dead, until he whined,
> "O sir — my eyes, — I'm blind, — I'm blind, — I'm blind" [ll. 12–18].

The long second line, with its seven stresses, which departs from the dominant iambic pentameter, denotes the violent change in the collective experience of the men. The subject, "The sentry's body," is withheld until the end of the sentence to reflect this disruption, and the body becomes a thing in a series of objects tumbling down the stairs. To the speaker, the sentry has become "it," no longer human until able to speak.

The remainder of "The Sentry" undergoes a complex and ultimately an emotionally satisfying process because of the feelings of guilt and responsibility which are revealed and explored. The sentry was initially dehumanized when thought to be dead; upon hearing him speak, the speaker once again gives him life. Kerr observes that when the sentry speaks, he "single[s] the officer out from the group (though he can see none of them) in an appeal *de profundis*, but the officer hears his voice as a whine, an undignified, unpleasant, and unwelcome noise."[4] The speaker suddenly introduces an "I" into the poem for the first time to distinguish himself from the rest of the men in the dug-out because of his rank:

> Coaxing, I held a flame against his lids
> And said if he could see the least blurred light
> He was not blind; in time they'd get all right.
> "I can't," he sobbed. Eyeballs, huge-bulged like squids',
> Watch my dreams still, — yet I forgot him there
> In posting Next for duty, and sending a scout
> To beg a stretcher somewhere, and flound'ring about
> To other posts under the shrieking air [ll. 19–26].

This passage displays Owen's ability to register the complexity in his speaker's response. As soon as the "I" enters this poem, the speaker engages in action and speech to decrease the emotional distance between himself and the man. The speaker realizes that the man has been blinded because of, in his mind, his own failure, and thus Owen introduces the nightmarish image of the bulging eyes that bridge the time between the event in the past and the speaker's present. This image of the ghastly face, "haunting [him] still" in September 1918, lies at the heart of Owen's recurrent nightmares that plagued him intermittently during the entire year and half of recuperation and surfaces in different forms in poems such as "Dulce et Decorum Est" and "Mental Cases," written before Owen's sustained examination of it in this poem.

Kerr states, "The speaker's rank, and his responsibility for what has happened, effectively isolate him and alienate him from the group, not only from the gibbering sentry with his repulsive blind eyes..., but also from the other soldiers...."[5] The speaker remains grounded within the details that have produced the nightmare in order to contend with the unresolved experience. Owen combines into a single sentence the paradox of forgetting and remembering that this poetic vehicle allows him to resolve: "Eyeballs ... / Watch my dreams still, — yet I forgot him there." Part of Owen's guilt stems from having forgotten the sentry's suffering in turning to other responsibilities — finding a new sentry, getting a stretcher, and moving to the other posts under his watch. He needs to forget the immediate problem of this dying man in order to uphold his duties on behalf of everyone else in the dug-out. Resuming these duties, however, becomes a source of guilt as well; to forget the man and to turn elsewhere is to sever the connection between the two of them — which the poem has established between all the soldiers, which the bombardment has disrupted, and which the speaker has sought to reconstruct through his words to the sentry. Unconsciously, he will keep the memory and connection alive through feelings of guilt manifested as nightmarish image of the eyes, but Owen's ability to write not just of the effects of the unconscious but also to recall the conscious decision to act in opposition to this memory enables him to go to work on the feelings of guilt. He conveys, along with guilt for having survived, the victory achieved through personal survival and the fulfillment of duty. In other words, the poem offers Owen the vehicle to write of his remembering of the sentry in a way that combines the memory with the necessity of forgetting.

The conclusion of the poem provides Owen with a further opportunity to remember and forget, and thus to package the experience from the past into a form he can assimilate emotionally in the present:

> Those other wretches, how they bled and spewed,
> And one who would have drowned himself for good, —
> I try not to remember these things now.
> Let Dread hark back for one word only: how,

> Half-listening to that sentry's moans and jumps,
> And the wild chattering of his shivered teeth,
> Renewed most horribly whenever crumps
> Pummelled the roof and slogged the air beneath,—
> Through the dense din, I say, we heard him shout
> "I see your lights!"—But ours had long gone out [ll. 27–36].

The futility of the line, "I try not to remember these things now," is clear. The existence of the memory in some form is unavoidable, but this ending shows the control the author seeks over the form that the memory will take. It is significant that he says, "I try not to remember," rather than, "I try to forget," particularly since his letter to his mother has revealed that he was the one who fought off the impulse to drown himself in the rising water. Trying to forget would be to attempt to act in order to rid the memory of these fifty hours from consciousness altogether, an impossible task. But to try not to remember is to control the persistence and recurrence of the memory. These final lines show the speaker engaging with the memory of the dying man in a way that will allow for the memory's inevitable existence but will temper its effect through the context within which the speaker places it and the interpretation for which he allows in retrospect. He claims to be "Half-hearing"—in effect to remember and forget at the same time—but his ear seems especially engaged in the moans, jumps, and chatters that cannot be shut out.

Though the speaker will "try not to remember," he will also "Let Dread hark back for one word only." That is, he will not change the subject to drive the memory back to the unconscious where it will recur through nightmare, but he will instead consciously give it voice. He grants the memory the final word: "how / ... we heard him shout / 'I see your lights!'—But ours had long gone out." This ending sanctions the death of the sentry as more than a wasted life. He had been unable to see the light when the speaker instructed him earlier in the poem, but now, when the actual lights around them all had gone out, the sentry sees light of a different sort, which the reader takes to mean his removal from suffering through death, perhaps to an afterlife. The final word he grants Dread, in other words, conjures up the memory of the sentry's death, but Owen conquers Dread by converting this memory into one with the possibility of value in the life lost. This possible value provides Owen with an alternative he had not explored in his year and half of war poetry preceding "The Sentry." The "I" establishes itself at the moment when the sentry is wounded and is thus distinguished from the collective body. He remains within the scene even as the sentry slips away toward death and whatever that offers while Owen himself rejoins the collective whole represented by the pronouns "we" and "ours," distinct from the voice and experience of the sentry. At the end of the poem, then, Owen is not isolated in personal nightmare but is back with the group of men that are his charge. Furthermore, though a part of this group, he also asserts his position as spokesperson for the men. In the line, "Through the dense din, I say, we heard him shout," the phrase, "I say" seems nothing more than a foot to fill out the line. However, this phrase provides Owen the opportunity to be the distinct poetic voice that speaks for all who have heard and seen, himself included. Owen has done much more in this poem than to retell the events listed in his letter where he had concluded his narrative with the fact of the blinding of the sentry. Poetically, he conflates the blinding of one man with the death of another not to change the facts but to represent the episode in a manner that allows for the memory of it to possess a therapeutic function. He strikes a balance between the feelings of responsibility that he can never ignore and the necessity of surviving and carrying on. And he imaginatively reconstructs the fact of the blinding, through the imagery of light, into an ending that offers the possibility for value within the experience.

This late poem reveals the method by which poetry could possess a therapeutic function for the sufferer of shell shock. Therapies which addressed symptoms of the condition could restore some control to the patient over his body but neglected the trauma within the mind. Owen, however, sees that to resolve the conflict at the heart of his reaction to the war he must return to the source of the trauma. To repress or ignore the terrifying memories of battle will result in their surfacing in nightmare, as Sassoon will vividly demonstrate in his poem "Repressions of War Experience." But the conscious control afforded through the vehicle of the poem allows Owen to subject the nightmare to the forces of imagination which can shape it and extract value from what had been solely traumatic. Dr. Rivers would instruct Sassoon on the strategies of such re-examination; Gurney, ignored by military and civilian authorities in the war's aftermath until his psychosis convinced his family they could ignore his troubles no longer, came upon the search for value within the memories of battle himself. For Owen, the process by which he arrives at this mature perspective upon the war occurs through a gradual finding of his poetic voice, a process begun by his therapist but completed on the poet's terms, a process which, sadly, leads to Owen's death at the end of the war.

Though no cases of shell shock are "typical," Owen's fell into a common pattern. The primary cause of Owen's trauma can be established as having been a single vivid and horrifying experience — the days spent in the dug out, in which he played the role of passive observer. Hibberd also chronicles an experience (Owen's letter to his mother about it has been lost) — in the trenches when Owen fell into a fifteen foot hole and was trapped for over a day, concluding that the event marked "the end of his 'exuberance' at being an officer who had done his honourable bit and survived."[6] But the event that precipitated the onset of his symptoms of stammering and disorientation would not occur for three more months, when a shell blast threw him into the air and left him face to face with a dead companion.[7] He provides "his own dearest Mother" with a description of the harrowing incident in April:

> For twelve days we lay in holes, where at any moment a shell might put us out. I think the worst incident was one wet night when we lay up against a railway embankment. A big shell lit on the top of the bank, just 2 yards from my head. Before I awoke, I was blown in the air right away from the bank! I passed most of the following days in a railway Cutting, in a hole just big enough to lie in, and covered with corrugated iron. My brother officer ... lay opposite in a similar hole. But he was covered with earth, and no relief will ever relieve him, nor will his Rest be a 9 days-Rest [*Letters* 452].

A week later, Owen's letters were addressed from the Casualty Clearing Station:

> The Doctor suddenly was moved to forbid me to go into action next time the Battalion goes.... I did not go sick or anything, but he is nervous about my nerves, and sent me down yesterday — labelled Neurasthenia.... [M]y nerves have not come out without a scratch. Do not for a moment suppose I have had a "breakdown." I am simply avoiding one [*Letters* 453].

Two days later he remarks to his mother, "Some of us have been sent down here [to the Clearing Station] as a little mad. Possibly I am among them" (*Letters* 454). The Casualty Clearing Stations, located near the front, had as their goal the rapid return of the soldiers to the trenches. Owen's condition, though, must have impressed his doctor, William Brown, as severe enough to warrant a lengthier stay and subsequent hospitalization, despite the determination to present himself to his mother as mentally intact.[8] These letters from the clearing station are characteristic of those chronicling his shell-shock. He acknowledges that there is some truth to the doctor's diagnosis, but he does so by avoiding any direct discussion of his condition and infuses his revelations to his mother with wit to suggest that he is in control of his faculties. In describing his ordeal in the shell hole, he stops short of describing the dead man beside him other than through subversions of military jargon.

At this point, Owen appears reluctant or incapable of putting the full extent of his suffering into words to his mother. Owen will be seen to eliminate his inability to confront his condition by means of the construction of strategies of self-revelation and self-healing achieved within the poetry which create for Owen a new, public voice. In June 1917, Owen was admitted to Craiglockhart Hydropathic Hospital Establishment, a healing ground for shell shocked officers, outside Edinburgh, Scotland. His most noticeable symptom was a stammer, displaying his inability to speak fully about the war or anything else. He remained at the hospital from June to late October 1917. After his release from Craiglockhart, classified as fit for light duty, Owen was stationed in Scarborough and later in Ripon where he lived an almost civilian lifestyle, retraining as an officer, writing poetry, and rebuilding his health. He returned to active duty on September 1, 1918 and served until he died in battle in the final week of the war. The months that made Owen the greatest poet of the First World War are those beginning with his hospitalization in June 1917 and ending with his death seventeen months later. It is a critical commonplace to see Owen's arrival at Craiglockhart as marking the turning point in his career — beginning his evolution from an imitator of the poetic styles of Swinburne and Keats to a poetic spokesperson for soldiers of the war. Leafing through the collected poems, one finds quite striking the shift in tone and subject matter during these initial months of recovery. In May of 1917 after having endured the experience in the dug out and the days face to face with a dead companion, he writes not about the experience but composes the sonnet, "How Do I Love Thee," in which he exclaims, "I cannot woo thee as the lion his mate." But written August of the same year as his psychological healing began, a poem like "The Dead-Beat" displays a radically different idiom: "Next day I heard the Doc's well-whiskied laugh: / 'That scum you sent last night soon died. Hooray!" (*Poems* 63, 121). The change from a late decadent to a modern did not occur overnight. This year marked Owen's finding of his voice as a spokesperson for soldiers incapable of telling their own stories, and this voice functioned as the means by which Owen achieved his recovery and return to the fighting. The shell shock which occurred four months after his entry into the trenches displayed symptoms of anxiety disorders, most commonly observed within the officer class. In order for Owen to recover he must confront the conflict between personal safety and the responsibility and guilt for the suffering of others which lies at the heart of his response to the war. Owen's poetry of convalescence will display the disparity of class but will lead also to the elimination of this distance, and by means of this process, he will assume the role of the public poet to speak against the war.

Much critical space has been devoted to the most formative relationship of Owen's poetic career, his friendship with Sassoon, whom he met at Craiglockhart in August of 1917.[9] Owen's daily discussions with Sassoon between August and October taught Owen the value of irony and the use of vernacular, rather than ornate, language in his poetry. Owen's letters provide ample testament to the impact the man and his verse had upon him, as Owen mustered the courage in August to approach the older poet and ask him to inscribe five copies of Sassoon's 1916 volume, *The Old Hunstman and Other Poems*. His excitement continues in a letter soon after this meeting:

> After leaving him, I wrote something in Sassoon's style ["The Dead-Beat"]. ...So the last thing he said was "Sweat your guts out writing poetry!" "Eh?" says I. "Sweat your guts out, I say!" ... He himself is 30! Looks under 25! ... Would you mind sending me *all the MSS* verse of mine in your keeping as soon as you can get at them? ... Cheero! I'm well enough by day, and generally so by night. A better mode of life than this present I could not practically manage [*Letters* 485–87].

Sassoon's poetic impact was almost immediate, and Owen sought approval for all of his work, which he modeled upon Sassoon's approach to the war. The tone of this letter suggests as well Sassoon's noticeable and positive effect upon Owen's mood, though the fact that Owen was only "generally" well enough "by night" suggests that he was settling into a pattern of nightmares which often accompanied the early stages of recuperation. When the period of hero worship faded and the two became friends, regarding each other as the superior poet, a more powerful force became the personal impetus for Owen's poetry — the very reason for his hospitalization, shell-shock. He was not forthcoming himself about the extent of his suffering, and he puts on a cheerful face for his mother, his most frequent correspondent, and for Sassoon who describes his first impression of Owen in *Siegfried's Journey* (1945): "He spoke with a slight stammer, which was no unusual thing in that neurosis-pervaded hospital."[10] But Sassoon confesses surprise after discovering the actual horrors which Owen had suffered and which Owen had never revealed to him nor had his demeanor revealed:

> I discovered that Wilfred had endured worse things than I had realized from the little he told me. On arriving at the Western Front he had immediately encountered abominable conditions of winter weather and attrition warfare. But of this he merely remarked to me that he wished he'd had my luck in being inured to the beastly business by gradual stages. His thick dark hair was already touched with white above the ears. As I remember him during those three months we spent together at Craiglockhart he was consistently cheerful.[11]

Even in the stance affected in his letters, Owen appeared intact, unlike those around him suffering from more visible hysterical disorders. Beneath this

facade lay the true extent of his emotional trauma, however. Norgate sur-
mises that Owen's symptoms were probably characteristic of anxiety neu-
roses; he was "tense, withdrawn, depressed, suffering from nightmares,
afflicted with a slight stammer."[12] Owen's poetry will engage in a similar con-
trast between the physical appearance of participants of the war and the psy-
chological torment cloaked by this appearance. The stammer from which
Owen suffered would soon leave, perhaps as soon as he began the process of
developing a confident poetic voice.

These nightmares, characteristic of the anxiety states, are the major
complaint Owen records in his letters: on August 15, "having ... some very
bellicose dreams of late"; on September 2, "disastrous dreams" (*Letters* 486,
490). Though after his release he appears to be somewhat healed, the dreams
return in a letter on June 24, 1918 from Scarborough: "War dreams have
begun again; but that is because of the flapping of the canvas all night in
the high winds; or else the hideous faces of the Advancing Revolver Targets
I fired at last week" (*Letters* 560). The persistence of these dreams, during
his stay at Craiglockhart and also many months after he was released "fit,"
in these first-person accounts of his experience, suggests lingering psychical
damage beyond that which his prescribed therapy could approach. Accord-
ing to Freud's theories, the repeated rumination in nightmares upon the
mangled faces he had witnessed in battle reflects Owen's struggle to master
the material of his memories, and the resurfacing of the image of the "hideous
face" seen here in the target dummies suggests that his therapy left the trau-
matic experiences untouched and as yet, unmastered. In discussing Owen's
first six weeks at Craiglockhart which eased the superficial manifestations of
his shell-shock, Norgate states, "Owen was by no means in such 'good shape'
as outwardly may have appeared. If the evidence of his writing is to be
believed, he had barely begun to articulate the deepest levels of his shell-
shock."[13] How exactly, then, was the process of healing enacted? To what
extent was Owen aware of his own need for rebuilding an identity if his let-
ters continued to claim that although shaken, he was never broken?

Sassoon's advice to "sweat your guts out writing poetry" has much in
common with the psychotherapy administered by Owen's primary doctor at
Craiglockhart, Arthur Brock, a proponent of ergotherapy, healing by means
of work and activity. The idea behind such therapy was "to encourage [the]
patients' involvement in a variety of practical projects and activities aimed
at restoring in them the healthy, 'normal' relationship with their environ-
ment which had been disrupted by war."[14] Practitioners of ergotherapy, such
as Brock, derived their theories from the thinking of the sociologist, Patrick
Geddes, who argued that fundamental sociological problems stem from
disrupted relationships between the "Place-work-folk" triad, which Brock

translated into the biological construct of "organism-function-environment."[15] When individuals felt alienated from their surroundings, they were unable to see how their efforts played an active role in harmonizing the individuals within the social system and their collective environment. Brock's theories shared much in common with those who saw shell shock as a flight from an intolerable reality; he argued that in the cases which came to be classified as shell-shock during the war, this alienation manifested itself through symptoms such as depression, paralysis, amnesia, or stammering. Brock took a tough-love approach to their cure, but his use of discipline distinguishes him from men like Lewis Yealland to whom Brock's stern demeanor suggested a resemblance. Men such as Yealland saw recovery from the condition as dependent upon the doctor's establishing command over the patient's illness, and the electrodes were the means by which the patient was brought back into the political order. To Yealland the means of "healing" lay completely within the hands of the doctor attempting to eradicate the symptoms; the role of the patient was to submit to the power structure of military authority. Brock's form of disciplinary treatment located the responsibility for recovery in the power of the soldier experiencing the psychological conflict. He postulated that these soldiers suffered from "ergophobia," or fear of effort, and had "allowed themselves to become weak."[16] Brock believed that rest would only exacerbate the malady by reinforcing the soldiers' feelings of helplessness. Rather, to heal, the individual needed to see that his actions could contribute to the health of the social body, and the doctor's role was to assist in this re-envisioning.

To counter the considerable force of inertia associated with ergophobia, treatment would be a regimented schedule of work. Brock's ideas, however, differed from other "work cures" which amounted to little more than busy work, such as basket weaving or necklace making, in his insistence that the efforts be expended not for the sake of exercise or distraction but for a moral purpose. The sufferer of shell-shock must see that his activity contributed to the health of his own body and to the health of the entire social body, in this case Craiglockhart. According to Brock, in fact, the person could not be healed unless he was able to see the value of improving the community at large. Almost as soon as Owen arrived at the hospital, Brock instituted a regimen of social activities for him. Owen became one of the founding members of the "Field Club" at Craiglockhart, an organization that studied and gave lectures about the natural environment around Edinburgh. On July 30, Owen delivered his lecture titled, "Do Plants Think?" in which he argued, along the lines of Brock's theories about organism and environment, that the apparatus for detecting and responding to sunlight, water, and temperature within plants was analogous to human sensory organs. Owen also participated in the Boys' Training Club, in which he worked with scout troops and headed a class in literature, tutored local boys in Edinburgh with their studies, toured the Edinburgh slums, and acted in plays put on by other patients. The activity that took up most his time, however, was editing the hospital magazine, *The Hydra,* which published announcements of hospital activities, editorials written by patients, and soldiers' poetry, including contributions from both Sassoon and Owen.

All this activity kept Owen extremely busy and, if the tone of his letters is any indication, happy during his stay at the hospital — at least on the surface. Sassoon goes so far as to claim in 1945 that "Dr. Brock, who was in charge of his case, had been completely successful in restoring the balance of his nerves."[17] Owen gives his mother a taste of the many roles he had the opportunity to play while recuperating:

> At present I am a sick man in hospital, by night; a poet, for quarter of an hour after breakfast; I am whatever and whoever I see while going down to Edinburgh on the tram: greengrocer, policeman, shopping lady, errand boy, paper-boy, blind man, crippled Tommy, bank-clerk, carter, all of these in half an hour; next a German student in earnest; then I either peer over bookstalls in back-streets, or do a bit of a dash down Princes Street,— according as I have taken weak tea or strong coffee for breakfast [*Letters* 480–81].

This letter demonstrates two possible effects that ergotherapy had upon Owen's recovery. On the one hand, he was feeling quite useful to the community of the hospital and of the city outside. His letters provide almost daily updates of places visited, people met, talks delivered, and lessons taught. He seems, however, to regret the short amount of time the activity leaves him to be a poet, and Owen reveals a sense of fragmented identity brought about as Brock's therapy forced him into several roles, all of which made use of his considerable skills and intelligence but which also denied a single identity to which he might hope to attach himself.

Like all therapies for shell-shock, Brock's method had as its ultimate goal the wounded officer's return to the fighting as soon as possible, even though those who studied the condition concluded that such an aim was misguided in terms of military expedience. Practicality seems to lie at the heart of Brock's method, but Kerr sees a humanistic element within it as well:

> Brock offered an explanation of their condition not as a shameful aberration but as a particularly sensitive, particularly tragic registration of a disease that was nothing less than the modern world; and his ergotherapeutic approach turned them back towards the world, rather than in upon themselves, for an understanding and some way out of their predicament.[18]

Brock believed that if the individual could perceive himself as in part dictating the moral course of the social unit at the hospital, then when he was reintroduced to the social body of a platoon, he would act and lead with moral authority for the good of all soldiers involved. This leap from hospital to the trenches is somewhat problematic. Brock had the responsibility for reintegrating these men as quickly as possible, and his no-nonsense approach yielded the desired results. And, granted, unlike the hypnotic or electroshock therapies which relied upon the doctor's control, ergotherapy did put the responsibility for healing in the hands of the patient. But like those measures, Brock's therapy did not approach the central trauma and conflict within Owen's specific experience which had caused his condition. Ignoring such trauma and conflict and dictating that the patient play multiple roles led Owen to a fragmentation, rather than a solidification, of identity. Brock as well did not have the personal experience of the trenches that lingered in the memories of the actual sufferers. Hibberd states, "Arthur Brock's RAMC uniform sat awkwardly on his bony frame and had never been near a battlefield; his authority came from his seriousness and learning, not from his rank."[19] While the soldier certainly could come to see the value, whether practical or moral, of overcoming the symptoms of shell shock while at the hospital, convincing him of the moral urgency of returning to fight for a cause in which few soldiers in late 1917 could believe posed a greater challenge.

Furthermore, Brock's theories did not make room for confronting any possible moral uncertainty about the value of leading a group of men to slaughter in an attack, and since the men at Craiglockhart were mainly officers, their shell-shock had been brought on not simply by having witnessed the horrors but having led their men into the horrors that they themselves witnessed. In other words, the psychological cause of shell-shock symptoms such as Owen's stemmed not from his alienation from the work that contributed to the moral strength of the social whole, but from his unconscious recognition that the "work" of leading his men led to the moral wrong of these men's destruction. Norgate feels that Owen "was acutely aware of his own apparent inability to do anything for these men — except, in giving orders, further to perpetuate their suffering."[20] Guilt for having acted as a leader in battle plagued officers as much as did their fear of acting again. While Brock's therapies began the healing process by showing the sufferers that their work could improve the social body, his therapies reveal their shortcomings when they are used to reintegrate the individual into a world where the business of work was perceived to contribute to upholding morally untenable ends.

So this "work-cure" left Owen somewhat in the lurch: he could resist the remedy and remain shell-shocked, incapable of doing anything; or he could participate once again in the business and activity of life to prepare himself for the activity of bringing more suffering upon himself and others in the trenches. Or he could search for another alternative. Poetry becomes for Owen the means to complete what Brock's methods had begun by enabling Owen to create a vision of his role as poet and spokesperson that would give his return to the trenches the moral purpose that the goals ergotherapy left out of the equation. Though his methods did possess this moral shortcoming, Brock also enabled Owen to begin the process of confronting these feelings of guilt and moral responsibility through therapeutic conversation. Though not as reliant upon these methods as was his colleague Dr. Rivers, Brock did utilize analytic discussion, though he "had less time for talking [because] his patients needed to work."[21] Brock felt that nightmares such as Owen's "were an expression of failure and guilt." But his approach to eliminating them is striking: "The way to deal with them was to face up strenuously to what they represented and resolve to do better."[22] Owen seems to have internalized such advice as he describes his efforts to assert conscious control over the workings of his unconscious mind. Months after his release, in a letter to his mother written February 18, 1918, Owen claims to "*bring on* what few war dreams I now have, entirely by *willingly* considering war of an evening" (*Letters* 534). Such a willed immersion in the images that have tormented him suggests Owen's decision to take control over his memories and experiences. If he can will the recurrence of the nightmares, he can bring the content of his unconscious to the surface where it will be subject to conscious, and as Owen had discovered by this point, artistic control. Brock suggests in *Health and Conduct* (1923) that his therapy had been successful in bringing on Owen's confrontation with his guilt. Brock calls Owen "one who having in the most literal sense 'faced the phantoms of the mind' had *all but* laid them ere the last call came; they still appear in his poetry but he fears them no longer."[23] The phrase "all but laid them" acknowledges room for Owen's further recuperation beyond that which Brock could administer. Brock suggests here that to place the offending images within the poems is a means to conquer the fears. He too could take credit for reaffirming for Owen the value of the struggle with one's consciousness that poetry could offer.

Shortly after Owen's arrival, Brock learned of his poetic interest and set him to work on a poem based upon the myth of Antaeus and Hercules, warning him in doing so that art must have a function and to "beware of Art for Art's sake."[24] The myth served as a metaphor for Brock's theories of ergotherapy, and he conducted his sessions with patients underneath a large mural of the mythological story. Brock discussed his explanation of the myth's significance in an essay printed in *The Hydra*:

In a wrestling combat [Antaeus] could not be overthrown as long as his feet were on his Mother Earth. When he was raised off the earth his strength rapidly failed, only to be renewed again at the first contact with the soil. Finally Hercules, seeing this, lifted him bodily up in the air, and holding him there, crushed him to death in his arms.

Now surely every officer who comes to Craiglockhart recognises that, in a way, he is himself an Antaeus who has been taken from his Mother Earth and well-nigh crushed to death by the war giant or military machine.[25]

When the patient becomes separated from his environment, Mother Earth, his strength fails. Connection once again with the world enables him to engage in the struggle with the forces that sought to disconnect him — in Owen's case, the war. During the last meeting between the two, December of 1917, Brock's first word to the poet was, "Antaeus!" (*Letters* 517). Owen attacked the project with enthusiasm; he resolved, in early July, 1917, "On The Hercules-Antaeus Subject ... I shall do a Sonnet" (*Letters* 476). Two weeks later, he had given up on the idea of restraining the topic to the sonnet form and reported to his mother, "About 50 lines are now done" (*Letters* 477). And the following day, he assessed his progress:

> These are the best lines, methinks: (N.B. Antaeus deriving strength from his Mother Earth nearly licked old Herk.)

> ... How Earth herself empowered him with her touch,
> Gave him the grip and stringency of winter,
> And all the ardour of th' invincible Spring;
> How all the blood of June glutted his heart.
> And all the glow of huge autumnal storms
> Stirred on his face, and flickered from his eyes [*Letters* 478].

Owen titled the poem "The Wrestlers" which grew to over ninety lines of blank verse. His selection of these lines as the strongest suggests at least a partial belief in the theories of Brock — that the earth or environment is the source of personal strength. However, the preponderance of description about Hercules at the expense of the poem's hero, as Hibberd has noted,[26] suggests also that the enemy of personal health, the war — rather than thorough self-examination through poetry — occupied the forefront of Owen's mind at these early stages.

This exercise proved to be significant for Owen's development into a war poet for two reasons: Brock's influence persuaded Owen to direct his energies to the considerable "work" of representing the war in poems, and the poem itself mirrored the struggle for emotional footing Owen himself was going through. The work of editing, teaching, lecturing, and acting may have helped to cure the symptoms of his stammer and depression, but it was his poetry, begun at Craiglockhart and continuing after his discharge and through his second tour of the trenches, that allowed for the complete confrontation of the shell shock which continued to manifest itself through feelings of guilt and nightmares. The role of the poet was the one he began, especially after his meeting with Sassoon in August, to adopt as his calling. In the letter from Scarborough in February, 1918, claiming to bring his night-mares on deliberately in order to provide himself with poetic material and inspiration, he explains: "I do so because I have my duty to perform towards War" (*Letters* 534), recognizing that it is within the content of these night-mares that the means of fulfilling this duty lies. To his cousin, Leslie Gun-ston, Owen claims about the importance of his work to his time, "I suppose I am doing in poetry what the advanced composers are doing in music" (*Let-ters* 531). Much as modernist music sought a new means of expressing the conditions of modern life, Owen saw the need for the construction of a new poetic voice to confront what he had endured. Furthermore, it was the need to confront his experiences from his first tour of duty that compelled Owen's verse to move beyond mere photographic reconstruction of war and beyond Sassoon's model of protest and satire. The ultimate vision to which Owen's progression of war poems strove was that of a completely unified world. He adopted Brock's notion of the individual's harmony with his environment, but only by working through the content of his battle dreams poetically was Owen able to achieve a vision of war where soldiers, the poet, and the land-scape of war were united in a common moral purpose.

This "duty" of poetry seems a likely way for this particular individual to undertake the process of reconstituting a coherent self. Poetry had pro-vided Owen with the single thread of continuity between his youth and his life as a soldier. He had been writing poems since 1909, most early ones showing the obvious influence of Keats and the Romantics, and he displayed a specific affection for the sonnet form. In fact, of the one hundred and three completed poems in Stallworthy's edition of *Poems of Wilfred Owen*, over one third are sonnets. More than twenty of these either were written and completed in their entirety at Craiglockhart or were revised from their orig-inal states, written at various points earlier, to their final forms during this hospital stay. Owen and Sassoon would engage in writing contests to con-struct quick sonnets in imitation of the propaganda being passed off as war poetry in the popular press. In a letter, he describes a meeting with Harold Monro about his poetry: "[H]e was 'very struck' with these sonnets. He went over the things in detail and he told me what was fresh and clever, and what was second-hand and banal; and what Keatsian and what 'modern'" (*Letters* 384). The sonnet form provided Owen with the forum to make the transition from a poet of imitation to one of modern creation. As countless poets before him have illustrated, the sonnet lends itself to and demands great control by the poet over the subject matter. The variant structures of the sonnet are suitable for poetic argument, for structures of point and counterpoint, and for ironic reversals of theme and subversions of the readers' expectations. And most significantly, the sonnet form offers the opportunity for closure, for the "last word" of the concluding couplet or the sestet to "answer" questions raised by earlier portions of the poem. All these characteristics of the form make it a likely choice for Owen, whose mental state upon arrival demonstrated the need for structure.

Owen's Search for a Language: The Poetic Confrontation with the Unspeakable

The first challenge confronting Owen as he began to approach the war within his poetry was the question of what sort of language could capture the experience which was unlike anything he had ever experienced or could anticipate. The language of the men he commanded caused him added concerns. When Owen arrived in the trenches in France, he writes to his mother as 1917 began about his initial impressions of the men he would lead in battle:

> We are 3 officers in this "Room," the rest of the house is occupied by servants and the band; the roughest set of knaves I have ever been herded with. Even now their vile language is shaking the flimsy door between the room [*Letters* 422].

The separation between himself and those beneath him in rank is apparent to him in differences in language; their cursings threaten to invade his upperclass sanctuary as would a barrage of shellfire. "Herded" with these "knaves," Owen believes he is in a world in which he does not belong. By the end of his life, Owen will claim to speak for those incapable of speaking for themselves, but during his initial exposure to trench life, the linguistic divide renders Owen incapable of communicating with the men who would one day die alongside him. When hospitalized months later, his own powers of speech affected by war, the initial struggle that Owen confronts is likewise a linguistic one. The evolution of Owen's poetic language to represent the war must work to eliminate the barriers of class between Owen's and his men's language, and must construct an idiom that can represent horrors that many thought inexpressible.

Perhaps because of these challenges, most of Owen's sonnets written at

Craiglockhart avoided discussion of the war altogether. Typically, these poems meditated upon conventional Romantic and religious themes through the use of Keatsian language, as in "Music," written at the hospital and shown to Sassoon: "I have been urged by earnest violins / And drunk their mellow sorrows to the slake" (*Poems* 75); or in "Maundy Thursday," composed in 1915 and revised under Sassoon's tutelage: "Between the brown hands of a server-lad / The silver cross was offered to be kissed" (*Poems* 86). His skill with the form provided Owen with the vehicle for his first successful poetic commentary upon the war, "Anthem for Doomed Youth." The poem, which decries the annihilation of a generation of men, describes the war by means of Owen's inability to imagine a language to represent it.[27] First, Owen describes the world of the battlefield in the octave:

> What passing-bells for these who die as cattle?
> — Only the monstrous anger of the guns.
> Only the stuttering rifles' rapid rattle
> Can patter out their hasty orisons.
> No mockeries now for them; no prayers nor bells;
> Nor any voice of mourning save the choirs, —
> The shrill, demented choirs of wailing shells;
> And bugles calling for them from sad shires
> [*Poems* 76; ll. 1–8].

The poem went through seven revisions between September and October, 1917 and emerged in its completed form through the guidance of Sassoon. Originally the sonnet had been much more jingoistic; the response to the call for prayer for the dying men in the first line was the "solemn anger of our guns," which Sassoon convinced him to change to the neutral "monstrous anger of the guns" because the poem was to be about the war's atrocities, rather than nationalism.[28] Sassoon allowed Owen to see and to articulate that the real enemy was not Germany but the senseless slaughter of the men. This textual debate between Owen and Sassoon and the extensive critical attention paid to the poem over the sources for the language reflect the difficulties Owen faced in this first serious grappling with rendering the war in poetry. He writes to his mother, "Sassoon supplied the title 'Anthem': just what I meant it to be" (*Letters* 496). His subject was to be "these who die as cattle." But the choice of this image, though reflecting the wholesale slaughter occurring on the Western Front, dehumanizes the men. The image recalls his sense evoked in his first letter from the trenches that he had been "herded" with his men the Other Ranks and illustrates how pervasive was the notion in Owen's consciousness of the separation between officer and enlisted men, evident in the "useful weeding" that Owen had previously hoped the war would effect.

Owen's initial strategy of representing warfare is to mediate the gulf between the home and Western fronts. He felt allied and alienated from both places, as did most soldiers, who were products of England, fighting for England, and desperate to return and be accepted by England. Nevertheless, these soldiers felt that the people at home were incapable of understanding their situation, and they felt as well that the war itself was becoming more and more useless. Owen employs the strategy of rendering both sides inarticulate to explain the meaning of the slaughter through their similar struggles to find the proper language for grief. The structural division of octave and sestet allows Owen to contrast the soldiers' and civilians' responses while simultaneously bringing them together in united mourning. The answer to this question of how to articulate the unspeakable, as posed in the octave, is that a sequence of incomplete responses or negations can at best approximate the experience: What passing-bells?— only guns and rifles as orisons; only shells as choirs; no prayers, bells, or human voices at all. The Romantic echo that critics have detected within the solemn language of the poem has a double effect: on the one hand, it serves as the idiom with which Owen had achieved a degree of comfort throughout his early poetic career, an idiom which he employs here to bring the war experience into an understandable form. But the emphasis upon negation and inadequacy also enables him to show, through the solemn tone, the impossibility of assimilating this experience into a poetic tradition.

Hibberd observes that the image of bugles in line eight prepares the reader for the turn in line nine to the homefront, where bugles would be a signifier of mourning as they would be on the battlefield.[29] At the homefront, as well, the poet observes a similar lack of adequate language to express the grief:

> What candles may be held to speed them all?
>   Not in the hands of boys but in their eyes
> Shall shine the holy glimmers of goodbyes.
>   The pallor of girls' brows shall be their pall;
> Their flowers the tenderness of patient minds,
> And each slow dusk a drawing-down of blinds
>   [ll. 9–14].

The poem locates the signifier of mourning — candles — not in the hands of boys (presumably sons orphaned by the slaughter) and thus not within poetic tradition. Mourning can be read in the tears of these survivors, or upon girls' brows, or within minds. The sequence of images recedes further and further from any linguistic or readable expression — from eyes, to brows, to minds — to arrive at "each slow dusk a drawing-down of blinds," an image which thwarts all linguistic connection and understanding between the mourner and anyone else. The poem is a success because of what Owen does not and cannot yet say. That is, the poem serves as an anthem for these doomed soldiers because of the poet's willingness to reject traditional glorification of them and to concede that their deaths defy, at this point, poetic categorization. The role of the poet is to give voice to both these sides, perceived as in opposition to one another, and to create a united expression through the decision to join them formalistically. The poem's greatest irony and greatest strength comes in the realization Owen offers that the anthem, which will seek to mourn properly, can be heard only as the sound of guns at the front and silence at home. Sassoon's typical response to the "unspeakability" of this war is to circumvent the problem through irony and understatement, to say the opposite of or less than what he means because the full meaning cannot be articulated. Gurney, feeling less obligation to convey the impact of war on anyone but himself, creates a unique language to suit his private purposes. But for Owen, whose recovery from shell shock and return to the fighting depends upon the resolution of his conflicted stance toward the war by vowing to fight and speak of this fighting, "Anthem for Doomed Youth" asks the unironic question of how to create a public voice.

As he shows in "Anthem," Owen's earliest poetic strategy in the creation of this public voice involves the removal of himself from the scene in favor of an apparent objectivity of perspective. In poems such as "S. I. W.," "The Letter," "The Dead-Beat," or "The Chances," Owen regards an event or casualty of the war in a way which emphasizes the war's power to isolate or incapacitate the individuals involved, rather than to unite them in a common cause or experience. These are the most straightforward poems of protest of Owen's body of work, and not coincidentally many were conceived during Owen's stay at Craiglockhart when the effect of Sassoon's techniques of irony and understatement upon his verse was strongest. A discussion of one poem of this type will illustrate the point. In "S. I. W." (self-inflicted wound), the speaker describes the process of disillusionment that drives a soldier to suicide, enumerating the stresses that lead to this response, such as the close shaves with bullets and the lies written to family telling them of his safety and comfort. The omniscient speaker assesses this man in terms that could speak for all those resisting the onset of shell shock:

> Courage leaked, as sand
> From the best sandbags after years of rain.
> But never leave, wound, fever, trench-foot, shock,
> Untrapped the wretch [*Poems* 137–38; ll. 15–18].

The impulse within the poem is to make this event unique to the individual, to argue that no matter how many others suffer similar fates, the relentless exposure to war has driven this individual to complete disconnection from humanity. The closing lines make the inexpressibility of what really happened to this soldier even more striking: "With him they buried the muzzle his teeth had kissed, / And truthfully wrote the mother, 'Tim died smiling'" (ll. 36–37). Sassoon could have written these lines: the poem delivers its message of a life wasted by calling upon readers to question the truth of their perspectives and suppositions about the war, and in that way the civilian readership might achieve a greater degree of sympathy with those in the trenches.

But this gesture does not involve Owen or his experience in any way that would aid in resolving the personal crises of identity caused by his shell-shock, other than to enable him to grow comfortable with an idiom of stark detail in describing the war. The role of the poet here is to present, and through the precision of the presentation, to explain how the fact of suicide has come about. The ending, "Tim died smiling," provides the poem with an additional function — to persuade those ignorant of the realities of war to interrogate the "facts" they receive. "The Letter" engages in a similar strategy, alternating between lines written from a soldier to his wife back home and the soldier's spoken reactions to an attack that leaves him dead at the end of the poem. The increasing disparity between his written words —"I'm in the pink at present, dear," or "We're out in rest now. Never fear" (*Poems* 114; ll. 3, 14) — and the intensifying attack underscores the immense divide between soldier and civilian. Owen's poem fulfills the journalistic function of bringing the civilian world's understanding of the events themselves a little closer to those who experience them. Although these poems do not possess the psychological complexity of later works with a first person perspective that attempts to assimilate more satisfactorily the events retold — and there is nothing to say that they should; they achieve their statements of protest effectively — these poems depict the relationship between the event and the words to retell the event, or between surface appearance and the psychological reality beneath.

Owen will utilize for more personal purposes in other portraits of the war a similar dichotomy between the symptoms of shell shock and the causes of the trauma. Much as the phrase, "Tim died smiling," while factual, asks the reader to inquire of the more complicated truth lying behind these words, such as the cause of his smile or of his death, Owen asks the reader to penetrate the surface of a non-linguistic set of signifiers in "Disabled" to understand the psychological suffering beneath the signification that is read differently by those who observe the survivor. This is a poem about appearances and depths of meaning beneath appearance alluded to but left unexplored by both the poetic perspective and by the soldier depicted in the poem. To the reader, to the poet, and to those who observe the crippled man sitting in a park, he appears alien to their experience:

> He sat in a wheeled chair, waiting for dark,
> And shivered in his ghastly suit of grey,
> Legless, sewn short at elbow [*Poems* 152–54; ll. 1–3].

The observers treat him in accordance with this ghastly appearance because they lack the language that would allow connection with this man: "All of them touch him like some queer disease" (l. 13). The speaker, however, does not move inward to speak for the essence of the man beneath this appearance who is instead defined in terms of absence and negation, as having an identity only in comparison to the whole man he once was and to the capabilities he once possessed. The poem does not give voice to his memories of the war, nor to any possible nightmares plaguing him at present; rather the objective speaker of the poem views the veteran as searching for connections to his pre-war self— one of sexual and physical potency — the man, of course, he can never again be:

> Now he will never feel again how slim
> Girls' waists are, or how warm their subtle hands....
>
> One time he liked a blood-smear down his leg,
> After the matches, carried shoulder-high.
> It was after football, when he'd drunk a peg,
> He thought he'd better join. — He wonders why.
> Someone had said he'd look a god in kilts,
> That's why; and maybe, too, to please his Meg ...
> [ll. 11–12; 21–26].

The values of sexuality, athleticism, and valor were all connected in the soldier's pre-war experience. Blood signified heroism in a football match, and thus he anticipated that enlistment would mark a continuity of these values, but at war, blood poured "down shell-holes till the veins ran dry," as a "leap of purple [that] spurted from his thigh" (ll. 18, 20). It is the same blood, but the war creates a different system of signification for valuing it. Furthermore, the experience of the war has denied the disabled survivor's reentry into the pre-war value system, which for the civilians has remained continuous, and thus the observers are unable to regard the soldier as they had before because all indicators of his heroism have now departed.

By avoiding the experience of war, except for the single image of the soldier's blood, Owen manages to bracket the war out of his and the reader's mind within a war poem; the war remains "in parenthesis" and for the moment controlled because of this avoidance. Like Yealland or even Brock, whose therapies for the shell shock focused upon the elimination of the symptoms and avoided the source of the trauma, Owen's focus upon the ruined body of the disabled soldier is vivid, but superficial. And just as Yealland's "cures" resulted in frequent relapses, the fact that the war is left unexamined in the poem suggests that Owen's confrontation with his war experience, yet to be undertaken, is the avenue which will yield poems with the greatest personal function. The war's absence from the poem makes it even more of a presence; the poem makes apparent the discontinuity through its very appearance on the page:

> And soon, he was drafted out with drums and cheers.
>
>   *   *   *
>
> Some cheered him home, but not as crowds cheer Goal.
> Only a solemn man who brought him fruits
> *Thanked* him; and then enquired about his soul [ll. 36–38].

The language of these lines evokes the public's attempt to ignore the unpleasantness that occurs in France between these stanzas. The cheers that mark his departure are echoed in the next metrical foot with the cheers for his return; "drums" achieves an inexact rhyme with "home" to attempt this continuity while acknowledging that these cheers are different than those for a heroic football player. Even the well-intentioned "solemn man," bringing fruits, lacks the language to sympathize or elicit a response from the soldier, and the gesture of thanking seems to miss the mark. Owen at this point lacks the language for the soldier's intervening years in France. His Craiglockhart poems, which begin the process of healing that continued for the entire year after his release, mark either the disparity between the degrees of understanding between the home and Western fronts, or in this case, between pre- and postwar England, as experienced by civilian and soldier who are likewise alienated from one another. To call these poems limited is not a criticism since each succeeds to establish this emotional distance between fronts and between Owen and the rest of the soldiers. These early war poems also predict later complications of the ideas implicit within the divide between language and experience, between appearance and psychological reality beneath such appearance. These poems posit a dialectic between what is whole and what is broken; between what remains intact and what once was. The challenge for Owen will be to move beyond such "Sassoonish" dichotomies to express a vision of the traumatic experience in all its horror in order to forge a poetic means of healing.

A later poem from Owen's mature period, "Mental Cases," written between May and July of 1918, engages in a similar juxtaposition between systems of signification in an effort to resolve the disparity between what a reader could see and what a reader would think impossible to understand. Distinguishing this poem from "Disabled," however, is Owen's increasing ability to infuse the signifiers of the broken soldier — crippled, impotent, or in this case mad — with language that does not thwart or render unspeakable the experience of war but which provides the reader with terms by which to understand what Owen's voice and perspective had kept off limits. The perspective at the beginning of the poem is like that of "Disabled" — an external and questioning speaker looks upon the human remnants of the war's devastation, a group of "mental cases" in a hospital. Owen takes for his subject exaggerated versions of the psychological affliction from which he himself had suffered. The poem begins:

> Who are these? Why sit they here in twilight?
> Wherefore rock they, purgatorial shadows,
> Drooping tongues from jaws that slob their relish,
> Baring teeth that leer like skulls' teeth wicked?
> Stroke on stroke of pain, — but what slow panic,
> Gauged these chasms round their fretted sockets?
> Ever from their hair and through their hands' palms
> Misery swelters. Surely we have perished
> Sleeping, and walk hell; but who these hellish?
>   [*Poems* 146–47; ll. 1–9].

The trochaic rhythm, here and consistently throughout the poem, lends the poem a solemnity fitting for its topic. The first line registers the same alienation between the speaker and the "mental cases" as that voiced by those who viewed the crippled soldier in "Disabled." But subsequent lines indicate that these are not men whom the war has made less manly; rather, the war has turned them into creatures that seem inhuman altogether. The speaker provides a catalogue of monstrous body parts: tongues, jaws, teeth, skulls, eye sockets, hair, and hands classify these men as human, but the speakers' descriptions of these human faculties connect the men with hell, an otherworldly state.

The questioning that marks this first stanza shows the speaker's desire to understand the identities of these sufferers, and to do so, he moves through a series of descriptions which, for all their horror, cannot come up with an answer that will define them in their entirety. The speaker of the poem appears to change in the second stanza to a voice capable of providing an answer: " — These are men whose minds the Dead have ravished" (l. 10). This voice functions to supply a different series of associations with the fragmented body parts of the mental cases:

> Memory fingers in their hair of murders,
> Multitudinous murders they once witnessed....
> Always they must see these things and hear them,
> Batter of guns and shatter of flying muscles.
> Carnage incomparable, and human squander
> Rucked too thick for these men's extrication [ll. 11–18].

The speaker of the first stanza has sought to understand the ghastly images of the men, and the speaker of the second provides this understanding by establishing the causal connection between the war and its manifestation of ravishment upon their bodies. The eyes, tongues, hair, and so forth appear as they do *because* they are the signifiers of memory and "human squander / Rucked too thick for these men's extrication." Memory offers the questioning voice an alternate explanation for the signifiers of the broken identity. In "Disabled," the crippled soldier was perceived as cut off in time from the man he was before the war, and memories of the war were avoided because of the pain, a defensive avoidance that Sassoon will suggest in "Repression of War Experience" exacerbates the trauma. By introducing memory in "Mental Cases," Owen introduces the possibility of temporal continuity between the war experience and its aftermath. To establish this continuity requires a return to the traumatic past through memory. As Eliot will suggest in 1922 in *The Waste Land*'s allusion to Dante's *Purgatorio*, healing can come only through immersing oneself in the flames of suffering.[30]

"Mental Cases" continues in the explanatory voice established in stanza two:

> Therefore still their eyeballs shrink tormented
> Back into their brains, because on their sense
> Sunlight seems a blood-smear; night comes blood-black;
> Dawn breaks open like a wound that bleeds afresh.
> — Thus their heads wear this hilarious, hideous,
> Awful falseness of set-smiling corpses.
> — Thus their hands are plucking at each other;
> Picking at the rope-knouts of their scourging ... [ll. 19–26].

These lines create an understandable logic within a poem whose subject matter seemed to defy such comprehension. The words "Therefore" and "thus" hammer home the syntactical wholeness of the poem and seek to establish such wholeness for the men. The result is not a familiar one to the questioning voice of the first stanza or to the reader, but it is logical because of the circumstances and explanations the rest of the poem provides. These mental cases are not alien or silent as they were at the beginning of the poem but can in effect be given voice by the poet's bringing them into a logical world. Sinfield detects Owen's ironic allusion to chapter seven of the Book of Revelation in the three-part structure of the poem which "provides a controlled intellectual structure [and] tempers the physical disgust, the visual hysteria, of the poem's diction.... Partly, Owen seems to be suggesting that these are the true Christian martyrs who have sacrificed themselves for the world."[31] In other words, Owen, through the ironic contrast between the established Biblical text and his own, is able to articulate what seemed ineffable in "Disabled"—the experience of war itself. And through a sustained allusion, he is able to give the poem a coherence that its question-answer form would seem to fracture. In the Biblical passage, one of the elders in John's vision of the worshipping multitudes asks him, "Who are these people all dressed in white? And where have they come from?" (*Rev.* 7:13). John does not know, and the elder provides the answer to his own question: "These are the ones who have survived the great period of trial; they have washed their robes and made them white in the blood of the Lamb" (*Rev.* 7:14). Sinfield is correct to argue that irony is the primary effect of this allusion; whereas those described in Revelation are those whom God has saved, the men observed in the poem are those whom experience has banished to a hell on earth. By echoing the rhetorical structure and the tone of the Biblical verse, Owen can suggest that the damnation of the mental cases is the opposite of the Elect's glory in salvation.

But the allusion provides another dimension to the poem which Sinfield has overlooked. In Revelation, the elder both asks the question and provides the answer when John cannot. If one were to question the divine inspiration for John's vision, Revelation allows for the reading that sees John as possessing both the question and the answer since he is the author and creator of the vision. Similarly, Owen's poem seems to possess two speakers — the questioning voice of the first stanza and the voice of explanation in stanzas two and three. But since the poem operates in part through the allusion to Revelation, Owen is creating a single speaker who appears ignorant of the answer to his question but then provides it. This situation mirrors Owen's own as a shell shocked poet. Though never as debilitated as these men and though he had recovered from his trauma to speak as they cannot, he nevertheless once was a "mental case" himself. Owen achieves double-voicedness through speaking as the voice that cannot understand the men in the first stanza since he is not one of them any longer. But his is also the voice that was once one of them, likewise hospitalized at Craiglockhart, who has had their nightmares and memories and has displayed the breakdown in identity that he is reconstructing in the poem. The portrait that Owen weaves resembles the extent of the psychosis to which Gurney will deteriorate a decade later. But in their experience of war and in the years when their war poems were written, neither Owen, Gurney, nor Sassoon would ever approach the state of these men. To do so would be to render each poet all but silent, as Gurney's final years will attest. But despite the distance between himself and the suffering, Owen, like Sassoon in "Survivors," reveals a degree of sympathy and understanding that is possible because of his own shell shock.

Owen concludes the poem by introducing a first-person speaker, which complicates things considerably: "Snatching after us who smote them, brother, / Pawing us who dealt them war and madness" (ll. 27–28). Owen's voice has been implicit within all the poems, of course, as the perspective from which the "objective" scene of the men who die as cattle, or the self-inflicted wound, or the death of the letter-writer, or the disabled soldier, has been observed. But the explicit use of the first person alters the poem from one of passing judgment upon the war to a statement of self-accusation. The poem, patterned on Revelation, is likewise a personal revelation of the poet's own feelings of guilt. Echevarria states, "Owen does not include himself among the victims but among the victimizers, ... where the burden of the responsibility is taken by the author who sees himself as an active cause for the state of the mentally diseased."[32] The speaker's address to an anonymous "brother" recalls a similar strategy in Owen's "Strange Meeting," which can be read as a dreamlike fracturing of the poet's identity so that he can see himself as both friend and enemy. Here, the use of "brother" reflects the division within the poem's speaker into a voice that questions and one that understands. In what way is the speaker of the poem guilty for what he has observed? The simple answer is the one that Owen will deliver in "Dulce et Decorum Est"— that all who have participated in and supported the war and its "old Lie" are guilty of the carnage it produces. By "dealing these men war" through the support of its supposed purposes, the speaker has also in part "dealt them madness." But the biographical fact of Owen's own "madness" and his connection through common experience to the men whom he here seeks to understand suggests, by extension, that he is not only placing blame on all participants in the war, but he is blaming himself somehow for the suffering he himself has endured. The poem does not fully explain why Owen might take such a stance, but an examination of his constructions of first-person speakers will provide the answer.

Owen's Speakers: The Introduction and Situation of the Self

For his poetry to possess a therapeutic function, Owen needed to undertake the process of examining his own psychological injury, an examination which would culminate in mature poems such as "The Sentry" in his final months. Owen began the more complex poetic strategy of creating first person speakers, of which "Mental Cases" marks a degree of maturity, during his stay at Craiglockhart, and he explored the possibilities of these speakers through his re-assimilation into the army in Scarborough and Ripon during 1918. Written at Craiglockhart hospital in October 1917 and revised in the early months of 1918, "Dulce et Decorum Est" remains Owen's most famous war poem. In a letter to his mother, he refers to it as a "gas poem," a description which emphasizes its photographic representation of a harrowing and realistic experience of warfare (*Letters* 499). Perhaps this photographic quality makes Owen, at first glance, resemble other contemporary poets of protest and propaganda. Yet these qualities of violence, detail, and anger in many ways date this poem as an expression of his early dealings with his psychological affliction. Johnston writes, "The negative, cynical attitude..., together with its emphasis on shockingly realistic details, represents an element in Owen's verse that is not really natural to it. He is sincere, of course, but neither cynicism nor purposive realism is a major factor in his true poetic vision."[33] Although the "true poetic vision" of Owen is something critics can only claim in retrospect that he had ever achieved since his life and work were cut so short, Johnston is right to see the poem as indicative of a moment of conflict in Owen's career after which he would move beyond the model of protest poetry learned from Sassoon. The poem's conflict occurs particularly in the relationship between its first and second halves, between the speaker and the soldier, between past and present, and between Owen and his directly addressed audience. Rather than regarding the poem as flawed or unnatural to his vision, though, it is more illuminating to see it in the context out of which it emerged — at the moment when Owen, hospitalized, began the process of subjecting his nightmares to conscious control in poetry.

Critics have rightly described this poem as "Sassoonish."[34] Gone is the archaic and elevated diction which lingers in "Anthem for Doomed Youth," and he chooses instead the idiom he had observed in Sassoon's volume *The Old Hunstman*. His letter of August 15, 1917 about Sassoon indicates that the young poet was ready for someone new to revere and imitate:

> I have just been reading Siegfried Sassoon, and am feeling at a very high pitch of emotion. Nothing like his trench life sketches has ever been written or ever will be written. Shakespere [sic] reads vapid after these. Not of course because Sassoon is a greater artist, but because of the subjects, I mean. I think if I had the choice of making friends with Tennyson or with Sassoon I should go to Sassoon [*Letters* 485].

Because of the similarities between the two observed in "Dulce et Decorum Est," Johnston may be correct to conclude that "If he had continued to write only on this communicative ... level, he would probably be viewed today as a talented imitator of Sassoon."[35] The anger within Sassoon's satires, while powerful, will function to resist personal exploration, even as its subject matter mirrors Sassoon's own experience. Owen would have soon exhausted the possibilities of "angry" poems such as this had he continued in this vein for the remainder of his brief career. Lane dates the poem as having been composed over a year prior to "The Sentry" and calls the two poems "superficially similar."[36] Stallworthy's updated chronology of Owen's compositions lends a value to this comparison of which Lane was not aware and which suggests that the similarity is less superficial than it is expressive of the poet's state of mind upon each poem's completion.[37] In actuality, "The Sentry," was conceived at the same time as "Dulce et Decorum Est," begun in August, 1917 and finished in October. The comparison offers even further insights into the progress Owen had achieved psychologically between Craiglockhart and the completion of this mature poem. Johnston and Lane overlook Owen's structuring within the poem which makes it a precursor of his great, psychologically complex, late works. Looking at the poem as a sequence of structural units will illustrate the formalistic emphasis Owen crafted into the poem which opens with two stanzas, one of eight lines and one of six:

> Bent double, like old beggars under sacks,
> Knock-kneed, coughing like hags, we cursed through sludge,
> Till on the haunting flares we turned our backs
> And towards our distant rest began to trudge.
> Men marched asleep. Many had lost their boots
> But limped on, blood-shod. All went lame; all blind;
> Drunk with fatigue; deaf even to the hoots
> Of tired, outstripped Five-Nines that dropped behind.
>
> Gas! GAS! Quick, boys! — An ecstasy of fumbling,
> Fitting the clumsy helmets just in time;
> But someone still was yelling out and stumbling,
> And flound'ring like a man in fire or lime ...
> Dim, through the misty panes and thick green light,
> As under a green sea, I saw him drowning [*Poems* 117–18; ll. 1–14].

On the page, the opening resembles a sonnet, the poetic form Owen uses more than any other. But while the Craiglockhart sonnets, with a few notable exceptions, avoided direct confrontation with the war, in this poem Owen chooses to confront the battle scene directly, and as a result, he modifies the form to suit such a psychological confrontation with the experience. The opening stanzas follow the rhyme scheme of a Shakespearean sonnet until the final two lines which fail to provide the concluding couplet, as Hibberd has observed.[38] Thematically, though, the opening conforms to a reader's expectations about the Italian variety of the form. The octave establishes the scene in great physical detail and creates a tone of fatigue and weariness. Lengthy lines, such as line two, evoke the tedium and difficulty of movement in the trenches and reflect the character of modern warfare that rendered the participants powerless and contributed to their shell shock. They are like "beggars" and "hags;" all senses have been overwhelmed by the physical realities of war, leaving them "bent," "knock-kneed," "limping," "lame," "blind," "drunk," and "deaf." If not classifiable as shell shock cases now, these men are not far from it. As Owen gives the men multiple physical and sensory characteristics through this description, though, these qualities render them impotent within their environment. Even the "tired" shells that fall behind them mimic their exhaustion.

Yet within these opening lines lies also the fact that this is a collective experience. As Owen displays in "The Sentry," this communal bond with his men functions as a potential weapon with which to combat his psychological trauma by enabling his sympathy for others' sufferings to become the cause for Owen's own self-healing when he becomes able to speak for both himself and them. All are bent double, and all are marching toward the same rest within these opening eight lines, but no man is suffering more than his neighbor. Therefore, all can experience another's pain because it is one with their own. But in the turn characteristic of the ninth line of the Italian sonnet, this collective experience abruptly changes. The poet records a voice as commanding, in the colloquial idiom Owen learned from Sassoon, "Gas! GAS! Quick boys!" The imposition of this voice at this stage of the poem, though serving as a necessary warning to the soldiers, establishes a difference between the speaker, the officer who speaks these words, and the rest of the men who hear them and react. The actions of the men abruptly change from a collective trudge to "An ecstasy of fumbling." The final stresses of the lines, all masculine in the octave, now alternate between masculine and feminine to suggest this heightened activity. The flurry of action does not lend the unit any collective power but emphasizes their helplessness from this specific form of attack. The speaker of the poem, whom we can assume to be the speaker of the command (and who, as an officer, has much in common with Owen), registers his vision of the one soldier who heard the command too late: "yelling out and stumbling, / And flound'ring like a man in fire or lime...." Just as the speaker's voice, which provides the warning and disrupts the unified experience of the group, establishes the distance between the officer and his men, the gassed private's experience separates him from the rest, including the officer, who are powerless to do anything but watch his individual suffering through misty panes of glass. The main clause of this "couplet"—"I saw him drowning"—highlights the separation and the immeasurable distance between them: the officer can only see, remember, and retell the event; the private can only drown, and neither can share the experience of the other. The conclusion of this "sonnet" shows through its *lack* of a concluding rhyme that the event remains unresolved in the poet's mind.

Whether its scene is one that Owen has imagined or one that he has taken from his own experience,[39] the poem enacts Owen's complex psychological response to having witnessed torment not unlike the soldier's drowning in gas. Anxiety states, such as Owen's, had the individual's perceptions of guilt at their root and were more common in officers than enlisted men. The guilt, therefore, is the result of some perceived failing in the officer's position of authority. Owen's structuring of the human relationships in the poem allows for him to explore this guilt. The officer's command to his men to put on the masks marks him as superior to his troops—in class, power, and responsibility. The suffering of others becomes in part the suffering of Owen himself. The gassed soldier's failure to follow the command has dictated that his experience will be different from the troops' as well, and consequently, Owen achieves a psychological identification with the sufferer on the basis of their common isolation from the collective body. While Owen cannot feel the same physical pain as this man, his psychological crippling assures him that he will continue to suffer because of this other man's fate. The "couplet" following the concluding "couplet" of the "sonnet" demonstrates the poet's present position: "In all my dreams, before my helpless sight, / He plunges at me, guttering, choking, drowning" (ll. 15–16). Owen has almost imperceptibly shifted the verb tenses from past in the octave, through progressive verbal forms in the sestet, into present tense in these lines. The visual image of the drowning man that provided the ending of the remembered experience provides the psychological link connecting Owen's past and present. These two isolated lines complete a quatrain begun by lines thirteen and fourteen, and the repetition of "drowning," at the expense of a conventional rhyme, emphasizes the persistence of the visual image within the poet's unconscious mind, which like the unfinished "sonnet" has remained unresolved, a recurrent nightmare. While Owen is unable to experience the same physical pain of having been gassed, his sympathy allows him his own form of suffering and gives voice to it in lieu of the voice silenced by the gas.

Hibberd observes, "The organisation and clarity of the first half is replaced by confused, choking syntax and a vocabulary of sickness and disgust, matching the nightmare which is in progress."[40] Indeed, the remaining twelve lines form a single, complex but controlled sentence:

If in some smothering dreams you too could pace
Behind the wagon that we flung him in,
And watch the white eyes writhing in his face,
His hanging face, like a devil's sick of sin;
If you could hear, at every jolt, the blood
Come gargling from the froth-corrupted lungs,
Obscene as cancer, bitter as the cud
Of vile, incurable sores on innocent tongues,—
My friend, you would not tell with such high zest
To children ardent for some desperate glory,
The old Lie: Dulce et decorum est
Pro patria mori [ll. 17–28].

Lane notes the striking rhetorical shift of this stanza, which moves from memory and nightmare to a direct address of the audience, and argues that "Owen's attention is, to some extent, outside the subject of the poem; his intention—certainly an admirable one—is to 'show' the horror to an all-too-uncomprehending audience on the home front."[41] The tone of the poem has shifted from one of horror to one of justified anger, but such a change leaves the reader wondering whether the second half is a satisfactory response to the first. That is, while the speaker who witnesses such atrocities, helpless to prevent them or assuage the pain they cause, surely feels anger in retrospect, the direction of this anger towards an ignorant populace removed from the experience deflects attention away from the real situation of the poem—Owen's personal confrontation with the traumatizing experience and his own feelings of guilt, not his audience's.

The source of Owen's Latin adage which concludes the poem and forms its title is also instructive in this respect. Owen quotes a line from Horace's Ode II in his third Book of Odes, and the rest of Horace's stanza which Owen did not include suggests that the impetus for this poem lay more in self-exploration than in political protest. Horace writes:

dulce et decorum est pro patria mori.
mors et fugacem persequitur virum,
nec parcit imbellis iuventae
poplitibus timidove tergo.

C. E. Bennett translates these lines to read, "'Tis sweet and glorious to die for fatherland. Yet Death o'ertakes not less the runaway, nor spares the limbs and coward backs of faint-hearted youths." Indeed, the ode as a whole is a meditation upon the virtue of "Endurance, and Fidelity to One's Trust," and opens with the plea, "Let the youth, hardened by active service, learn to bear with patience trying hardships."[42] While the end of Owen's poem's sentiment, earned in part by the recreation of the horror in its opening stanzas, is one of protest against the war, this allusion to Horace suggests that part of Owen's need to write the poem came from the fear that having broken down in battle, he was one of these "faint-hearted youths." He had only four months of "active service" before his collapse, and implicit within the self-conceptions of survivor's guilt of shell-shock sufferers were the suspicions that personal cowardice might have played a role in making one prone to breakdown. Realistically, there was nothing the speaker in Owen's poem could have done beyond issuing his warning which saved the majority of the platoon. Part of the challenge, initiated through this poem, is to recreate the traumatizing experiences so that the poet can re-envision them in ways that will resolve the feelings of personal failure. The first half of the poem, then, has charted new psychological territory for Owen by immersing him in the memory that haunts him while writing, but the second half, with its rhetoric of anger, illustrates that like the unresolved sonnet embedded within, the poet's crisis of responsibility, though exposed poetically, remains an open wound.

This is not to call the poem a failure by any means. It exists as a representation of the state of his healing from shell shock caused by experiences such as this one, and one imagines that he could not have posited the possible value in death in the conclusion of "The Sentry" without having written this poem first. But whereas the speaker of the later poem remained within the poem's narrative to confront the traumatic experience and to struggle to extract a possible value from it, Owen in "Dulce et Decorum Est" engages in a rhetorical shift outwards to the audience outside the poem which functions to save him from wallowing in the nightmare too deeply. Within this concluding stanza lie further elements that predict the course that later poems will chart in his reconstitution of a coherent voice resulting from a sustained analysis of the content of the traumatic memory. This fragmentation of identity is mirrored in the perspective which the speaker takes toward the gassed soldier. Fussell states, "Owen's favorite sensuous device is the formula 'his _____,' with the blank usually filled by a part of the body."[43] Within the rhetoric of anger directed toward the ignorant "Second Front" of England, Owen registers the gassed soldier as a catalogue of useless body parts — "white eyes," "hanging face," "froth-corrupted lungs" — rather than as the whole person sharing in the collective experience before the attack. Despite the graphic detail about the soldier's fight for life which captures both Owen's and the reader's eyes, this stanza is more concerned with Owen's own mental anguish. He does not ask the "you" of the poem to imagine what being gassed feels like; rather he asks the audience to imagine pacing behind the wagon with the man in it, to watch his eyes, and to hear the obscene sounds as he nears death. In other words, Owen is calling to the reader to sympathize with him by sharing in his nightmares and by experiencing vicariously Owen's own torment of the graphic and lasting vision. Caesar discusses the psychological motivations for such a strategy within the poem: "Suffering authenticates the morality [of the poem], ... Owen becomes the hero of his own poem, and suffering is glorified as the means to wisdom."[44] Owen's implicit association of his own suffering with that of the dying soldier makes both men heroic for what they have endured, and furthermore, asserting this relationship through a poem enables Owen to achieve and express a degree of the sympathy between the two lost when their different experiences within the event caused their fates to diverge. Yet, by the end of this early poem, Owen remains with his recurrent nightmares still intact. His ability to elevate his suffering to that of the dying soldier enables him to acknowledge the survivor's guilt at the heart of his shell-shock, but as the lack of formalistic resolution to the poem suggests, he is yet to resolve the true source of his trauma. Much as our last vision of the soldier is of a heap of broken body parts, we see Owen at this point still broken in mind, having now exposed the trauma in a controlled forum which will lead him to the reconstruction the identity lost through war experience. Ending the poem upon the justified anger at "The old Lie" of patriotism that led himself and other young men to battle shows that Owen's personal struggle is far from over.

"Insensibility" represents another response to the question of how best to construct a poetic vehicle to assist in coping with both the war experience and the resulting mental affliction. Stallworthy dates this poem as written either during Owen's last days at Craiglockhart — in November, 1917 — or during his retraining at Scarborough in January, 1918.[45] Though slightly revised in April to its final form, the timing of its initial composition seems particularly significant for understanding the state of mind of the poet at this pivotal moment. In early September 1917, Owen writes to his mother of a consultation with Dr. Brock: "I asked him (for the first time) when he meant to have me boarded [released]. He said there were no instructions given to him yet; and wasn't I quite happy where I am? Very well ... I still have disastrous dreams, but they are taking on a more civilian character, motor accidents and so on" (*Letters* 490). This is Owen's last mention of nightmares before confessing to his mother in February of 1918: "I *bring on* what few war dreams I now have, entirely by *willingly* considering war of an evening. I do so because I have my duty to perform towards War" (*Letters* 534). Much seems to be going on during this transition from shell-shocked, hospitalized patient to a soldier, fit enough to be released and to begin light duties. The first of these letters reveals a restlessness and a desire to return to active duty, but the persistence of nightmares indicates that Brock and the staff at

Craiglockhart were prudent in keeping him for a while longer. The content of these dreams suggests, one might argue, a degree of progress as well, as Owen's unconscious had begun to remove the haunting experience from the context of war and to "civilize" it into a more familiar form. But nightmares, however "civilian," display that he was not free from the trauma. Paradoxically, Owen's letters suggest both his desire to become "well" enough to return to France and his willful determination to keep the experience that rendered him shell-shocked alive in his mind through "deliberate" invocations of the nightmares. It is difficult to know just how seriously to take his precise prescription for bringing on dreams — "proper thinking before sleep" (*Letters* 533) — or to know how effective this habit was in yielding the sort of dreams that helped him to keep his "duty toward War" at the forefront of his mind. But the self-consciousness in this letter about this duty and his efforts to sustain it demonstrate his desire to keep the memory alive while sustaining it in a form subject to his conscious control.

"Insensibility" provides an instance of Owen's effort to transform war into a controllable form through conscious patterning and imagination. The poem was composed at some point between the dates of these two letters — between the end of hospitalization when Owen was free from the visible symptoms of shell shock and his near-civilian lifestyle of "friends, oysters, and antique shops" in Scarborough before returning to fight.[46] The poem engages in the very question with which Owen struggled at Craiglockhart and again during these months of transition: how best to satisfy the demands of the various roles he found himself playing — of soldier, civilian, and most of all, poet. Where could he, attracted to all these positions, find himself most "whole?" Caesar states, "Here Owen seeks to ironically contrast the justifiable 'insensibility' of the troops with the unjustifiable 'insensibility' of the home front.... Between the insensibility of both 'men' and civilians is the sensibility of [Owen], officer and poet...."[47] Owen devotes the first three stanzas to defining the insensibility of soldiers and its cause:

1

Happy are men who yet before they are killed
Can let their veins run cold.
Whom no compassion fleers
Or makes their feet
Sore on the alleys cobbled with their brothers....

2

And some cease feeling
Even themselves of for themselves.
Dullness best solves
The tease and doubt of shelling....

3
Happy are these who lose imagination:
They have enough to carry with ammunition....
Having seen all things red,
Their eyes are rid
Of the hurt of the colour of blood for ever.
And terror's first constriction over,
Their hearts remain small-drawn.
Their senses in some scorching cautery of battle
Now long since ironed,
Can laugh among the dying, unconcerned
                    [*Poems* 122–24; ll. 1–5; 12–15; 19–30].

The use of "happy" throughout the poem is clearly ironic. The opposite of misery in the trenches is not conventional happiness but rather this state of insensibility where the soldier remains alive by casting away the emotional faculties, such as compassion, self-consciousness, imagination, fear, or sensitivity, which would make him aware of his own and others' suffering. The "Insensibility" of the title names the protective measure which characterizes the shell shocked soldier's shutting down of his senses by which the war experience could be understood. The device of half or para-rhyme, used for varying effects throughout Owen's verse, lends the entire poem a dull and muted tone to evoke this defense of shutting oneself off from the overwhelming sensory experience. Lines achieve only partial resolution through consonance, as in "feeling / shelling" or "themselves / solves." The meandering rhyme scheme of the stanzas, where lines remain unmatched for four lines or more, recalls Frost's "After Apple-Picking," another poem of monotony and weariness. There is a certain pragmatism to the soldier, as well; survival dictates that he carry ammunition, so imagination becomes a luxury, and this half-rhyme creates a juxtaposition of the possible tools, with differing degrees of value for his survival, that the soldier has at his disposal.

Kerr assesses the soldier depicted in these stanzas: "In order to function, that is, in order to work efficiently, a kind of disintegration has taken place within him. To avoid breakdown he is broken down, mentally dismembered.... The result is a monster: brute, machine, corpse, madman: but it is also the good soldier, and he is still alive."[48] Owen, facing the fact of his imminent return to the trenches, paints the portrait of the man he once was before his breakdown and also of the man he could become once again. But to become such an automaton conflicts with Owen's desire to embrace the identity of a poet, gifted with all the faculties the efficient soldier must cast away, an identity which would give his participation in this war a moral purpose. Owen must risk returning to his emotionally crippled state, plagued with nightmares, if he wishes not simply to experience the horrors but to come to terms with them poetically. He contrasts the description of the "insensible" soldier with that of the poet:

5

We wise, who with a thought besmirch
Blood over all our soul,
How should we see our task
But through his blunt and lashless eyes?
Alive, he is not vital overmuch;
Dying, not mortal overmuch;
Nor sad, nor proud,
Nor curious at all.
He cannot tell
Old men's placidity from his [ll. 40–49].

The existence of "thought" for the poet causes "blood over all [his] soul." To be sensible and reflective about the war experience, he believes, leads to an intensification of personal suffering. Silkin highlights the patronizing element of Owen's contrast between the "wise" poet and the insensible soldiers which, though accurate, should not detract from the honest questioning of his position in relation to the soldier which experience might make him again.[49] The increasingly short lines describing the soldier (ll. 44–48) point to his inability to speak for himself and his need for the voice of Owen to speak for him.

The relationship between the soldier and the poet, the insensible and the sensible, remains, for now, in a state of paradox: "How should we see our task / But through his blunt and lashless eyes?" To see and communicate means that Owen must see through eyes incapable of poetic vision. The uncertain position of the poet here recalls the conflicted address that concludes "Dulce et Decorum Est" where Owen calls upon the audience not to imagine the gassed soldier's suffering but to imagine being an observer of such suffering. The poet is an intermediary between the soldier and the homefront, a spokesperson but potentially a fellow sufferer himself. The question remains, within this poem, one of perspective — "How should we see?" Owen has progressed from the perspective of "Anthem for Doomed Youth," where the men were to be seen as cattle, and the poet must grope to find an idiom, but the resolution to the paradox is not yet complete. As if uncomfortable with such an unanswered and yet unanswerable question, Owen deflects the conclusion of the poem by means of a description of the ignorant populace in England where the ignorant are not blissful but are "cursed ... dullards whom no cannon stuns" (l. 50). The shift in tone from personal questioning to righteous anger resembles the change in "Dulce et

Decorum Est" from the nightmare state to the rhetorical address of the reader. The poem concludes:

> By choice they made themselves immune
> To pity and whatever moans in man
> Before the last sea and the hapless stars;
> Whatever mourns when many leave these shores;
> Whatever shares
> The eternal reciprocity of tears [ll. 54–59].

Owen achieves, through this shift, no final resolution or answer to the question he poses to himself, but he articulates a clearer vision of what his role will be. His "sensibility" enables him to possess "whatever" moans, mourns, and shares, as part of a natural landscape, where the sea, stars, and shores are unified with the reciprocal tears of the sufferers and the ignorant populace. The desire within this conclusion has perhaps been learned from Dr. Brock's emphasis upon Mother Earth, a desire for unification between all the elements of the war-torn landscape, soldiers and civilians included.

Another poem, whose dates of composition and revision closely overlap those of "Insensibility," is "Apologia Pro Poemate Meo," written in Scarborough at the end of 1917. Owen achieves a partial response to the question left open at the end of "Insensibility" of how to see the experience of the war — as both soldier and poet — as an experience of suffering and of glory. Backman describes the strategy of the poem: "Owen exploits the technique of paradox, or stark contrast.... A series of central religious or artistic concepts ... are reinterpreted in terms of his war experience."[50] The poem begins, "I, too, saw God through mud,—/ The mud that cracked on cheeks when wretches smiled" (*Poems* 101–02; ll. 1–2). The "too" in this first line raises initial questions: Welland argues that Owen is responding to Robert Graves' poem, "Two Fusiliers," told through the voice of a soldier who describes two comrades "closely bound / ... by the wet bond of blood."[51] If true, Owen's response to the older, established poet is telling as Owen both establishes the "I" as primary perspective for the retelling of this experience and equates his central speaker with an authentic poetic voice. From the onset, we see a speaker with much greater confidence than that of the unresolved questions concluding "Insensibility" — confident enough to claim to see God through mud. Owen seems to anticipate this juxtaposition in his letter to his mother of January 4, 1917, days after arriving in the trenches:

> After those two days, we were let down, gently, into the real thing, Mud. It has penetrated now into that Sanctuary my sleeping bag, and that holy of holies my pyjamas. For I sleep on a stone floor and the servant squashed mud on all my belongings; I suppose by way of baptism [*Letters* 422].

Upon entering the trenches, he describes the mud as infiltrating and polluting his civilian notions of comfort, described in religious terms to suggest that the experience of war corrupts all that he once knew to be pure and good. In the poem, though, God emerges through the war experience, and emerges to Owen the poet alone. In other words, Owen the poet claims to reverse the process of disillusionment experienced by soldiers, himself included, by envisioning the war experience, with all its grim reality, as the means of envisioning God.

The poem begins with the statement of the speaker's privileged vision, but Owen is more concerned with using this vision to elevate the experience of the men, through religious metaphor, to capture the experience which the soldiers found themselves incapable of articulating:

> [I] witnessed exultation —
> Faces that used to curse me, scowl for scowl,
> Shine and lift up with passion of oblation,
> Seraphic for an hour; though they were foul [ll. 13–16].

Owen compares the face of the soldier to one's exultation at receiving the Eucharist, suggesting that all soldiers experienced such ecstasy but lack the metaphor to convey it. The "I" of the first line (and of the first lines of alternating stanzas throughout the poem) establish the speaker as apart from the common soldier and as the sole voice and perspective capable of his vision. Yet, at the same time, by speaking for these men and by giving their experience voice, Owen approaches the experience of the men once again. He imagines that the curses, which upon entering the trenches were the most troubling reflection of the distance Owen perceived between himself as officer and the men beneath him, have disappeared. The poem reaches its climax in its sixth stanza as the "I" shifts from the visual to the aural:

> I have perceived much beauty
> In the hoarse oaths that kept our courage straight;
> Heard music in the silentness of duty;
> Found peace where shell-storms spouted reddest spate
> [ll. 25–28].

Compare this passage to one written in January 1917 to his mother:

> [T]here is the universal pervasion of *Ugliness.* Hideous landscapes,
> vile noises, foul language and nothing but foul, even from one's
> own mouth (for all are devil ridden), everything unnatural, broken,
> blasted; the distortion of the dead, whose unburiable bodies sit
> outside the dug-outs all day, all night, the most execrable sights
> on earth. In poetry we call them the most glorious [*Letters* 431].

In the letter, Owen is resisting the pull of those he outranks to become one with their ways. He sees their words as a threat to all he brought into the trenches and seems embarrassed by his own capacity to use such language. Now, having been removed from the world to which he prepares to return, and recollecting the experience for the poem, he recalls and imagines beauty in the curses because of their function in uniting the men as expressions of communal courage. Silence is music, and shell-storms create peace in ways that defy understanding to anyone not experiencing them.

The poem succeeds further in articulating the bond between ranks of men in a voice which invites, but ultimately thwarts, the reader's participation, a gesture which marks the poem's greatest power and its ultimate limitation. Johnston claims, "In 'Apologia,' ... Owen dwells upon the exclusive nature of his experiences as soldier and poet. The new experiential basis of his poetry really becomes an experiential bias, which, though it seems to invite pity, coldly forbids sympathy and understanding."[52] As he has in "Dulce et Decorum Est" and "Insensibility," Owen concludes by addressing the reader:

> Nevertheless, except you share
> > With them in hell the sorrowful dark of hell,
> > Whose world is but the trembling of a flare
> > And heaven but as the highway for a shell,
>
> You shall not hear their mirth:
> > You shall not come to think them well content
> > By any jest of mine. These men are worth
> > Your tears. You are not worth their merriment
> > > > > [ll. 29–36].

In his prior addresses to the reader, Owen's tone of anger toward the audience stemmed in part from the audience's propagation of "the old Lie" which allowed them to ignore the sufferings of the soldiers. Here the tone of anger emerges from the speaker's emphasis upon "worth," in his passing judgment on the reader in the final lines, which his perception of moral inequality between the two worlds of soldiers and civilians justifies in his mind. There is no place for the "eternal reciprocity of tears" in this poem. The reader has been invited to listen to silence for its music; to see exultation in foul faces; to see God through mud with the poet. But once these striking and paradoxical connections are achieved, Owen asserts the impossibility of understanding all the reader has been led to believe the poet can express to an uninformed audience. Owen asserts the value of returning to the experience by his glorification of it, but in taking a step closer to articulating the inexpressible, nightmarish world to which he will return, he makes the connection between the poet (and thus the soldier) and the civilian world even more difficult to achieve.

But Owen is willing to sacrifice the understanding of the civilian world for the achievement of solidarity with the men he will lead once again. He sanctions the tears that civilians might shed but thwarts any sympathetic relationship between soldier and civilian which would enable the two sides to exist on the same moral level. Tears, arguably a feminine sign of grief, suggest that those not in the trenches are not granted entry into complete understanding of the men because civilians are not all men. One need not insist upon this distinction in gender, however, because the civilian and military experiences of the First World War were different enough. But reading "Apologia" alongside "Greater Love," a poem composed at almost the same time,[53] enables the question of gender and sexuality to be raised in each. "Greater Love" defines the love between soldiers, achieved through sympathy and common experience, as "greater" than conventional definitions of love, represented here through stock images of red lips or voices singing like wind. Johnston summarizes the impact of these contrasting loves: "[T]he poet evokes the familiar imagery of the one in order to bring fresh meaning to the other. The contrast, therefore, is more than a revelation of pathetic discrepancies; it is the redefinition of a spiritual concept in terms of its lesser physical counterpart."[54] Written alongside "Apologia" and at this late moment in Owen's process of reassimilation into the fighting, "Greater Love" engages many of the same psychological conflicts. The reception by soldiers after the war suggested that Owen was able to articulate something through the poem which he had not previously achieved; Hibberd observes, "several reviewers of the 1920 edition of his poems, including experienced soldiers such as Blunden, singled out ['Apologia' and 'Greater Love'] as the truest and most beautiful in the book."[55] He sustains throughout the poem the second person address to the reader who engages in conventional, implicitly heterosexual, love, and at every stage, the symbols of the reader's love, such as "red lips," are judged inferior to the symbols of the soldiers', such as "the [red] stained stones kissed by the English dead" (*Poems* 143–44; ll. 1–2). Owen echoes the idea from "Apologia" of music heard in soldiers' silence:

> Your dear voice is not dear,
> Gentle, and evening clear,
> As theirs whom none now hear ... [ll. 15–17].

Once again, the reader is shut out of the relationship between poet and the soldiers, and any conventional response, to hear nothing in silence, is devalued in comparison to the silence's capacity to lead to sympathetic understanding. As in "Apologia," the situation of the soldier attains its moral superiority through Owen's associations of it with Christianity:

> And though your hand be pale,
> Paler are all which trail
> Your cross through flame and hail: [ll. 21–23].

The love of the men is greater because of the sacrifice they express; they die for one another, as Christ died for mankind. The last line of the poem, however, signals Owen's begrudging movement towards inclusion of the ignorant outsiders into his message: "Weep, you may weep, for you may touch them not" (l. 24). This is extraordinarily ambivalent: Owen both grants and denies the reader the right to sympathize with the suffering. The poem has dealt in symbols of emotion throughout, comparing the symbols of love and judging the soldiers' more authentic, and tears become symbols for both groups' degrees of sympathy. Owen allows the reader to shed real tears, presumably to display pity for the suffering, but Owen defines these tears as symbolic representations of the distance that remains between the men and the audience whom they are still not worthy of touching.

This sequence of four poems, whose compositions and revisions overlap one another between October of 1917 at Craiglockhart, through July of 1918 at Scarborough, marks Owen's tactics for reassimilation into the war experience that both broke him mentally but to which he now felt compelled to return. The poems display his struggles to achieve comfort with his relationship to the troops he would soon rejoin, moving from the nightmares that result from his failure to save a companion in "Dulce et Decorum Est" to love in "Greater Love" which excludes in part those who do not participate in this world of men. That Owen was homosexual is beyond question; the extent to which his homosexuality was expressed remains a matter of conjecture, complicated by the fact that his brother, who controlled his estate after his death and wrote Owen's three volume biography, *Journey from Obscurity* (1963–1965), sought to keep this dimension of his brother's life from public knowledge.[56] Certainly, his friendship with Sassoon was instrumental in providing Owen with not only a poetic mentor but with someone understanding and perceptive of Owen's concealed sexuality, and Sassoon presented Owen when he left Craiglockhart with a letter of introduction to Robbie Ross, one of Oscar Wilde's most loyal supporters, which allowed Owen to experience before returning to the war a social circle in London in early 1918 where homosexuality was acceptable and the norm. Hibberd discusses the friendship between Owen and Charles Scott Moncrieff which began when the two met at Graves' wedding in 1918 and which led Moncrieff to write a series of love sonnets to Owen, to which

Owen never responded, but Hibberd also warns that most "evidence" of Owen's love affairs during 1918 before his return to the war is either speculative or biased.[57]

Despite this uncertainty about the facts of Owen's sexual life, the fact of his orientation does inform his war poetry, "Greater Love" most vividly.[58] Stephen discusses the relationship between the emotion of love and the feelings of sexual desire. Both Owen and Sassoon, he claims, write poems "where the overwhelming emotion of love totally demotes any need to talk of physical consummation. The tenderness and overwhelming desire of the man in a heterosexual relationship to protect his love are transferred to the officer's care and compassion for his men...."[59] Sassoon will express feelings of love in his poems, "Banishment" and "The Dug-Out," which engage in the sort of transference which Stephen discusses. But Stephen's assessment answers only part of the question about the relationship between Owen's sexuality and the psychological healing that would allow him to rejoin the men he expresses such love for in "Greater Love." The love within the poem is a feeling of emotional harmony between men that does not demand sexual expression to be authentic. Sacrifice for one another is the "consummation" between soldiers in the poem, symbolized by "stained stones kissed by the English dead," "limbs knife-skewed," "[voices] whom none now hear," and "hearts made great with shot" (ll. 2, 7, 17, 20). Stephen perceives an impulse to protect within the officer's position, which he equates with the conventionally masculine role in a heterosexual relationship. But what makes the love between soldiers "greater" and more ideal to Owen is that the emotional sympathy which men within the same physical situation of warfare can experience has the potential to transcend the class distinctions between officers and enlisted men. The officer still must command his men, but Owen's acceptance of his own homosexuality enables him to direct his desires into feelings of emotional connection with those whom he had once regarded as his inferiors. Through this sublimation of desire, he can lead by means of notions of equality and sympathy, rather than through belief in superiority and perceptions of the burden of responsibility, which in part has made his shell shock to affect him so deeply. "Greater Love" has defined the love between soldiers largely through what it is not — heterosexual love, but the only images of this love arrive as symbols of soldiers' sacrifice after they have died. For complete visions of this harmonious relationship between men at war, one can look to Owen's poems that, because his life would end, will end his poetic development with prophetic elegies written for himself as well as for his men.

"Strange Meeting" and "Spring Offensive": The Nightmare and the Dream

Because forces beyond Owen's control dictated that his poetic career would end on November 4, 1918, it is inviting to read a shape into his body of work which envisions his final war poems as a culmination of trends at work in his earlier representations of the war. Owen's evolution of a language appropriate for the war and his developments in first-person speakers have shown his maturation but have also shown their shortcomings as complete expressions of Owen's poetic stance upon the war. These poetic developments have charted his psychological confrontation with the war that brought his therapy begun at Craiglockhart toward completion and marked his readiness to return to the war as a "whole" man. Owen's letters concerning his return reveal that he envisioned the return not as an endpoint but as a new beginning. In a letter to his mother marked "Strictly Private," Owen reveals the final stage yet to be fully realized: "I came out in order to help these boys — directly by leading them as well as an officer can; indirectly, by watching their sufferings that I may speak of them as well as a pleader can. I have done the first" (*Letters* 580). The poems "Strange Meeting" and "Spring Offensive" allow Owen to do the second (as he had done in another of these late poems, "The Sentry") by allowing final confrontations with the meaning of his nightmares and by enabling his poetic statement of the meaning of his involvement in the war. In "Strange Meeting" he immerses himself within a sustained vision of his nightmare for the purpose of self-revelation. And in "Spring Offensive," he achieves his ultimate vision of the moral purpose of war poetry by allowing his processes of imagination to elevate the subject of war to the heroic.

"Strange Meeting" survives as Owen's most moving elegy of the war, even though manuscript evidence suggests that the poem was never completed in a form with which Owen was satisfied. Critical approaches to the poem have been numerous and wide-ranging.[60] While intertextual references create layers of meaning in many of Owen's war poems, their cumulative effect here creates a work in many ways apart from the concerns of his typical battle poems. We are not in the world of mustard gas, mud, or rats; we are not asked to observe a physical reality that allows for Owen's meditations upon the war's sufferers. In a poem like "Dulce et Decorum Est," readers glimpse Owen's nightmares which he would not describe in letters, but in "Strange Meeting," Owen takes the reader deep within the nightmare world from the very first phrase of the poem, "It seemed." The allusive quality of the text suggests this place as timeless and removed from a physical reality that would situate the poem in France in 1918. As never before, Owen explores a realm that is purely psychological, in which a dead man, whom Owen had often described and pitied, is given the chance to speak. Stallworthy dates the poem as written in the March 1918, a full six months before Owen would return to the fighting.[61] He spent most of the first six months of the year "in a calm period of home service," finishing his convalescence while awaiting final orders to resume combat duty.[62] Despite this distance, the war was alive in his mind during the moment of the poem's conception. March 21, 1918 began the wave of German onslaughts on the Western Front, the main thrusts occurring at St. Quentin and resulting in the loss of land the Allies had spent years acquiring. Hibberd writes of this German offensive, "The daily rate of losses was higher in those few weeks than in any other battle of the war. Any hopes Owen had entertained about peace negotiations or his own demobilization vanished immediately. [Owen wrote,] 'I must buck up and get fit!'"[63] Though not called to duty for a few months, the urgency of the national situation demanded that he prepare himself. He began this preparation by shoring his own fragments together; initial drafts of "Strange Meeting" combined a number of partially completed poems accrued over the war years, such as "Cramped in That Funnelled Hole," and "Earth's Wheels Run Oiled with Blood." The psychological impetus of the poem, the confrontation of its first-person speaker with the meaning of the war in the form of the dead soldier, marks the final stage of Owen's facing up to the psychological trauma experienced almost a year before, to which he might soon subject himself again. Hibberd states, "Among the thousands of poems written during the Great War, there are very few about the poet-soldier meeting his dead victim, fewer still in which the two men talk to each other, and perhaps none expect 'Strange Meeting' in which the killer stands his grounds, accepting the truth of what he has done."[64] The motivating force behind the creation of Owen's alter-ego within the poem is the desire to resolve the fatal paradox he perceived in his relationship to the war: to return meant to achieve an authentic voice as a poet but also ran the risk, if not the inevitability, of death. To remain safe and alive, on the other hand, meant failing to fulfill his poetic potential and, metaphorically, the death of his poetic identity.

"Strange Meeting" was written concurrently with another poem of descent into a metaphorical hell, "Mental Cases," both of which made use of the same fragment, "Purgatorial Passions." Evidence suggests that Owen intended the two to be companion pieces in the collection which he envisioned publishing but would never materialize, *Disabled and Other Poems*.[65] The allusion to Revelation provides the structural framework for "Mental Cases," and both poems also owe much to Dante in their subject matter and diction describing the hellish descent. "Strange Meeting" marks an intensification of Owen's journey taken in "Mental Cases," where the speaker, who seems fragmented into questioning and answering voices, possesses both the questions and the answers which he seeks. By the poem's end, the speaker assigns blame to himself for the men's suffering to suggest a degree of self-learning achieved through his observation and ultimate understanding of these alien forms. "Strange Meeting" represents further psychological exploration than that achieved in "Mental Cases" because of Owen's strategy to allow the phantom here to speak, rather than to speak for the silent as he does elsewhere. A further quality which distinguishes "Strange Meeting" from Owen's oeuvre is its speaking out against all wars, not simply against the one which spawned the meditation. However, the poem's setting comes from Owen's own war experience:

> It seemed that out of battle I escaped
> Down some profound dull tunnel, long since scooped
> Through granites which titanic wars had groined
> [*Poems* 125–26, ll. 1–3].

His letters reveal his most traumatic war experiences to have involved burial and descent. The lengthy letter of January 1917 that chronicles the event retold in "The Sentry" describes his ordeal in an underground dug-out in No-Man's Land. In March 1917, Owen fell about fifteen feet into a ruined cellar, suffered a concussion, and was trapped for over a day. And in April 1917, Owen survived days of shelling by hiding underneath a railroad embankment, covered in corrugated iron, with the dismembered remains of a fellow British soldier feet from him. The underground setting recurs in other poems, as well, such as "Purgatorial Passions," "Miners," "A Terre," and "Exposure," a recurrence indicative of Freud's notion of a desire to master the traumatic experience through repetition. An early draft of "Strange Meeting" had established the setting even more precisely in the trenches: "It seemed from that dull dug-out, I escaped / Down some profounder tunnel...."[66] The revision removes the specific markers of this war from the poem to create its universal message, but the underground setting connects the speaker's experience with Owen's, particularly those which induced his trauma, and with those of every man fighting in this specific war.

Though Owen never describes the tunnels which connected trenches and led to dug-outs, they were a part of trench life. The trench system was a vast configuration of disorienting twists and turns in which soldiers lost all sense of direction when moving through them. Most often men relied upon the sky to keep themselves oriented, but even the movement between front, supporting, and reserve trenches depended upon connecting alleys and tunnels so that the men could avoid exposing themselves to sniper fire by coming above ground.[67] Fussell, who termed the trench existence a "Troglodyte World," states, "Coming up from the rear, one reached the trenches by following a communication trench sometimes a mile or more long. It often began in a town and gradually deepened. By the time pedestrians reached the reserve line, they were well below ground."[68] Entering the trenches means exiting the civilized, familiar world. The war of the poem is at once the Great War, which is Owen's frame of reference, as well as all "titanic wars" which have left their indelible marks upon the landscape. The underground existence of the soldiers establishes the setting as potentially real to heighten the impact of the world of dream that the poem soon enters with the introduction of the speaking dead. Owen's subtle blending of the worlds of reality and dream in this opening recalls the speaker's assessment of the hospital wards in "Mental Cases": "Surely, we have perished / Sleeping, and walk hell" where the speaker, very much awake and cognizant of his surroundings, interprets the experience in much the same way that dreams relive and reshape actual events — through the cloaking and illuminating effect of metaphor and allusion. There, the speaker is in a world for which he lacks a satisfactory language, and to describe the scene, he compares it to a circle of hell which Dante may have overlooked. By creating such a metaphoric linkage between the mental ward and hell, Owen is able to build to the moral question of blame that concludes the poem.

In "Strange Meeting," Owen creates dreamlike metaphors to serve a similar function of exploring his personal culpability for suffering such as that which his dead counterpart will describe. The vagueness of the reality in the poem's opening enables the entire poem to serve as a metaphor for the speaker's war experience when, sleep-deprived and fatigued, the boundary between wakefulness, nightmares, and sleep were hard to pinpoint. The speaker moves even further toward the ambiguous:

> Yet also there encumbered sleepers groaned,
> Too fast in thought or death to be bestirred.
> Then, as I probed them, one sprang up, and stared
> With piteous recognition in fixed eyes,
> Lifting distressful hands, as if to bless.
> And by his smile, I knew that sullen hall,—
> By his dead smile I knew we stood in Hell [ll. 4–10].

The question of the feasibility of such a scene is irrelevant because the psychological function of providing an unconscious representation of anxieties gives dreams value that outweighs any impediment to understanding that dreams' detachment from conventional reality might create. Still, thus far in the poem, the speaker has encountered nothing that would locate the poem entirely in the world of dream. Perhaps the speaker means that this place is *like* hell, a metaphor to convey the prolonged suffering of the speaker and these men. Owen brings the actual trenches into the realm of metaphor and dream in his description of this "profound dull tunnel"—after all, a group of men huddled together in a trench could mark either an potentially aggressive army or a mass grave in this war. Sassoon will describe a sleeping man in "The Dug-Out" as occupying a similarly ambiguous place between life and death, and his meditation upon the human form becomes one of Sassoon's most successful statements of sympathy. The movement of Owen's speaker through this tunnel has led him to what appears to be a grave filled with men who appear either dead, asleep, or hovering between these states: they are "[t]oo fast in thought *or* death to be bestirred" (italics added). The distinction between life and death in the poem depends on the existence of consciousness and thought; too much thinking leads to a state indistinguishable, to the speaker, from death. This odd dialectic, "thought or death," suggests that this poem is as much concerned with Owen and his individual experiences as it is about the horrors of all war. Shell-shock is a reaction, in effect, against too much mental activity; overwhelmed by the sensory experience of war, unable to resolve the conflicting roles war dictates that the soldier play, the men flee through their psychological syndromes. Yet, the shell shocked soldier finds himself unable to stop his mind from remembering and reliving the memories. Extreme cases, such as those in "Mental Cases," become catatonic; the body is all but dead while the mind continues on without any hopes of applying thought to useful purpose.

Welland was the first to see the poet's self-examination, rather than protest, as the subject of the poem: "The imaginative force of 'Strange Meeting,' of course, resides in the fact that it is not a friend or an enemy that the soldier meets so much as an *alter ego*."[69] Owen's revisions to the poem make this intention likely. An early draft contained the line, "I was a German conscript and your friend," which would have both thwarted the universality of the anti-war message and would have eliminated the possibility that the poem represents Owen's struggle with anything more than sympathy for someone suffering a similar fate.[70] Since this war made rare the hand-to-hand combat which would allow the enemy to be an individual rather than an anonymity across No Man's Land, shell shock was more likely to ensue because of one's inaction in preventing a companion's death than it would as a result of having killed a member of the enemy army. The reflexive actions of the speaker and his "double" compound the idea that the speaker is seeing himself in this phantom. Since the first line establishes the dream-state, it is fitting that he come upon "encumbered sleepers" likewise dreaming. As the speaker probes the body, the phantom arises and probes the speaker's mind by staring "[w]ith piteous recognition in fixed eyes." The phantom "reads" the speaker in order to recognize him, and reflexively, the speaker reads his smile and realizes that "we stood in Hell." The recognition of their situation in Hell is achieved only through the sequence of reflexive actions wherein the "I" and "he" which distinguished the two in the early lines merge into the "we" at the end of the stanza. Complete sympathy with other soldiers, such as that depicted through this reflexivity, is the ideal relationship in "Greater Love," and in "Dulce et Decorum Est" and "The Sentry" this bond has been disrupted by the war. Here, such sympathy is sustained through the course of the poem.

In addition to representing his bond with fellow soldiers, the relationship between the speaker and his double represents Owen's troubled relationship with his own past in the war, for which he seeks resolution through the workings of the metaphorical dream and conversation with this symbol of himself. As he continues to read his double's face, however, the speaker expresses the problem in "reading" and understanding the bodily signifiers which Owen has displayed in previous poems, like "Anthem for Doomed Youth" and "Disabled":

> With a thousand pains that vision's face was grained;
> Yet no blood reached there from the upper ground,
> And no guns thumped, or down the flues made moan.

These lines establish the pains ingrained as having no traceable cause. Neither blood nor guns can be seen nor heard in this present moment, cut off from the conventional time of the war, and the speaker can see only the aftermath of the "thousand pains."[71] The poem completes the struggle within Owen's work of finding the language with which to represent the war. Early war poems, like "S. I. W." and "The Letter," displayed the ironic disparity between written language and fact. "Disabled" and "Mental Cases" worked to bridge this distance by locating the facts of war upon the broken bodies of its victims, but to explain this bodily language, Owen encountered, in "Disabled," the disruption of time that could not be filled in, or the need to borrow a traditional language, as in "Mental Cases." Through sublimating himself into the figure of the double in "Strange Meeting," Owen unifies this disruption between the bodily signifiers and their meanings. By projecting his experience onto the other and giving this other, in effect, his voice, Owen articulates the previously off-limits span of time charted by personal memory.

To explain the source of these "thousand pains," the signifier which lacks the concrete explanation to connect the past with the present, Owen enters terrain not yet attempted poetically as the double offers his story which will describe:

> ... the undone years,
> The hopelessness. Whatever hope is yours,
> Was my life also; I went hunting wild
> After the wildest beauty in the world,
> Which lies not calm in eyes, or braided hair,
> But mocks the steady running of the hour,
> And if it grieves, grieves richlier than here.
> For by my glee might many men have laughed,
> And of my weeping something had been left,
> Which must die now. I mean the truth untold,
> The pity of war, the pity war distilled [ll. 11–26].

The double conflates his experience with the speaker's and identifies both of them as poets. Since the poem can be read as the speaker's dream, he in effect is giving voice to his own poetic experience. And since in this dream, the speaker envisions that his poetic double has died, Owen is representing his own anxieties about the death, or perhaps the silencing or ineffectiveness, of his poetic voice. This "wildest beauty in the world" will not be found in conventional images such as eyes or hair; rather, the beauty is marked by the poet's feelings of loss and grief. It "mocks the steady running of the hour" because the ideal beauty somehow is apart from the impermanence of time; it is eternal. It "grieves richlier than here" by causing greater suffering and loss for the poet than even the loss felt through untimely deaths such as he envisions in the dream of this mass grave. But the reality of the war has marked the end of the double's quest for this beauty because the war has killed him. He regrets that men will not laugh or weep along with his words and that fate has decreed that he no longer represent "the pity war distilled" through poetry. By creating this double of himself, Owen is exhorting himself to speak about the war in a manner different than he has spoken of it since entering Craiglockhart. His creation of a voice which laments the inability to speak "the truth untold" reflects Owen's belief in the moral necessity of his calling. He must return to the fighting not simply to reaffirm his responsibility to the men he feels he has failed in war (though this is certainly part of the impetus), but must return to forge an expression of "the pity war distilled" lest the truth remain untold. Part of the psychological reconstitution of Owen's identity relies upon his embracing of this role. The moral force impelling him is one greater even than self-preservation. He recreates himself as a dead man to express yet another paradox within his role as spokesperson for the silent: to keep silent and to keep away from the war is a metaphoric death for Owen's poetic identity, but to achieve the authentic voice through his return is to submit to a physical death and silencing of this authentic voice. Shell shock results from the individual's unconscious desire to save himself. Overcoming shell shock in order to return to the place from which he had escaped demands that Owen construct a purpose for this return that can outweigh the threat of death or relapse.

The quality that elevates the poetic identity within Owen to a state outweighing his comfort in survival is the prophetic power that the double articulates in the following lines:

> Now men will go content with what we spoiled,
> Or discontent, boil bloody, and be spilled.
> They will be swift with swiftness of the tigress.
> None will break ranks, though nations trek from progress.
> Courage was mine, and I had mystery,
> Wisdom was mine, and I had mastery:
> To miss the march of this retreating world
> Into vain citadels that are not walled.
> Then, when much blood had clogged their chariot-wheels
> I would go up and wash them from sweet wells,
> Even with truths that lie too deep for taint.
> I would have poured my spirit without stint.
> But not through wounds; not on the cess of war.
> Foreheads of men have bled where no wounds were [ll. 26–39].

This passage displays Owen's fears about what will be lost with his death and what would be lost without his attempts to achieve his poetic potential through his return. Without the poet to represent the war from the inside, he prophesies, the public would receive the wrong message, and the implications would be grave: "nations [would] trek from progress." The poet has both the wisdom to speak of the war and the courage to do it; he has mastery of his poetic ability and curiosity about the mysteries of life to explore them by means of poetry. The quality that gives poetry for Owen its true moral purpose is its capacity to heal and cleanse in war's aftermath. Blood clogs chariot-wheels and halts the progress of nations, but the poet is gifted with truths that are both natural, from "sweet wells," and pure. This cleansing according to Owen is a natural baptism. Poetry brings about healing not upon the physical wounds but upon the real source of pain and suffering — in the mind, in "[f]oreheads of men [which] bled where no wounds were." For the poet, healing others through poetry is part of the process of healing oneself.

To read the poem as Owen's self-examination provides the ending with further paradox. The double addresses the speaker with words that tell of his murder and beckon him to join him in the grave:

"I am the enemy you killed, my friend.
I knew you in this dark: for so you frowned
Yesterday through me as you jabbed and killed.
I parried; but my hands were loath and cold.
Let us sleep now..." [ll. 40–44].

By delivering the last words of the poem, the ghost appears to be both accusing the speaker and forgiving the speaker for having murdered him, and in the end, inviting him to join him in death. The pronouns "I" and "you" which establish difference between the two as he narrates the murder that occurred "yesterday" are harmonized here in the final line with the return to the collective "us." As a dream about the aftermath of a realistic event like the murder of this enemy, even though Owen never committed such face to face killing, the poem charts Owen's self-accusation and self-forgiveness for his participation in the butchery of the war. Absolving himself for such blame is certainly part of the healing process that Owen must undergo, but Owen's poetry has revealed more complicated notions of responsibility than guilt for killing Germans, and the paradoxical line, "I am the enemy you killed, my friend," points to these complications. Owen has been both friend and enemy to his own men in leading them in battle because his command has sought to protect but has overseen their suffering. "Dulce et Decorum Est" displayed a moment of such guilt, where the speaker warns the men about the gas attack but can do nothing to prevent the suffering of one soldier, and "The Sentry" has recreated Owen's experience where his commands tried to move the sentry out of harm's way, though he was still blinded. Here Owen comes face to face with such a man, in the guise of a dead comrade, and can immerse himself in his responsibility for his suffering to put the guilt and the man to rest. These closing lines reveal further complexities by bringing the fact of Owen's imminent return to the trenches to bear upon the poem when the ending is read as the words of Owen's alter-ego in poetry speaking, rather than the ghost of an actual enemy. Owen is both friend and enemy to himself as a poet because of his firm resolve to go back to France — friend in enabling himself to achieve the voice of the war that he believed was his purpose; enemy in bringing his death upon himself through this decision. As a battle between competing impulses within himself, Owen reveals his victorious side. His return will be self-murder, but it will also be his achievement of a resolute identity with all doubt about his duty to his men and his poetry put to rest in the poem's closing call to sleep. The poem illustrates both the life and death of a poet who will prophesies that he will die but, by having spoken, will also live on.

Owen's death at the hand of German machine guns on November 4, 1918, gave final shape to his poetic career, whether we like it or not. Though he would certainly have had more to say about the war, particularly about his situation in the aftermath had he survived, his final poetic utterance, "Spring Offensive," survives as a fitting closing commentary upon the personal relationship Owen had undergone with his past, his companions in battle, his attitudes about war, and his role as a poet. Though "Smile, Smile, Smile" has been dated as the last complete poem he wrote and parts of "Spring Offensive" had existed for a few months, the final stanza of "Spring Offensive" was composed later, in October 1918, and remains as the final word upon all he had endured.[72] Like "The Sentry," a poem like "Spring Offensive" could result only after the poet had returned to the conditions of combat from which he had escaped through shell shock. Owen bases the subject matter of the poem upon his participation in an offensive assault on the German lines at Savy Wood in March of 1917. And as he had in "The Sentry," Owen searches his personal past for the subject matter for the poem, but this poem allows Owen's vision of the war experience to be transformed from one of nightmare to one of glory. In Owen's Preface which was to have introduced his collection, *Disabled, and Other Poems*, he claimed, "This book is not about heroes. English poetry is not yet fit to speak of them."[73] Hibberd assesses Owen's approach to the subject matter of this poem, written after the Preface, by stating, "he began to fashion a kind of poetry that would be fit to speak of heroes while denying heroic qualities to the war itself."[74] Envisioning the war's participants as heroic, and by extension, his poetic record of such heroism as likewise a heroic role, Owen embraces an identity in battle that can ward off a relapse of shell shock by making the once intolerable reality tolerable. Since the poem exists as Owen's final statement upon the war, it is unavoidable that we read it as the culmination of his vision; as Simcox states, "this is the poem in which he comes to rest."[75] The problem becomes how to see this final vision of the war as emerging from the poetry that has led to it. That is, with a body of war poetry unequivocal in its condemnation of the war, how is Owen able to make the imaginative leap that allows for the creation of a poem like "Spring Offensive," where the depiction of battle, at first glance, appears steeped in traditional qualities of heroism and glory in death — precisely the values Owen claimed the war was not about?

   Owen is able to achieve a feat which seems at odds with his belief about war by making his men the poem's focus and by making the enemy which the men assault in the poem the natural world, rather than the Germans. He represents battle in a manner which challenges the idea felt by soldiers and civilians alike that since the war lacked a noble purpose, the lives lost must have been in vain. The poem represents this specific battle in terms which remove almost all markers of time and place. If we knew nothing of Owen's other work which is precise in its setting in the First World War, the military jargon of the title, the soldiers' "pack-loads," and one mention of "bullets" late in the poem are the only details that situate the poem in any concrete time or place. Much as "Strange Meeting" suggested its connection to the trenches of the First World War but did not insist upon it in order to establish the real, of dream, "Spring Offensive" rids itself of the context of this war to speak of a universal "War." But beyond its attempts at universality, the poem also marks a development beyond the concerns of "Strange Meeting" and "The Sentry" by removing of any explicit speaker and creating an omniscience in the true meaning of the word — one which imagines the perspective of God. The poem begins with the description of a reclining mass of men:

> Halted against the shade of a last hill
> They fed, and eased of pack-loads, were at ease;
> And leaning on the nearest chest or knees,
> Carelessly slept [*Poems* 169–71; ll. 1–4].

This opening recalls the scene in "Dulce et Decorum Est" in which the platoon trudged through the trenches as a unit, but the title of this poem suggests that these are not passive sufferers but are men preparing for assault and directed action, and these lines establish that they are waiting not to be slaughtered in the trenches but for the opportunity to mount an offensive in the open air. The passive verb forms suggest the presence of someone who has allowed them to halt and ease themselves of their loads, but Owen is leaving this presence — the commanding officer — out of the poem. The officer figure who has come to represent Owen himself in prior poems is absorbed into the collective group who feed, lean, and sleep as a united body without distinctions of rank or class.

The first line of the poem establishes the opposition that the poem as a whole will explore. The men are "[h]alted against the shade of a last hill." The use of the word "against" posits the conflict between the men who exist within a natural landscape and the landscape itself which will act against their actions. Welland characterizes this dichotomy as a "contrast between the unnaturalness of what these men are doing and the natural background against which they are doing it."[76] Owen emphasizes the men's bodies and the relationship between them; the chest or knees of each man serves as comfort to the next. He complicates the poem through the introduction of consciousness which will act in opposition to their bodily existence:

> But many there stood still
> To face the stark blank sky beyond the ridge,
> Knowing their feet had come to the end of the world.

> Marvelling they stood, and watched the long grass swirled
> By the May breeze, murmurous with wasp and midge;
> And though the summer oozed into their veins
> Like an injected drug for their bodies' pains,
> Sharp on their souls hung the imminent ridge of grass,
> Fearfully flashed the sky's mysterious glass [ll. 4–12].

What is most striking about this stanza is Owen's ability to craft an individual's unique response to the natural landscape while attributing it to a collective body. These men are aware that during their impending assault, many will lose their lives, but the poem makes explicit that no man is isolated from the rest through any single individual's isolating thoughts, such as those that lead to the self-inflicted wound in Owen's early war poem. The reader enters the mind of a man who stare at the foreboding sky and knows that his "feet had come to the end of the world." However, Owen is not content to leave the description as one in which a man must face his personal moment of crisis. Rather, the poet pulls his camera back, so to speak, to reveal "many" undergoing the same thought process, all of whom Owen unites in a sequence of collective actions and thoughts.

This tactic is a significant development from "Dulce et Decorum Est" or "The Sentry" which exposed Owen's lingering conflict with his war experience as the war's tendency to disrupt the collective body by either killing the individual or leaving him, as it did with Owen, isolated and wallowing in responsibility. The tone of these collective thoughts is reverent as well as foreboding. Owen is locating within the landscape both restorative potential — summer as "an injected drug for their bodies' pains" — as well as destructive power, suggested by "the imminent ridge of grass." The emptiness perceived in "the stark blank sky" lends it an unsympathetic attitude toward them and predicts their deaths. But "the sky's mysterious glass" is perceived to have "[f]earfully flashed," a description which makes the sky itself the fearful party. This fear, attributed to the sky in this line, is more likely reflective of the men's projection of their own fears upon it, but the fluidity of agency in these contrasting lines about the sky points to the element of sympathy that for Owen is the redemptive force of the poem and the war experience. Here Owen creates an complex image of the sky emblematic of a natural world that has the potential to both maim and redeem the men. Fussell has discussed the prevalence of imagery of the sky within poetry of the First World War, and he observes that conventionally, the poet contrasts beauty of the sky with the ugliness of war for ironic effect to allow for statements of protest against the war.[77] Here, the image is used not for protest but in the manner which Gurney will explore in many of his postwar poems looking back upon his experience — to create a canvas upon which the imagination can project subjective emotion.

The poem then tips the balance of nature's imagined agency towards
that of redemption and sympathy:

> Hour after hour they ponder the warm field
> And the far valley behind, where buttercups
> Had blessed with gold their slow boots coming up;
> When even the little brambles would not yield
> But clutched and clung to them like sorrowing arms.
> They breathe like trees unstirred [ll. 13–18].

Owen's perspective imagines the natural world as endowed with sympathetic
feelings toward the men who march through it, but one might say that he
attributes power to a landscape which it cannot have. The buttercups leave
their mark on their boots as they walk by; they are not blessing the men.
The men are getting tangled in the brambles; the brambles do not clutch or
cling to them. However, when the poet gives nature this capacity to act upon
the soldiers, the landscape can even turn the men into part of the natural
order itself: "They breathe like trees unstirred." It is the voice of the poet,
though not overtly present in the form of an "I" but with voice nonetheless,
that constructs the metaphors that establish the moral center of the poem.
Hibberd observes, "He does not refer to himself in 'Spring Offensive' yet
the poem came—as naturally as leaves to a tree—out of his inner life."[78]
The natural world, a morally neutral realm, is transformed into a force that
blesses and protects the men by bringing them into closer contact with
nature.

These opening stanzas predict the men's inevitable turning against the
landscape in the assault that will form the second half of the poem. Estab-
lishing this agency within the natural world enables the poet to attribute the
violence that is about to occur to this agency as well.

> So, soon they topped the hill, and raced together
> Over an open stretch of herb and heather
> Exposed. And instantly the whole sky burned
> With fury against them; earth set sudden cups
> In thousands for their blood ... [ll. 27–31].

The communal force, which gave the men their collective strength when
contemplating the prospect of the assault, sustains the group here at the
moment of the attack. But Owen exposes the limitation of this collective
force by isolating the word "Exposed" at the beginning of the line, which
"heralds the dramatic abruptness with which the counter-fire bursts on
attackers and readers alike."[79] Nature, "an open stretch of herb and heather"
on the other side of the hill, acts against them to expose them to the bar-

rage, despite any strength gained from racing together. And the poet gives nature the role of killer as well, as the same sky defined ambiguously — "stark," "blank," as well as "fearfully flash[ing]" and "mysterious"— now "burn[s] / With fury against them." According to the poet, all of nature's ambiguity is gone, as is nature's sympathetic appeal to refrain from the assault, represented by the clutching brambles. Nature is unquestionable in its role as the men's enemy; its "fury" suggests an anger at the actions of the soldiers and punishment for having disobeyed the implicit "command" not to have attacked. But almost immediately, nature becomes redemptive once again, setting "sudden cups / In thousands for their blood." Owen struggled with this image through a number of drafts; at one point it read, "and soft sudden cups / Opened in thousands for their blood."[80] Settling upon this version of the line completes the pattern of nature's agency, but it raises the question of why the earth, acting so furiously against the men and elsewhere so sympathetically, is powerless to prevent the slaughter. The best it can do, when all is said and done, is to catch the spilled blood into holes that the "sky [which] / Burned in fury against them" has been responsible for creating in the first place.

This complicated pattern of nature's shifting allegiances does display a connection to the personal issues Owen explored through the poem. The easy route would have been to vilify the Germans and to proclaim the heroism of his men because of their bravery in the face of their human adversaries. But Owen's knowledge of the futility of the war would imply also that their lives had been lost in vain, the blood on both sides shed for no purpose. Because he is participating in the war on behalf of the warriors and not the cause, Owen elevates the casualties of the fighting through an imagined connection to a transcendental realm: "...and the green slope / Chasmed and deepened sheer to infinite space" (ll. 31–32). The poem has posited a shifting relationship between the men and the natural landscape that they attack in the poem. This image, though, takes the relationship out of the natural world altogether. The image hinges upon the word "sheer." The shells have pounded the slope, and the result is a decimated landscape. The word makes room for the possible meanings of "shining," or "pure," or "altogether," or even "diaphanous." Such ambiguity in word choice establishes a value for the fighting that elevates it beyond considerations of life or death to a supernatural realm. He writes to his mother on October 5, 1918, after having experienced new fighting, "I can find no word to qualify my experiences except the word SHEER.... It passed the limits of my Abhorrence. I lost all my earthly faculties, and fought like an angel" (*Letters* 580). Owen lacks the language to convey the ecstasy of fighting and survival; in "passing the limits of [his] abhorrence," the experience has taken him beyond the morality allowing him to judge it in conventional terms. In his mind and in his memory, he has transcended the earthly and entered another realm altogether. In the poem, such feelings of transcendence are projected onto the image of the slope that serves as a portal to this heightened perception.

However, these are perceptions caused by human feelings of exhilaration. Owen's imagination can elevate them to such heights, but he must contend with the brutal facts of battle in the poem as well. A letter written to his younger brother Colin from the Casualty Clearing Station in May of 1917, having succumbed to shell shock and describing his experience in Savy Wood that became the basis for the poem, indicates why Owen constructs this complex moral universe in his last poem of his war experience:

> The sensations of going over the top are about as exhilarating as those dreams of falling over a precipice, when you see the rocks at the bottom surging up to you. I woke up without being squashed. Some didn't. There was an extraordinary exultation in the act of slowly walking forward, showing ourselves openly....
>
> Then we were caught in a Tornado of Shells. The various "waves" were all broken up and we carried on like a crowd moving off a cricket-field. When I looked back and saw the ground all crawling and wormy with wounded bodies, I felt no horror at all but only an immense exultation at having got through the Barrage [*Letters* 458].

When Owen retells the experience in letter form, the distinction between himself and others is unavoidable: "I woke up without being squashed. Some didn't." Moments before, all had been connected in "extraordinary exultation" of "showing [them]selves openly." He echoes this exultation in the poem by the experience of all racing together to face the sky's fury. After the shelling which Owen survives, however, he is able to sustain the feelings of "immense exultation at having got through" which outweigh any "horror" that the ghastly image of "crawling and wormy ... wounded bodies" would leave upon his consciousness. This response displays a remarkable frankness in discussing such a recent and traumatic event. The facts of battle have created the division of the collective group into "I" and "they" in this letter. For Owen, the transcendent feelings of "exultation" at having survived establish a personal continuity between the before and after stages of the raid. In the letter, he displays none of the "survivor's guilt" that will characterize his shell shock, but the disparity between his own exultation and the agony he witnesses in the rest provide ample room for such guilt to develop as the experience takes root in memory. In reshaping the events that form the letter into "Spring Offensive," Owen removes this distinction between "I" and "they" through an omniscient perspective. Without a first-person speaker to narrate the events, all are seen at a distance, and all are equal, at this moment, because of their common physical and emotional responses to the event.

The removal of the self from the poem is not merely a convenient way to elide confronting the personal responsibility that has plagued other poems. Instead, Owen crafts this objective perspective to locate the responsibility for the slaughter in the hands of an omnipotent power. In doing so, Owen is releasing himself from the duty to save the men, a duty that the war has proven is beyond his complete control, and instead is establishing his sole responsibility to the men to be that which he argued in his letter he was returning to fulfill: "watching their sufferings [so] that I may speak of them as well as a pleader can" (*Letters* 580). But in this battle, as in all battles, the split between the survivors and the fallen does occur:

> Of them who running on that last high place
> Breasted the surf of bullets, or went up
> On the hot blast and fury of hell's upsurge,
> Or plunged and fell away past this world's verge,
> Some say God caught them even before they fell [ll. 33–37].

These are the men who die. Owen has prepared the reader for the movement from the description of the war as a battle between man and nature to this analysis of the moment of death. He has created the moment of the battle as marking "the end of the world" in the soldiers' minds early in the poem (l. 6) so that "the last high place" at this moment of judgment is simultaneously the crest of the hill and a metaphor for the summit of their earthly lives before they "fell away past this world's verge." The sky which "burned / With fury against them" (ll. 29–30) is taken one step further to become "the hot blast and fury of hell's upsurge." The power given to nature has made it superhuman; the next logical step is to locate this power acting against the men in the realm of the supernatural. Owen's vision enables him to chart this progression and to sanction the lives lost. In the previous stanza, "earth set sudden cups" for the blood; now "God caught them even before they fell." Nature, which has comforted them in death, has evolved into the saving Grace.

But this stanza contains another possibility. The entirety of the poem has been the poet's vision; the absence of an "I" establishes an apparent objectivity, but such an absence makes room for the expression of poetic imagination to recreate the experience through the subjectivity necessary for such an appearance of objective truth. The poet avoids the definitiveness offered by God's salvation in this closing line by the phrase, "Some say." Lane argues, "The 'Some' who can so easily assimilate the fact of the soldiers' death are not those who were there as witnesses...."[81] But an earlier letter suggests that those that claim God's presence on the battlefield may include the poet. Owen had claimed to his mother in May, 1917 from the hospital shortly after his first tour of duty, "Christ is literally in no man's land. There men often hear his voice..." (*Letters* 461). This letter is either a statement of personal faith or his acknowledgment of his and all men's need to believe. The poem questions this belief in its final stanza which serves as Owen's ultimate poetic utterance to give voice to silence:

> But what say such as from existence' brink
> Ventured but drave too swift to sink,
> The few who rushed in the body to enter hell,
> And there out-fiending all its fiends and flames
> With superhuman inhumanities,
> Long-famous glories, immemorial shames —
> And crawling slowly back, have by degrees
> Regained cool peaceful air in wonder —
> Why speak not they of comrades that went under?
> [ll. 38–46].

Here Owen establishes the alternative to death: a harrowing of hell that has resulted in survival only through "out-fiending all its fiends and flames / With superhuman inhumanities." Because the poem has established the forces of nature and the forces beyond the natural as those dictating death, to have survived means that the individual has overpowered such forces and, by thus becoming "superhuman," has become "inhuman" in a way as well. To regain "cool peaceful air" is to survive this descent into hell, but for most men it is to live not to tell about it. It seems fitting for Owen that his last words in his last poem about the war would come in the form of an unanswerable question which, as Lane states, "casts a deep shadow over the whole poem."[82] By asking the question as the culmination of the process that builds to it, Owen in effect supplies the answer for those incapable of uttering it themselves through the imaginative reconstruction of battle that is the poem. He has charted the war experience, condensed here into the battle of "Spring Offensive" to represent the whole war, as a movement through the natural realm to a transcendent realm of both horror and glory. The poem is this ultimate paradox: It speaks of comrades who went under by representing the progression toward the vision of the transcendent at the moment of death, experienced by the fallen and by the survivors, including Owen who has felt both "abhorrence" and "exultation" and "has lost all earthy faculties" in battle. But its conclusion which questions not only the silent survivors but questions the whole vision preceding the question gives expression to Owen's ultimate truth of war — its inexpressibility.

It was a question he hoped to have time to answer more fully had he not died shortly after writing this last stanza. Owen's final written words on October 31, 1918, to his mother reflect the mood of this last poetic statement:

> It is a great life. I am more oblivious than alas! yourself, dear Mother, of the ghastly glimmering of the guns outside, & the hollow crashing of the shells.
> ...I hope you are as warm as I am; as serene in your room as I am here; and that you think of me never in bed as resignedly as I think of you always in bed. Of this I am certain you could not be visited by a band of friends half so fine as surround me here [*Letters* 591].

These are the men who have almost survived the duration of the war. Some would die alongside Owen in their final mission, and some would survive, dividing this collective whole once again. The strength Owen possesses to render himself "oblivious" to the guns and shells comes from the collective force of this "band of friends," many of the same men he led in January 1917 and described then as a herd of foul-mouthed cattle. The ability and conviction of his envisioning of the battle in "Spring Offensive" to imagine such value in such destruction stems as well from the collective silence of these men who "speak not ... of comrades that went under." The poem completes Owen's psychological progression by displaying his ability to invert the effects that his nightmares have had upon him. Those visions kept him trapped within the events of his past, regretting past actions and his inability to change the past to alleviate the guilt produced. Only through confrontation of the guilt, as accomplished in "Strange Meeting" and "The Sentry," has Owen been able to forgive himself and to engage within a present moment not tainted by memory. "Spring Offensive" achieves its power and creates a definition of heroism for the men because of its willed disconnection from the past, despite its basis in prior experience, and its creation of a transcendental world where a battle is waged between the human and natural worlds, with God and the poet as the final voices of judgment. Owen could not have written such a final poem as this, had he developed the language and the conceptions of selfhood enacted in all of his prior work upon the war. These poems were preparations for establishing the voice that has re-envisioned the war and carved out of its ruined physical and psychological landscape a new definition of the heroism of its participants, living and dead.

CHAPTER THREE

"Strange hells within the minds war made": Ivor Gurney and the Poetic Reconstitution of Identity

---

Childhood and the Preparation for War and Mental Illness

> That blood, those chromosomes ... drew him to the absurd
> Disordering of notes, to the garrulity of the word,
> Instead of the forms that already his youthful passion
> Had prepared for the ordering of both self and nation.[1]

Charles Tomlinson, writing almost sixty years after Ivor Gurney's death in 1937 and over seventy years since the early twenties when the poet produced most of his best work, points to the essential irony and enigma within Gurney's life and artistic career. The mental illness that would lead to his institutionalization has created the conception of the mad artist, the vision of the poet and composer that lingers for those who have not forgotten him altogether. By the late 1920s, mental illness had rendered Gurney effectively silent as a poet and musician and had largely destroyed the coherence of self and artistry that has established his limited legacy. During his period of greatest lucidity and productivity — during the years following the First World War — Gurney showed interest in the creation of forms, both poetic and musical. Tomlinson's poem suggests further that these forms were part of the enterprise of self-creation inextricably connected to Gurney's sense of place.[2] An especially sad irony of Gurney's mental illness comes in the limitations in psychological understanding and psychotherapy offered to him during the time in which he lived and wrote. His participation in the war caused his doctors to assess the mental instability at first as "Nervous Breakdown from Deferred Shell Shock" and only later to change this diagnosis to what has come to be called paranoid schizophrenia.[3] And more recently, today's scholars continue to debate how exactly Gurney's illness should be classified, arguing that his symptoms and his periods of intense productivity of verse and music, coupled with periods of crippling depression, point to a diagnosis of bipolar disorder with psychotic episodes.[4] If not for limitations in methods of treating his illness and a lack of financial resources to enable such treatment, Gurney might have functioned coherently enough to allow for the artistic creation which tapered off when he was locked up for good. Contemporary medicine, through combinations of medication and psychotherapy, in all likelihood would have enabled Gurney an existence, however fragile, outside the confines of the insane asylum.

Much of the writing that resulted from these "asylum years" (1922–1937), particularly in the 1930s, is notable for its lack of structure and organization. Hurd begins his biography with a representative letter from this period to "the London Metropolitan Police Force," the institution responsible, Gurney believed, for the electrical impulses he perceived as controlling his movements in the asylum. The rambling letter reads in part:

> [B]ut I eat little, though drinking much tea, and working late with too much light. But I slept by my work often, washing my body every morning and trying not to go to bed. Seeing many dawns; writing much, walking much; almost any active employment I would have taken, at 5/— a week and keep. An enema was used, but I eat little, drinking much; working much; sometimes walking 17 miles at a time. I took a dog out for walks (for kindness), saved it from eating; kept its health, and sometimes beat it, but was kind to it.

Gurney closes, "Asking for Death, Release, or Imprisonment. An end to Pain. I. B. Gurney."[5] Some poems from this period appear to be letters that Gurney simply has broken up into lines of more or less equal length, such as "The Retreat" which provides a detailed account of Gurney's participation in battle during the war. It reads in part:

> I fired straight at the middle one.
> No move; now at the right side of the left one.
> No move; again between the right one and middle one ...
> When up there dashed my Platoon, crashing branches down
> And off went Germans as swift as deer....[6]

The poem contains over a hundred occasionally rhymed lines of similar description. While the poem offers some of the most vivid accounts of the war Gurney would pen, it seems more a narrative that Gurney would tell his fellow soldiers back in the safety of the trench that evening, or would recount in a letter home, rather than an experience to which the poet has applied imagination to wrest the story into a meaningful shape. In letters and poems from the asylum, Gurney's command over the recollection of the events that comprise his tormented past has been reduced to accumulating the details and listing them without any sense of selectivity in their order or degrees of importance. The cause of such deteriorating quality of poetic output is the deterioration of selfhood which accompanies his increasing disconnection to reality as his psychotic episodes intensified. Gurney himself recognizes that his condition has reduced him to a broken semblance of the artist of his youth. "Chance to Work" clocks in at over three hundred lines of rhyming couplets, a form which does offer Gurney some means for stabilizing the thought within, but it functions for the poet as an autobiographical confession of the hardships life has dealt him. The poem concludes:

> [I] Would pray for death, beneath which Chance, Change; this life
> Is horror, and bad horror. For here now no strife
> With self or evil is possible, nor yet is brief
> The minute. Pain or Wearing without relief [*Collected Poems* 265–73].

Mental torment, Gurney confesses, has made the double battle of his artistic life — the "strife / With self or evil," the demons within or the challenges without — impossible.

Samuel Hynes calls Gurney, "One of the finest poets of his generation, … better, I'd say, than Owen, better than Rosenberg, better than the young Graves, more powerful, more wide-ranging, more original in his rhetoric."[7] How was a poet of this stature reduced to such "garrulity of the word?" To what extent should we blame "the strife / with self" or "the strife / With … evil" — the First World War — for the end result of the immense talent and potential from his youth that we glimpse in these sad letters and poems of his final period? Did Gurney's art aim to resolve such strife, or did it function simply as the means to represent it? In some respect, art (because of its capacity to represent, to provide structure to and thus potentially to offer understanding of, reality) is inextricably linked to every stage of his biography, and some preliminary facts will prove relevant to a discussion of his time at war. Ivor was born in 1890 to parents who ran their own tailoring business and who had "gained a tenuous foothold on the ladder of middle-class comfort and respectability."[8] By all accounts, his father David Gurney was a pleasant and hard working man, but his mother, Florence, appears to have been much more troubled and troubling for young Ivor. She was prone to bursts of anger, and her overall temperament seems to have been one of emotional detachment from all of her children — Ivor, as well as from his younger brother Ronald, his elder sister Winifred, and younger sister Dorothy. W. H. Trethowan argues:

> Gurney seems to have inherited not only his musical ability from his mother but also his mental instability.... Although there is no suggestion that Florence Gurney herself ever suffered from schizophrenia, descriptions of her personality suggest that she could certainly be described as schizoid, a term indicating certain personality traits such as coldness, aloofness, undue sensitivity and a tendency to develop persecutory attitudes. As is well known, such a personality is often the precursor to schizophrenia but does not always develop fully in this direction.[9]

Thinking today suggests that Gurney's illness, however it is classified, likely had a hereditary component, but in addition to these "chromosomes" alluded to in Tomlinson's poem, the presence of his mother probably exacerbated the psychological difficulties Gurney experienced as a youth. Trethowan argues that Gurney's eventually incapaciting illness was schizophrenia, linking it genetically to his mother's schizoid condition, but regardless of the diagnosis, the familial link is significant. Hurd describes Florence as continually badgering her husband for his minor misdeeds and resisting the independence of her children that accompanied their growing up. Winifred recalls, "She possessed us as babies, but couldn't do so later and her iron rule led to nagging. Life for us was something akin to a bed of stinging nettles.... The pity of it was that Mother did not seem to enjoy her children, and so far as I could see she did not win their love. Worse still, Father was not allowed to give us as much love as he had for us."[10]

While the mother caused difficulties for each of the children, Ivor's sensitivity seems to have caused him to bear the brunt of them and to search for an outlet. Ivor soon devoted himself to the development of his unique musical ability. At age nine, he competed for a place in the Cathedral Choir in Gloucester and was accepted. As a result of the lack of nurturing found at home, Ivor began to turn inward for comfort during these pre-adolescent years. Exposed to literature by a family friend with an extensive library, Ivor read far more complex books than would be usual for a boy of his age, and he began writing short organ works and songs which became more complex and accomplished through his teenage years. As this stage of his artistry intensified, his behavior became increasingly odd. He often stayed out all night and slept in barns or under the stars. His sister recalls, "The truth was, he did not seem to belong to us...."[11] He would starve himself for periods of time "and then suddenly purchase great quantities of apples or buns and consume them voraciously.... At home, and even in other people's homes, he would creep into the pantry and stuff himself with all manner of unsuitable foods — half a pound of butter, or some ill-considered jumble of leftovers."[12] Despite digestive troubles no doubt brought on by this bizarre diet, Gurney appeared content and harmless, and his family granted him the latitude to continue with this behavior.

His output of musical compositions increased with such impressive quality that Gurney applied to and was accepted at the Royal College of Music in London where he remained between October 1911 and his entry into the war in 1915. Gurney's teachers found him brilliant, with potential for greatness as a composer, but also difficult and at times exasperating. One instructor, Sir Charles Stanford, called him "unteachable" and kicked him out of class after Gurney responded to the suggestions made to one of his pieces by saying, "Well, Sir Charles, I see you've jigged the whole show."[13] Hurd, a musician himself, assesses Gurney's mental state at this point by focusing both upon the quality of the music produced and even its appearance on the page: "The major flaw ... is the tendency to let the line degenerate into a mere scrabble of buzzing semiquavers that leads nowhere in particular.... The confusion and illegibility is such as to suggest ... a mind that is, in some respects, already out of touch with reality."[14] As a young man in his early twenties, he fits the romanticized stereotype of the genius: very much in a mental world of his own, breaking with convention in order to discover original means of expression, but in danger, in doing so, of losing contact with the stabilizing, conventional forms which served to anchor him and his creativity to reality.

The stresses of composition and his more recent forays into the creation of poetry took an emotional toll upon him. He suffered from extended periods of deep depression, as he describes when writing about hearing a performance of Vaughan Williams Sea Symphony, "I crawled out of bed to hear it, and afterwards went back for three days more — but it was worth it."[15] He returned to his home of Gloucester in May of 1913 to recuperate and avert a complete breakdown, a move which seems to have provided relief for the time being. He writes from home to Marion Scott, his friend from the music school: "My brain, heart, nerves, and physique are certified sound, but that I am overworked and run down" (Letters 4). In late June, he seems to have turned a corner towards stability once again, "Well, I had a pretty bad time of it for the first 6 weeks, and then an increasingly better time of it; and I am still on the mend..." (Letters 6). He returned in the fall of 1913 to resume his studies, where he remained when war was declared in August

1914. No letters survive to reveal his thinking about the war during its first months. He did attempt to enlist alongside the thousands of men who were swept up by the patriotic fervor at the onset, but Gurney was rejected because of poor eyesight. In February 1915, he tried again, when British authorities were "less fussy about the nature of its cannon fodder."[16] He was drafted on February 9 and hastily scribbled a postcard home that read, "Private Gurney (5th Gloucester Reserve Battalion) sends you greetings" (*Letters* 12).

Selfhood and Service: Private Gurney's Experience in the War

What is most peculiar about Gurney's troubled life is that of all his various stages of experience, the years of his service in the British army from 1915–1918 show him achieving relative mental balance and writing music and primarily poetry (since conditions in the trenches made musical composition difficult) of great lucidity. During the unprecedented and mechanized slaughter of a large proportion of a generation of European men, when the Western world seemed to be at war with the foundations that characterized its civilization, Gurney found his participation within the war to be an opportunity for forging an individual purpose and identity as a soldier. Far from dismantling the pre-war identity as the stresses of combat would do in the psychological wreckage of many of his peers, the war itself functioned to solidify the fragmented and misdirected individual who had struggled to find his place in the pre-war world. The war did result in a change of personality for this individual as it had for many others, but in this unique case, the change — at least temporarily — was for the better.

Because so much of the time in the trenches was spent in idleness, Gurney became one of many soldiers who wrote numerous letters home. Never close to family members, Gurney corresponded most frequently with Marion Scott, who wrote him equally often. These war letters provide a detailed impression of Gurney's life in training, in France, and in hospitals where he was treated for a bullet wound in the arm in April 1917 and for gas during the battle of Passchendaele in September 1917. They display the experience of a private soldier whose daily physical reality was much like those of his fellow soldiers in the Fifth Gloucester Regiment but whose psychological struggles seem unique to him. He returns often to the idea that the war will serve as an opportunity to repair his fragile psychological state by means of the discipline of army life. He writes to his friend, the poet F. W. Harvey in February 1915, shortly after enlisting, "Let's hope [the war will] do the trick for both of us, and make us so strong, so happy, so sure of ourselves, so

crowded with fruitful memories of joy that we may be able to live in towns
or earn our living at some drudgery and yet create whole and pure joy for
others" (*Letters* 12). This letter reveals Gurney's anxieties about class limita-
tions and his desire to transcend these boundaries through art. Since he is
not from the upper class who became the officers, Gurney will remain a pri-
vate and, should he survive the war's duration, will return to the life that his
lower middle class upbringing predicted. He hopes that the war will pro-
vide him with the mental stability to make the best of a life of "drudgery."
He suggests that the capacity for his imagination to make something out of
his situation is the predictor of his future happiness, not the simple and
seemingly limiting facts of a mundane life.

Letters throughout the war convey similar hopes. He describes the war
as a means of escape from more personal horrors of his civilian existence,
again in February 1915: "I feel that nowhere could I be happier than where
I am.... It is indeed a better way to die; with these men, in such a cause;
than the end which seemed near me and was so desirable only just over two
years ago. And if I escape; well, there will be memories for old age; not all
pleasant, but none so unpleasant as those which would have come had I
refused the call" (*Letters* 14). Later that spring, he writes, "I am convinced
that had I stuck to music, complete health would have been a very long job.
This life will greatly help.... It is hard, and always am I tired, but struggle
through in a very much happier frame of mind than that I have had for some
time — probably 4 years" (*Letters* 17). Before his entry into the physical real-
ity of the trenches, this hope for healing could sustain him. The routines of
meals, drills, and rest provided structure for Gurney during these months of
training, a structure he hoped would continue when introduced to the actual
fighting.

His battalion arrived in the trenches at Riez Bailleul in June 1916, dur-
ing the most chaotic and violent stage of the war, when patriotic thoughts
of national purpose that had energized the country were beginning to erode
in the consciousness of those experiencing the fighting. They were stationed
near the Battle of the Somme, which was about to begin but which Gur-
ney's regiment avoided until the end of the campaign in December 1916. The
Fifth Gloucesters were entrenched to the north near Ypres, and as Denis Win-
ter states, "Anywhere near Ypres was always bad."[17] Gurney participated in
intense fighting which had a psychological impact upon him during his time
in the trenches, and he writes about battling the fronts of both selfhood and
the battlefield: "The only thought that disturbs me ever, is that all my con-
tinual striving and endeavour to become a fit and full man ... may be ended
by a German bullet or bayonet" (*Letters* 71). Despite periods of dangerous
exposure, Gurney quickly perceived the major key of the war: "Guns are

going in the distance, and every moment there is the chance of a strafe (we have had one, not a bad one) yet the note of the whole affair is boredom" (*Letters* 90). In the face of danger, Gurney's nerve appeared to be strong, and he felt connected to his fellow man: "Men go one by one, some with nice blighties, some with the Eternal Discharge. But on the whole we are a cool lot. Some of us ... amazingly cool" (*Letters* 128). And in September 1917, he writes, "By the way, I ... have got the name for being extremely cool under shell fire. It may be so to the view, but could they read my mind sometimes! So you see, neurasthenia leads one to a strange praise. By conquering fear-of-Life one may learn at once to love Life and to scorn death together; but neither has come yet in reality" (*Letters* 328). Elsewhere, as this letter from April 1917 demonstrates, Gurney seems to doubt his conviction that the army will be a healing experience: "We should all lapse into neurasthenia were we not driven" (*Letters* 238). The real core of danger for Gurney lay within: the difference between himself and his fellow soldiers may not have been visible, but he recognized it as a fundamental mental weakness which made him prone to nervous collapse. The stability of army life provided a potential scaffolding for building a stable identity, but the weakness of this structure was internal and surfaced in letters. Furthermore, the argument put forth by Blevins that Gurney's eventual illness would be best termed bipolar disorder, rather than schizophrenia, receives further support from these war letters documenting his trench experience. Blevins writes, "Had Gurney possessed the withdrawn and potentially dangerous antisocial behaviour of a schizophrenic, it is unlikely that he would have made friends or that he would have made it through basic training much less become a reliable soldier at the Front."[18] And even though schizophrenia could arguably have surfaced later, throughout Gurney's life, he shows as he does here an awareness of his fragile state, rather than the assured convictions common to schizophrenics that their deluded perceptions of reality are sane. Boden writes, "a schizophrenic is usually unaware that he is mentally ill, believing his perception of life to be quite normal. Gurney, on the other hand, was only too well aware that he was sliding into the abyss."[19]

Gurney's letters do not engage with much detail in descriptions of the carnage he was witnessing on a regular basis, in part because such descriptions were thought by his superiors to be bad for the morale of those back home: "It is difficult in these letters to interest you, and yet avoid trouble with the Censor" (*Letters* 128). Hoffpauir argues for a different explanation: "Gurney was not overwhelmed by the horrors of the war he experienced. He achieved a certain detachment.... When he complained of the war it was in different and less dramatic terms than those of the more emotional poets."[20] Oddly enough, Gurney's year and a half in battle shows him to have been a hardy soldier, despite his sincere confessions of psychological vulnerability in his letters. The detachment seen in the letters, whether as a result of the censors or of Gurney's emotional removal from the experiences he witnessed, denies contemporary readers of a detailed vision of the sufferings of Gurney and the rest of the Fifth Gloucesters, except in the most general terms: "[W]e suffer pain out here, and for myself it sometimes comes that death would be preferable to such a life. Yet my chief thought is that I have found myself unfitted for Life and Battle, and am gradually by hard necessity being strengthened and made fit for some high task" (*Letters* 168). Even seen against the background of mud, exhaustion, and pain, Gurney continues to represent the struggle he is undergoing as a battle with that part of himself that has proved to be incapable of dealing with the business of living. This self-concern is more central to his thinking than the actual suffering brought on by the circumstances of war. This "chief thought" is a personal one — not about the horrors or absurdity of war, but about the struggle to achieve and maintain an internal coherence. Only through experiencing this pain and working through this struggle, according to Gurney, can he alleviate the mental anguish. The sentiment throughout his war letters never is hope for the victory of the British army, or a successful assault, or contempt for the enemy; as he says, "In the mind of all the English soldiers I have met there is absolutely no hate for the Germans" (*Letters* 215). Rather, it is an almost obsessive hope for the coherence of self that might emerge out of all the pain.

Gurney's letters from France show as well the development of another form of self-healing — beyond what he had envisioned army life as effecting — the reconstruction of the identity that had offered the greatest stability before the war, the artist. The army might offer structure imposed from without, but artistic creation became the "high task" which offered the chance for Gurney to will these structures upon the raw material of both his physical and psychological realities, to create forms from within. He provides an even more definitive belief in the value of art in a moving letter to Marion Scott in December 1916:

> After all, my friend, it is better to live a grey life in mud and danger, so long as one uses it — as I trust I am now doing — as a means to an end. Someday all this experience may be crystallized and glorified in me; and men shall learn by chance fragments in a string quartett [sic] or symphony, what thoughts haunted the minds of men who watched the darkness grimly in desolate places. Who learnt by the denial how full and wide a thing Joy may be, forming dreams of noble lives when nothing noble but their own nobility (and that seemed tiny and of little worth) was to be seen. Who kept ever the memory of their home and friends to strengthen them, and walked

in pleasant places in faithful dreams. And how one man longed to be working to celebrate them in music and verse worthy of the high theme, but did not bargain with God, since it is best to accept one's Fate when that is clearly seen [*Letters* 171].

This extraordinary document serves as an *ars poetica* for the poet, conceived with remarkable clarity in the midst of such squalor, destruction, and self-doubt. The dense passage of artistic purpose reveals many dimensions upon which Gurney's war poetry, written during and after his time in France, sought to deliver. There is an acknowledgment that the process of artistic creation will take some time; for these "crystallizations" and "glorifications" of war experience to have validity in speaking for "the minds of men who watched the darkness grimly in desolate places," the artist requires the passage of time to grant him the perspective to wrest the experience into shape.

Within this letter as well lie suggestions of the lengths to which Gurney committed his imagination to go in order to create beauty not only out of the ugliness of war but out of the torment in his mind. In a landscape where "nothing noble but their own nobility ... was to be seen," the artist enters the terrain of "dreams of noble lives." Denying himself joy by wallowing in mud and death enables the poet the vision of "how full and wide a thing Joy may be," never appreciated until it is denied. Throughout Gurney's poetry of war exists the desire to turn the facts of battle and trench life into something they do not appear to be, or to turn his eye toward beauty existing within the ugliness as a means of blocking out the ugliness and thus making the beautiful even more so, and by doing so, redeeming the experience of war. Gurney's statement is a complex vision of both the function and personal need for such an art. It displays the commitment to transform his experience through the application of an ordering consciousness. This in itself might not seem a revolutionary credo and indeed might be a generic definition of art, all of which is, in one sense, a distortion of the truth. But, as his poetry will show, the belief within this vision that good will emerge out of all the suffering, in addition to providing the poet with the means to restructure and control experience, threatens also to allow the imagination to enter a realm divorced from reality.

Simultaneously, the poems themselves engage in the reconstruction of Gurney's "private" vision of the life of the private.[21] Poetry written about the trenches becomes a pursuit that allows the poet to apply his will to the forging of a vision of selfhood out of the war landscape. As the introduction has explained, the social class structure of peace time fed directly into the army life. The educated upper and upper middle classes were trained as officers who led the volunteers and conscripted men from the lower rungs of British society, ranks which included Private Gurney. Eric Leed describes the reality that the officer class encountered:

> They learned, first of all, that their attitude toward the social significance of war, toward the nation, toward the meaning of combat was rarely shared by the [men] who made up their companies. More importantly, they often concluded that their conception of the war as a community of fate in which all class differences would be submerged was an "illusion," a function of their initial innocence and idealism.[22]

The war was not the great leveler of class systems; efficiency demanded that class roles become as apparent during wartime as they had been during peace, if not more so because of the close quarters. Undoubtedly the private class endured the greatest physical trials while in the trenches, living only by means of the food, clothing, and tools given to them from the higher-ups or sent from home; sleeping, when they slept at all, in whatever space they could clear for themselves; and obeying the orders of either their lance-corporals, responsible for about fifteen of them, or their subalterns, supervising about sixty.[23] Though such a life was hard, the private class of soldiers did not have to concern themselves with one of the results of war that became the officers' burden — sending men below them in class to their deaths.

Donald Davie writes, "Because he is not of the officer class, [Gurney] feels no responsibility for the horror, hence no guilt about it, and so his revulsion from it is manageable."[24] The private's life had a definite practicality to it; he took for his goal keeping himself alive when stationed at the front trenches; resting and preparing for a return to the front when stationed in reserve. Much time was spent at work at dirty, menial chores, such as digging trenches, stacking sandbags, and pumping the ever-present rainwater. The men lived alongside lice, maggots, and rats. When the private was sent on a dangerous mission in an assault, his goal was survival, and if he were to be hit, he hoped for a "Blighty" wound, a "cushy" one, not life-threatening but enough to send him home for good. Waterman says of Gurney, "[h]is was not to reason why, but only to do as he was told, and to try not to die...."[25] Gurney reveals in a letter the image he struck as a private:

> I never shave, wash late in the day if I please, and wear horrid looking sandbags round my legs because of the mud. When the [Sergeant-Major] tackled me about looking so like a scarecrow — or rather ... "Come, come, Gurney, look more like a soldier for the Lord's sake." "Well, He doesn't seem to be doing much for *my* sake, and anyway I'm not a soldier. I'm a *dirty civilian*" [*Letters* 115].

Gurney did what he was told while in service, but the letter reveals that he never considered himself entirely part of the purpose of the war, though he benefited from its regimented and ritualistic daily activities. This detached stance seems typical of the private who envisioned himself as a pawn in a game played by men who had little to do with the concerns of the private's day to day existence. Winter quotes a veteran private of the war: "I remember being asked on leave what the men thought of Haig. You may as well have asked the private soldier what he thinks of God. He knows about the same amount on each."[26]

Such an existence, apart from the political purpose of the war (as were most men by late 1916) and not altogether fitting in with his companions, forced an introspective individual like Gurney in upon himself. Gurney began to send poems to Marion Scott in November 1916, and by February 1917, Gurney had revised the works, assembled them into suitable order, and written a Preface to his first collection, *Severn and Somme* (1917). In the Preface, Gurney includes in his dedication:

> ...and last but not least — 5 Platoon, B Co, 2/5 Glosters; who so often have wondered whether I were crazy or not. Let them draw their own conclusions now, for the writing of this book it was that so distracted me.... I fear that those who buy the book ... to get information about the Second-Fifth will be disappointed. Most of the book is concerned with a person named Myself ... [*Letters* 213].

Unlike many "war" books published concurrently with this one, Gurney's primary purpose is neither protest against the war nor patriotic invective in favor of it. As the title of the collection suggests, Gurney's world is split between the reality of war experienced alongside the Somme and the memory of his youth along the Severn River, to which he escapes in imagination and in art. To borrow the terms laid out in his previous letter, the Somme River landscape reminds him and teaches the reader through "denial" of beauty of the beauty of his past alongside the Severn. His prior letter had established also that his purpose was in part so that "men shall learn ... what thoughts haunted the minds of men." Here he claims a much more personal motivation. This is one of the saddest lessons that Gurney's poetry teaches us, here in his early volumes and more poignantly in his postwar work: Gurney confesses that such an obsession with selfhood and self-representation is the means of averting the "craziness" his companions suspected, and such self-representation in art functions as the only distraction and therapy possible to avert and control the thoughts that haunted his own mind.

Although many of the poems in *Severn and Somme* display Gurney's complete imaginative escape from his surroundings to construct a nostalgic

glimpse of his homeland, the poems which engage directly with the facts of
his present experience in France give an indication of the personal concerns
that his war poems will address more fully after the war. The poems that
provide the ending to this collection are a sequence of five sonnets which
Gurney claimed he:

> intended to be a sort of counterblast against "Sonnetts 1914," which
> were written before the grind of the war and by [Rupert Brooke,] an
> officer (or one who would have been an officer.) They are the protest
> of the physical against the exalted spiritual; of the cumulative weight
> of small facts against the one large.... Old ladies won't like them, but
> soldiers may.... I know perfectly well how my attitude will appear,
> but — They will be called "Sonnetts 1917" [*Letters* 210].

One of these sonnets is called "Pain":

> Pain, pain continual; pain unending;
> Hard even to the roughest, but to those
> Hungry for beauty ... Not the wisest knows,
> Nor most pitiful-hearted, what the wending
> Of one hour's way meant. Grey monotony lending
> Weight to the grey skies, grey mud where goes
> An army of grey bedrenched scarecrows in rows
> Careless at last of cruellest Fate-sending.
> Seeing the pitiful eyes of men foredone,
> Or horses shot, too tired merely to stir,
> Dying in shell-holes both, slain by the mud.
> Men broken, shrieking even to hear a gun.
> Till pain grinds down, or lethargy numbs her,
> The amazed heart cries angrily out on God
> > > [*Collected Poems* 36].

The sonnet seems molded out of the sentiments revealed in his war letters,
in which he has constantly identified himself as one "[h]ungry for beauty"
through his description of trench existence as "a grey life in mud and dan-
ger" where "we suffer pain" (*Letters* 171, 168). Gurney employs the device of
repetition that he will complicate in postwar poems, here repeating the sin-
gle words "pain" and "grey" to give the sense of both the monotonous exis-
tence and seemingly endless exposure to and experience of human suffering.
Repetition functions as well to suggest the incapability of language to cap-
ture the ineffable nature of the horror, as if the poet and private has a lim-
ited number of words in his arsenal for expression. Indeed, the physical
depiction of the scene outweighs any hope for spiritual redemption, as Gur-
ney claimed about the sonnets. The landscape, all of the components of

which are described as equally grey, does not allow for contrast between figure and ground. From a distanced perspective, the sky blends into the men who blend into the mud. The "grey bedrenched scarecrows" are not even granted humanity by the poet because the entire experience has eliminated the possibility of a humanity or imagination that might elevate it from this reality. Dying in shell holes, men achieve the status of horses through this unending process of suffering, a juxtaposition that recalls Wilfred Owen's opening line in "Anthem for Doomed Youth," written only a few months later: "What passing-bells for those who die as cattle?"[27] This time, however, the poet is one of these "beasts" himself, a private, not an officer who purports to speak for him.

Though Gurney does not seem to have heard of Owen until 1922, after Owen's first collection was published (*Letters* 529), the closing lines of the poem, with the half-rhyme of "mud" and "God" recalls Owen's "Apologia Pro Poemate Meo" with its beginning, "I, too, saw God through mud —."[28] But Owen's juxtaposition of God and mud shows the place of the imagination within the poem; the poet possesses the capacity to turn an image of ugliness to something divine, whether imagined or perceived. Gurney, at this stage in his war poetry, does not offer the possibility of transforming the mud or anything within this scene into a vision redeemed by his imagination. He does create a sonnet out of all this mess, a creation that points to the imagination of the poet who applies form to the disorder, but the use of the form functions primarily to respond to Brooke's war sonnets with their elevated diction, emblematic of the stage in the war before things got this ugly. "Pain" is notable for the absence of a first person perspective that might be capable of asserting an imaginative order upon the ruined landscape. The soldiers in the poem, when they are given any qualities that make them human, are depicted as men without means to control their environment, through body or mind: "Not the wisest knows, / ... what the wending / Of one hour's way meant." The only action taken by the men in the poem, other than the endless trudge of the collective body, is to die or, in the closing line, to "[cry] angrily out on God." This final plea is ironic as an active assertion of the will; it is a desperate gesture that reveals the ultimate passivity and helplessness of the common soldier.

The Preface to *Severn and Somme*, which claims the book "is concerned with a person named Myself," does not apply overtly to the perspective of this sonnet, and the role of the speaker in the others that make up Gurney's sonnet sequence on the war ("For England," "Servitude," "Homesickness," and "England the Mother") is minimal.[29] The self that Gurney is representing through first person speakers in this book is the man who recalls and desires a return to the pastoral world of Gloucester in such poems as "Hark,

Hark, the Lark" or "West Country." One might surmise that the war is too close to be rendered in a form for Gurney that at this point would enable him to see his place within it with any great psychological depth. The thrust of the Preface's claim to explore a self comes to fruition in Gurney's treatment of the war after it begins to recede into memory. The title of Gurney's second collection, *War's Embers* (1919), suggests the effect of the passage of time between the events of war and their retelling — the war burns on in memory. Though some of the poems were written during his hospital stay for a bullet wound in April 1917 and most of the book was written from France before his gassing at Passchendaele in September of the same year removed him from the trenches for good, the war poems within the collection display a mind that is beginning to impose upon the experience, and expose to the reader, greater psychological complexities in the war's reconstruction. Gurney's most famous war poem, "To His Love," comes from *War's Embers*:

> He's gone, and all our plans
>   Are useless indeed.
> We'll walk no more on Cotswold
>   Where the sheep feed
>   Quietly and take no heed.
> His body that was so quick
>   Is not as you
> Knew it, on Severn river
>   Under the blue
>   Driving our small boat through.
> You would not know him now ...
>   But still he died
> Nobly, so cover him over
>   With violets of pride
>   Purple from Severn side [*Collected Poems* 41].

Unlike "Pain" and several of the war poems from *Severn and Somme*, the role of the "I" is central to the poem's attitudes toward the war experience, seen here through his relationship to the dead soldier. The title suggests that the dead soldier has left a lover back in England, and the first stanza informs her that neither the speaker, presumably a friend from the dead man's youth, nor she will resume the peaceful and pastoral existence in Gloucester after the war because of the violence that has intervened and disrupted such a life.

The complexity of the poem's speaker is revealed in the second stanza when he posits a difference between himself and this woman in degrees of understanding this death. This difference is caused by the moment of death separating past from present and by the speaker's privileged proximity to this man, physically and psychologically, that comes from having experienced the same life at war as he has. With this difference comes a moral superiority of the speaker, a right to speak these words to the distanced lover. He locates the difference between himself and the woman upon the dead body: "His body that *was* so quick / *Is* not as you / Knew it.... / You would not know him now...." The world of the Severn River, an escape for the poet in the poems of *Severn and Somme*, is seen now as a thing of the past, unable to redeem the brutal reality of the present. But the speaker must contend with this reality somehow. He too has been part of this pastoral past, and if he is to survive, this is the world to which the speaker hopes to return. He orders the lover to "cover [the soldier] over / With violets of pride / Purple from Severn side." Because he died "Nobly," this gesture, the speaker concedes, is a valid one for the perspective of the lover whose limitations of experience has left her ignorant in part of all the death entails. But from the perspective of the speaker, the perspective that really matters in revealing the poem's function for him, this response to the dead rings false. The use of the word "Nobly" is ironic; the fact of the matter is that the body has been mangled beyond recognition. The man died obeying orders and fighting for his country, but the poem questions how authentically noble such values are. Silkin states, "'Nobly' is not merely the individual soldier's attribute; it is the propagandistic aura that the state awards the dead in an effort to persuade the living to continue their efforts."[30]

The speaker seems to share the scorn for such empty values of patriotism; the gesture of covering, or to be redundant "cover[ing] over," implies such a falseness. But the poem has yet to offer the speaker himself a means of coping which the concluding stanza then delivers:

> Cover him, cover him soon!
> And with thick-set
> Masses of memoried flowers —
> Hide that red wet
> Thing I must somehow forget [ll. 16–20].

Silkin states, "[B]y ending the line on the adjective 'wet' he transforms it momentarily into a noun, which reinforces the rawness. The man is no longer a person but a 'wet thing.' This is what Gurney must — and because must, cannot — forget."[31] The rhyme as well shows this difficulty; the speaker cannot forget the image of something wet that once was alive. Though complete forgetting of the experience may not be possible nor even desirable, the poem shows the mind's capacity to distance itself from the source of emotional pain. The sentimentality and nostalgia of Severn and childhood have disappeared in the poem, either because they offer no practical way of resolving the grief or because these memories of what once was are in part source of the pain. Flowers are not symbols of gratitude for his laying down his life or ways to keep his memory alive. They are practical tools to obliterate one redness with another that is easier for the mind to assimilate. The speaker adopts a stoic stance that refuses in the end to admit that the dead soldier was ever a man; the war has changed him into an object that the speaker lacks the word to name. Of course, the dead soldier, or someone like him, must remain in Gurney's mind as the recollecting poet for the poem even to be written. The mechanisms of distancing reveal the extent to which the war lives on in memory for Gurney, despite the poem's claims to the contrary. The gesture of forgetting is the poem's final note, and the graphic nature of the "red wet thing" ensures that the speaker, and the poet, cannot forget what has been seen. As the war itself becomes a thing of the past, Gurney's postwar verse will engage in even more complex and personal methods and needs of remembering.

The War Poems of the 1920s: Gurney's Postwar Return to the Private Experience

The war soon would become memory for Gurney. On September 12, 1917, during the disastrous blood and mud bath of the Third Battle of Ypres, which the soldiers called Passchendaele, Gurney was gassed. He tells Marion Scott, "One cannot smell the new gas. One starts sneezing. The old has had a heavy hothouse Swinburnian filthy sort of odour — voluptuous and full of danger" (*Letters* 326). There he remained under observation for the better part of the war's final year. Even as his days in the army drew to a close, Gurney showed that his capacity to resist a relapse might be waning. From the hospital in January 1918, he appears depressed and confesses, "I am just dry — my strength being taken up by endurance" (*Letters* 390). When forced to remain in bed, he loses the comfort that duty and activity provided to ease his mind. He complains of "the old nervous trouble" and an "unsettled state of mind" and soon thereafter, fears "slipping down and becoming a mere wreck" (*Letters* 410, 425, 430). And on March 28, 1918, to Marion Scott, comes the strangest letter of all:

> And yesterday I felt and talked to (I am serious) the spirit of Beethoven.... [W]hile playing the slow movement of the D major, I felt the presence of a wise friendly spirit; it was Old Ludwig van all right.... Bach was there but does not care for me. Schumann also, but my love for him is not so great. Beethoven said among other things he was fond of me, and that in nature I was like himself as

a young man.... What would the doctors say to *that*? A Ticket certainly, for insanity. No, it is the beginning of a new life, a new vision [*Letters* 418].

In some respects, the letter is an aberration. Gurney, whether or not he believed this meeting occurred, mentions it nowhere else in his letters. By 1929, however, Gurney will claim to be the author of Shakespeare's plays and the composer of Beethoven's Symphonies.[32] And one can see this initial delusion as marking the beginning of the pattern that would come to dominate Gurney's thinking and self-conception. Gurney's confused beliefs in his authorship evidence increasing confusion of identity which by the end of the 1920s would spell the effective silencing of his voice. Trethowan points to a similar loss of authority over his musical composition of the twenties which "shows a loosening of internal structure and lack of cohesion.... Each bar considered individually makes harmonic sense: it is only the ability to define and organize material, and to construct a coherent whole, that is altogether lacking."[33] While Trethowan argues that such symptoms are telltale signs of schizophrenia, Blevins convincingly counters that delusions and hallucinations are symptomatic also of bipolar patients suffering through the most intensely manic phases of that condition.[34] And the Beethoven letter does occur within a period marked by great productivity and great clarity, but it nonetheless points to the forces that Gurney was up against which would only intensify from this point on. The poetry that emerges from this transitional phase between war and his most severe battle with mental illness makes vivid the struggle that had consumed Gurney all his life for a stability of identity. In these postwar poems, he returns to the war, the period that provided him paradoxically with the greatest pain and pleasure, both of which he seeks to recombine in his imagined visions of beauty and selfhood to be found against the backdrop of war.

In 1919, when he was discharged from both the army and the hospital where he recuperated from the gas, Gurney's doctors diagnosed him as having suffered from "Deferred Shell Shock."[35] Gurney's doctors were responding to the fact that upon the ending of the war, which he experienced in a hospital bed in England, Gurney was beginning to display the early warning signs that the odd behaviors, suicidal tendencies, and delusions, which would lead to his institutionalization three years later, were resurfacing. But because of the state of psychological thinking at the time and their lack of awareness of his prior mental history, these doctors, having seen many minds crippled by the war's impact, attributed this mounting mental instability to the delayed effects of what he had both seen and lived through in France. As the biography has shown, it would be a gross misrepresentation of the facts of Gurney's life to claim that the war was the sole source of his malady. Unlike the experiences of officers such as Sassoon and Owen, whose psychological problems were caused by the war experience, Gurney's suffering was not the direct result of the war's capacity to fracture a pre-existing identity which the poet sought to reconstruct or rehabilitate through poetic self-representation. War, ironically, provided temporary relief from the varying degrees of mental illness that plagued his life. Contemporary medicine and thinking about the nature of severe mental illnesses like Gurney's tell us that with or without the war, Gurney was likely to have broken down. Both schizophrenia and bipolar disorder have been shown to have a clear physiological basis, unlike shell shock even when its manifestations are somatic in nature. A genetic tendency towards mental illness is oftentimes exacerbated by periods of emotional stress, so that the likelihood of an individual's suffering is increased when something as momentous and disruptive as two years of trench warfare is combined with the genetic predisposition. The years in France certainly did nothing to suppress the illness; it is more likely that, despite his feelings of security and purpose in the battlefield, the war dictated that before long Gurney would succumb in full to the condition that was pointing toward this crisis point in 1919.

It is not the purpose of this discussion to argue that the war was or was not the primary cause for the disintegration of identity Gurney displayed during his bout with the disease. It is enough to observe that the chronology and timing of the war and the recurrence of his illness make the stress of combat a likely contributor. Though one might argue that Gurney's struggles ensued because of the war, it is just as likely that without the memory of war as an anchor, however precarious this role might seem to us now, Gurney's dissociation of self would have ensued even more quickly. This discussion will examine Gurney's strategy of using poetry as a means of engaging in a type of poetic "self-therapy" by returning to the time when he felt most whole — his years in the trenches — to reconstruct this self of the private soldier that, once the war was over, was no longer available to him in life. Gurney's postwar work engages directly with the war experience, more so than the two volumes written during Gurney's two year stint in France with the Gloucester Regiment. The poems that Kavanagh has collected as *Rewards of Wonder*, Gurney's planned collection of poems composed most likely during the first half of the 1920s, reflect the poet's later perspective upon the war in which he redeems the ugliness of the experience through imagination.[36] Recent investigations in Gurney scholarship have debated the chronology of the compositions within this remarkably prolific period. Lucas states that "in 1924 [Gurney] listed the titles of no fewer than seven books which he claimed to have written or were on the stocks, [including] *Rewards of Wonder*...."[37] Walter and Thornton's introduction to the recent collection of previously unpublished poems by Gurney from this period, titled *80 Poems or So*, argues convincingly that this volume, which does not directly represent the war, and not *Rewards of Wonder*, was the one that publishers rejected, and that *Rewards of Wonder*, while a planned volume, was composed most likely between 1921 and 1924, straddling his commitment to the asylum in 1922, and existed only in a form circulated among a few of Gurney's sympathizers.[38] Unfortunately, it is difficult to date many individual poems from this period with precision. Having returned from the war, Gurney no longer included poems in his letters for safe keeping which would provide accurate dates, and the manuscripts of the poems show few conclusive dates themselves. Yet these most recent findings make the role that the composition of war poetry played in the 1920s for Gurney even more poignant: as his condition worsened, as family and medical authorities grew, arguably, less sympathetic and more resigned to Gurney's permanent incarceration in the asylum, reconstructing the war experience in verse became an even more crucial link to the days when Gurney felt most whole.

Rewards of Wonder, as well as numerous earlier poems uncollected during Gurney's lifetime written between the war and his confinement in the asylum in 1922, when Gurney returned to Gloucester and survived off the support of his brother Ronald and the patronage of musical and literary admirers, shows Gurney's increasing tendency to return through imagination to his years as a private in the trenches in France. The physical and temporal distance from France has allowed him to achieve, as he suggested in the Preface to *Severn and Somme*, the psychological distance for a mature perspective looking back upon the war. These poems display his strategy of fighting against his resurfacing mental illness, and the stylistic difficulties of syntax and meter perhaps display the poet's struggles to wrest the memories of warfare into satisfactory shape. The poems function as momentary stays against his own personal confusion, havens of nostalgia for his war years as his mental state began to deteriorate, much as Gloucester functioned nostalgically during the war. Within individual poems, furthermore, Gurney reconstructs his memories of the private soldier's tactics for creating an imaginative space of safety and security within the dangerous landscape of the trenches.

Gurney hints at his strategy of representing the war through the title of his postwar collection. In the war poems of this volume, Gurney searches his memories of the war experience for "rewards," for moments of beauty and wonder to be found within the ruined landscape. The imaginative treatment of these moments elevates them to states in which they appear to the speaker and to the reader as apart from the war that is their background. In "Pain," Gurney painted a picture of war that saw grey upon grey upon grey, with no place for the consciousness or imagination of a speaker to differentiate between elements of the experience. In these later poems, though, Gurney posits the capacity for the imagination to act as a line of defense for the poem's speakers against the perils of war. This recurrent theme crafted into the poems provides Gurney with the means of creating formal poetic constructions which function to defend him against the encroaching chaos of mental illness during this period between war and madness.

The poems share also the common element of precision in the time and place of their settings. Titles such as "June Night," "Billet," "First March," "Laventie," "Crucifix Corner," "New Year's Eve," "Near Vermand," and "Riez Bailleul" all establish exact physical or temporal locations which anchor the poems to the realities of warfare so that Gurney can grant the speaker, and thus himself, the poet who recollects the experience, the latitude to allow the imagination to wander and create. The first poem in *Rewards of Wonder* is "First Time In":

> After the dread tales and red yarns of the Line
> Anything might have come to us; but the divine
> Afterglow brought us up to a Welsh colony
> Hiding in sandbag ditches, whispering consolatory
> Soft foreign things. Then we were taken in
> To low huts candle-lit, shaded close by slitten
> Oilsheets, and there the boys gave us kind welcome,
> So that we looked out as from the edge of home,
> Sang us Welsh things, and changed all former notions
> To human hopeful things [*Collected Poems* 69, ll. 1–10].

Gurney suggests that the first image seen in the trenches will be the dominant memory of his time there. Before he had any experience to mark the origin of his trench life, he had the "dread tales and red yarns" from other soldiers upon which to base his expectations. He marks the shift in the second line with the word "but," to create the opposite of speculation that his actual experience provided. He remembers a "divine / Afterglow" which sanctions their movement below ground with purpose, and there they find a colony which the poet reconstructs through images of protection. At first, the speaker perceives himself as an invader into this "Welsh colony;" the men are "hiding in sandbag ditches" and they are "whispering consolatory / Soft foreign things." It is unclear to the reader, and perhaps to the speaker himself, whether these whispers denote a realm of secrecy and exclusion, where the Welsh men console one another and where the language is their own, or a place of calm where the gesture of consolation is extended outward to welcome the new men. The speaker is entering the scene with presuppositions about what he will find, and such defense mechanisms make him understandably wary of complete trust of this "foreign" world.

The movement of the poem and of these new men continues inward to a womblike, protective center. The speaker enumerates the details of the "low huts candle-lit," the shade of "slitten / Oilsheets," and the "kind welcome," which remove the suspicion from his initial perception. These layers of protection within create a physical scene that functions metaphorically for the psychological comfort to be found through human contact. That is, the physical scene allows for the possibility of such a transformation, but it is the mind of the speaker which accepts the welcome and allows his expectations to be transformed. The formation of such community and reciprocity establishes a regional identity within the dug-out. The songs of "Welsh things" cause the speaker's belief in "human hopeful things." And although Gurney and his fellow soldiers are from Gloucester, the boundary dissolves between Gloucester and neighboring Wales within this makeshift existence; Gloucester and Welsh men alike "looked out as from the edge of home." These lines describing home, song, transformation, and hope arrive at the exact center of the poem. Through formal reconstruction of the event, Gurney is allowing the poetic structure to underscore the desire, as a soldier, for such an anchoring structure of protection and the desire, as a civilian reliving the memory, for such stabilizing forms to provide structure to consciousness. Gurney's neat couplets further reinforce the physical protection found in the dug-out and the psychological comfort provided by the poem.

After arrival at this central image of home and hope in line ten, Gurney ends the sentence mid-line to sustain the moment of comfort. But the fact remains that despite the "home" to which imagination has transported the speaker, the war is going on around them, and the imaginative construction must contend with such a reality. Even within their shelter, the men have "looked out" toward the war "from the edge of home." The tightly woven couplets give way to a looser rhyme scheme as the war itself enters the poem and consciousness of the new arrivals.

> And the next day's guns
> Nor any line-pangs ever quite could blot out
> That strangely beautiful entry into war's rout;
> Candles they gave us, precious and shared over-rations —
> Ulysses found little more in his wanderings without doubt.
> "David of the White Rock," the "Slumber Song" so soft, and that
> Beautiful tune to which roguish words by Welsh pit boys
> Are sung — but never more beautiful than there under the gun's noise
> [ll. 10–17].

Despite the gunfire which cannot be completely ignored, the speaker asserts the power of the imagination and memory to combat the weathering effects of the war. Memory, in fact, is more lasting and possesses a power that guns can never match. Gurney's allusion to Ulysses in this passage connects the private experience to the archetypal search for home and provides added reassurance that this beginning of trench life will result in a successful return to the land the poet loves. As the poem draws to a close, Gurney expands the length of lines, beyond the iambic pentameter that has been the dominant rhythm of the poem, to emphasize the capability of imagination and memory to resonate far longer than the sound of gunfire. This loosening and lengthening of lines recalls the ending of Tennyson's "The Lotos-Eaters," based upon an episode of *The Odyssey*, where Ulysses' men succumb to the temptations of complete psychological escape from their situation of wandering in search of home.[39]

The Welsh songs, which persist in memories of the "first time in" and are recreated poetically through alliteration like "'Slumber Song' so soft," function as siren songs to Gurney to silence the sounds of warfare around him, threatening the imaginative haven within. Unlike the temptations of Ulysses and his men, however, such songs do not distract Gurney from his goal of safety and survival. Rather they become the means of defense against the forces of war that would destroy him. The final line gives the value of the experience even greater weight: the songs achieve their beauty in memory because of the entire context out of which they were sung. Only "under the guns' noise" do the songs reach their pinnacle of meaning to Gurney. The music or the guns alone can be only themselves; the poem proclaims that, paradoxically, the combination of music and gunfire makes the music more beautiful than itself. And thus, the poem argues that the entire imaginative process redeems the moment of entry into the war experience by creating beauty out of it. Furthermore, he may hear or recall the songs at a later date to return him to the original scene through memory. In all these ways, music is not merely distraction for the poet during the war or after it, to get his mind off of what might happen should he leave such a protective environment. Through a poem written after the war, Gurney simulates a temporal return to the experience through which he hoped to become most whole, the war itself.

So significant was this experience to Gurney that when it occurred in June 1916, he wrote four letters to different friends at home, providing them with many of the same details that he recalls years later in the poem. He writes to Catherine Abercrombie of the delightful experience with the Welsh men in the same exuberant tone that marks the poem, but the tone of the letter changes later on:

> Every now and again a distant rumble of guns reminded us of the
> reason we were foregathered. They spoke of their friends dead or
> maimed in the bombardment, a bad one, of the night before, and
> in the face of their grief I sat there and for once self forgetful, more

or less, gave them all my love.... This Welshman turned to me passionately. "Listen to that damned bird," he said. "All through that bombardment in the pauses I could hear that infernal silly 'Cuckoo, Cuckoo' sounding while Owen was lying in my arms covered with blood. How shall I ever listen again...!" He broke off, and I became aware of shame at the unholy joy that had filled my artist's mind [*Letters* 92].

"First Time In" has argued for the permanence of the experience, particularly the songs, in memory, and the poem that has emerged from the memory in 1919 is evidence that the experience has had a lasting impact on Gurney. The poem ends upon the note of the song, upon the moment of that first night when voices of men equal in rank but superior in war experience kept the soldiers protected from the sounds of the front, but Gurney does not involve in the poem the sentiment he felt the next day. In fact, in the letter, he expresses a degree of shame at having elevated the previous evening's events to such heights in his mind. The letter and morning reveal that the casualties of war are the constants in the trench experience. Flights of imagination and belief in the permanence of such moments are luxuries that the war might afford, but the machinery of warfare will eventually drown out such imaginative constructions and reveal their temporality. The Welsh songs that were made beautiful through the accompaniment of gunfire modulate into the Cuckoo's song in the letter, which does not eliminate the sound of gunfire but brings the bombardment that killed Owen, the friend of the Welsh solider, back into this soldier's consciousness. Gurney has engaged in selective memory in the poem; he does not distort the truth of the experience as much as he fails to tell the entire story. But he does so for a reason: looking back upon the war in its aftermath, Gurney sees that his poetic imagination is his most valuable resource for providing order to his mind, and thus he recreates an experience where such imagination and faith in its power have shown their capacity to comfort.

The letter shows the ways in which the poem stops short of complete disclosure. The war of course cannot be completely ignored or evaded through the mind, so Gurney visits this initiatory experience into the trenches a second time to acknowledge the presence of the war more fully. He calls this poem "First Time In" as well, inviting comparisons to the first "first time." This version of the experience follows the same plot as the first, but Gurney supplies much more detail in this sixty-four line poem of rhyming couplets. The speaker approaches the trenches, sees sights of "iron and lead rain, sandbags rent in two," and hears his heart speak as if to say, "'Here men are maimed and shot through, hit through'" (*Collected Poems* 87–89, ll. 13–14). He arrives at the shelter and company of Welsh soldiers, once again at the center of the poem and the experience, where "home / Closed round us" (ll. 31–32). The actual words of these knowledgeable and comforting men get greater treatment, and Gurney and his fellow Gloucester soldiers receive advice on "line-mending," "Minnewerfers," and "grenades." The poem employs the jargon of the trenches — "duckboards" "wire," "billets," "signallers," "dug-outs" — to recreate Gurney's initiation and immersion within the physical and linguistic reality of the experience, that which he calls "the really, really / Truly line" (ll. 29). Winter writes of soldiers' common language, "United by a common jargon, by shared secrets and experiences, ... men belonged to platoon or section as to no other aspect of their war life."[40] The recollection of the evening underground is much the same as in the first version. The borders between Wales and Gloucester disappear, and Gurney recalls the same songs that contribute to his conclusion about the value of this moment and its permanent place in memory: "What an evening! What a first time, what a shock / So rare of home-pleasure beyond measure / And always to time's ending surely a treasure" (ll. 52–54).

The significant difference between these two "first times" occurs in the poem's ending, when Gurney speaks of the time which has elapsed between the war and its poetic reconstruction:

Since after-war so surely hurt, disappointed men
Who looked for the golden Age to come friendly again.
With inn evenings of meetings in warm glows,
Talk: coal and wood fire uttering rosy shows
With beer and "Widdicombe Fair" and five mile homeward —
Moonlight lying thick on frost spangled fleet foot sward,
And owl crying out every short while his one evil word.

At any rate, disputeless the romantic evening was —
The night, the midnight; next day Fritz strafed at us,
And I lay belly upward to wonder: when — but useless [ll. 55–64].

Gurney has proclaimed that the memory will be "always to time's ending surely a treasure," and the number of times he has returned to it in writing, in poems and letters, points to such a value. But this ten line "coda" of sorts questions the value of this treasure. The syntax and punctuation make complete understanding of these lines difficult; two possible readings emerge from the first grouping of lines. Either this description of "hurt, disappointed men" who meet at inns has occurred between Gurney's time in the trenches and the conception of the poem after war, or this image is created within the mind of the speaker while still involved in the war as an idyllic vision of the future and the home to which he hopes to return, when "the golden Age [comes] friendly again." The significance of this description comes in the connection of its images with those that have characterized Gurney's experience with the Welsh men. The "warm glows" and "rosy shows" of the fire and the room recall the candle-lit shelter in France and the "Afterglow" that surfaces in both "First Time In" poems. The talk and especially the singing of the men in inns is a clear parallel to the soothing talk and singing of the Welshmen. And even the owl with "his one evil word" seems to suggest the persistence of the Cuckoo's song from Gurney's letter about the experience that pointed to the limits of art to alter the truth in any lasting way.

The poet, whether recalling his idea of postwar life imagined from the trenches or relating the postwar experience, emphasizes the resonances of this initial experience within his representation of postwar life, good and bad. Gurney is revealing the desire for continuity between these phases. Jeremy Hooker observes, "After the war, however, he could not find his ideal community except as a memory or a dream...."[41] The ideal for Gurney would be the persistence of the "home-pleasure beyond measure." In reality, though, the war is the more powerful force and will seep into recollections of the experience unless imagination acts to shut it out for the moment that is the poem. The closing lines provide the answer to the ambiguity; the strength and resonance of the imagined construction does not seem to matter much to Gurney at the end when the war assumes control over the experience. The night was Romantic to be sure, but the guns of the Germans are real and dangerous. From his perspective on the ground and on his back, safe for the moment from gunfire, the romanticized memory of the previous evening does not seem so important or capable of drowning out this gunfire. Gurney, when writing this poem, suggests the imagination and the planning for the future is, as he says in "To His Love," "useless" at the end. And with the benefit of hindsight, he can recollect in the early 1920s what the postwar reality has been like for himself and men like him; Lucas writes, "the promise that evening held out, of a new society, has not been fulfilled.... Gurney has to face the defeat of those hopes which the meetings of war had helped to engender and strengthen."[42]

Gurney has other sets of poems paired by title, two poems called "Near Vermand" and two versions of "Riez Bailleul" which display conflicting emotions depending upon the poet's perspective at that moment. But these are places, and places change with time and allow for the different descriptions and accompanying emotions of the two representations. "First Time In," however, establishes not only a place but a single time, and since each poem is told through the perspective of a speaker whose perceptions resemble Gurney's as spelled out in his letters, the reader expects an experience the reality of which he is not able, much less invited, to challenge. By ending them each on such different and discordant notes, Gurney exposes the uncertainty

of both representations. He affirms the power of the imagination to offer
relief and quickly questions this capacity in the subsequent poem. The ulti-
mate implication of such a unique strategy, though, is not to undermine the
validity of the sentiment of either poem, but to create a space and function
for poetry to serve the private needs of Gurney at the given moment of the
poem's creation after the war. He suggests through the inclusion of both in
Rewards of Wonder that no poem need be "true" in some objective sense, but
that both poems speak to the same "truth" of the war. His imagination can
sustain him in times of need depending on the degree to which he believed
in the imagination's capacity to sustain him. After the war, when his grip
on reality and emotional state fluctuated between lucidity and conversations
with Beethoven, such fluctuations in poetry are not surprising. In the end,
imagination remains stable as Gurney's primary resource for remaining
grounded; the will with which he posits the imagined version of experience
against evidence to the contrary varies.

The "First Time In" poems display a resource other than immersion in
selfhood that can buoy the strengths of the individual private — the collec-
tive strength of the unit, here represented through the harmonious voices of
the Welsh soldiers. Gurney returns to many memories of other such collec-
tive activities in his postwar poems. In "Of Grandcourt," the pain of the
individual is seen as the pain of the group:

Through miles of mud we travelled, and by sick valleys —
The Valley of Death at last — most evil alleys,
To Grandcourt trenches reserve — and hell's name it did deserve.
Rain there was — tired and weak I was, glad for an end
                                    [*Collected Poems* 100].

It is not much of an imaginative leap for the poet to assume that his expe-
rience is that of his companions on the endless march. The speaker projects
his feelings of fatigue upon the "valleys" and "alleys" he sees on his way to
the Grandcourt trenches, and the lines recall the sentiment of "Pain," now
seen from the perspective of a speaker who articulates the suffering of his
silenced peers. In "Billet," the poet is not the spokesperson but gives voice
to a man who in turn gives voice to the collective body:

But one Private took on himself a Company's heart to speak,
"I wish to bloody hell I was just going to Brewery — surely
To work all day (in Stroud) and be free at tea-time — allowed
Resting when one wanted, and a joke in season....
Then God and man and war and Gloucestershire would have a reason,
But I get no good in France, getting killed, cleaning off mud."
He spoke the heart of all of us — the hidden thought burning, unturning
                                    [*Collected Poems* 76].

Spoken language in the poem establishes sympathy and equality, in rank and in experience. The officer must lead and, even if respected or admired by the men beneath him, displays the markers of his elevated class, such as differences in language and relative comfort in the trenches, unlike these privates. Winter writes of all that united the soldiering class: "The group helped each carry the guilt of killing, allowed the pooling of verbal aggression which eased the burden of dependence and fear.... Above all, the group allowed a sense of purpose not present in the actual war situation...."[43] These moments within the poems show how such communal life and suffering could be turned into great strength; the other members of the platoon hear their thoughts — their similar desires, memories, and resentments — articulated in a form they were not aware of sharing before the utterance. Despite this potential strength to be gained from comrades, however, Gurney reveals himself as a soldier somewhat out of the collective loop. His letters show affection for the men who were his equals, but little loss for those whom he knew and whom the war claimed, and he admits that he is one whom his companions regarded as a bit odd: "I pass with my comrades as one who is willing to be friendly with almost anybody; looks depressed, but makes more jokes than anyone around here...; but has an itch, a positive mania for arguing, and discursing on weird and altogether unimportant subjects" (*Letters* 65). He mentions few of his companions by name in letters from the war, and he appears to have been a loner in the trenches as he had been in England as a youth.

So, he adopted personal methods in the trenches for coping with the stress of battles, strategies his postwar poems replicated. In several of the poems of *Rewards of Wonder* and in others uncollected but written before his committal to the asylum in 1922, Gurney symbolizes the desire for an imaginary transformation of the war experience through the image of the sky. Waterman writes, "And always in his poetry is the infinitely varying sky."[44] This recurrent image is a logical choice for soldiers who lived underground for years in a "troglodyte world."[45] Fussell argues, "When a participant in the war wants an ironic effect, a conventional way to achieve one is simply to juxtapose a sunrise or sunset with the unlovely physical details of the war that man has made."[46] Gurney's employment of this image is a little different. His purpose is not to protest against the war by drawing the reader's attention through irony to the destruction war has caused. Rather, his purpose is a personal one — both to escape in his mind, for a moment, the destruction all around him and to draw strength from visions of beauty that exist in natural world. These lines from "First March" show such a private escape:

> Barely frostbite the most of us had escapen.
> To move, then to go onward, at last to be moved.
> Myself had revived and then dulled down, it was I
> Who stared for body-ease at the grey sky ...
> [*Collected Poems* 75].

The collective body of men has endured the physical hardship, but Gurney singles himself out as having shifted his gaze elsewhere in search of "body-ease" from the reality of the physical moment. The sky is a resource that the imagination of the soldier can tap for strength to enable him to confront the brutal physicality of the trenches again.

Such searching of the stars for relief is understandable, given the facts of the soldiers' experience. Unable to lift his head above ground level in fear of sniper fire, the soldier saw the sky as the only image available which was not part of the ugliness all around him in his home in the trench. The sky became in effect a blank canvas for the poet's projection of emotion. The war ravaged much of the natural landscape, the rivers and the woods around them, and thus these images could not sustain a poet's attempts to project his desires for comfort and relief, feelings always at odds with his physical reality. The stars and sky remained untouched and unchanged and offer the possibility of an imaginative return to the soldier's pre-war existence. In these lines from "Crucifix Corner," the imagery of stars has value for the poet because of their familiarity:

> Transport rattled somewhere in southern shadows,
> Stars that were not strange ruled the lit tranquil sky,
> Arched far and high.
> What should break that but gun-noise or last Trump?
> [*Collected Poems* 80].

When everything else around him portends danger, the "stars that were not strange" enable Gurney's emotional return to feelings of safety. And the stars can offer glimpses of real beauty as well, as in these lines from "Half Dead":

> Half dead with sheer tiredness, wakened quick at night
> With dysentery pangs, going blind among dim sleepers
> And dazed into half dark, illness had its spite....
> Yet still clear flames of stars over the crest bare,
> Mysterious glowing on the cloths of heaven.
> Sirius or Mars or Argo's stars, and high the Sisters —
> the Pleiads — those seven [*Collected Poems* 81–82].

Reaching the beautiful description of the stars as "Mysterious glowing on the cloths of heaven," the reader has all but forgotten about the dysentery pangs a few lines earlier. The naming of the stars seems a game the speaker might have played as a child, and his ability to recollect them now connects him to this simpler time. The long final line of the passage reflects the desire that the stability offered by this naming continue beyond the momentary relief it offers. As in "First Time In," Gurney creates an image of beauty that relies upon the background of war and suffering against which it is contrasted. The stars would be more likely to be seen simply as stars if not for the context of dysentery that prompts the imagination of the speaker to create such a sustained image. The context of the Welsh songs made them more beautiful than the songs themselves in memory. The stars seen in this total perspective of the landscape of war allow the speaker both to acknowledge the reality and to depart from it momentarily, and through this imaginative process the stars paradoxically become more beautiful than themselves.

Even the scene of intense fighting depicted in "The Silent One," finds a place for the imagination.[47] But the immediacy of battle makes imagined escape secondary to the necessity of confronting the real bullets raining around the speaker. The poem illustrates, with characteristic precision and wit, the pragmatic view of a private during battle and, according to Bergonzi, "matches anything in Sassoon and Owen in its terrible directness."[48] Gurney weaves the technique of repetition and echoing through the entire poem, which begins with its title:

The Silent One

Who died on the wires, and hung there, one of two —
Who for his hours of life had *chattered* through
Infinite lovely *chatter* of *Bucks accent:*
Yet *faced unbroken wires;* stepped over, and went
A noble fool, faithful to his stripes — and ended,
But I weak, hungry, and willing only for the chance
Of line — to fight *in the line, lay down under unbroken*
Wires, and saw the flashes and kept unshaken,
Till the *politest* voice — a *finicking accent,* said:
"Do you think you might crawl through there: *there's a hole.*"
Darkness, shot at: I smiled, as *politely* replied —
"I'm afraid not, Sir." *There was no hole* no way to be seen
Nothing but chance of death, after tearing of clothes.
Kept flat, and watched the darkness, hearing bullets whizzing —
And thought of music — and swore *deep* heart's *deep* oaths
(*Polite* to God) *and retreated and came on again,*
Again retreated — and a second time faced the screen
                    [*Collected Poems* 103, italics added].

The poem represents the various relationships Gurney confronted and relied upon in his struggle for survival, the first being between the speaker of the poem and the dead soldier on the wires. Gurney displays both his sympathy for this man and the limitations he must place upon this sympathy in the poem's opening lines. Gurney characterizes the man through the description of his voice, the music of his "Infinite lovely chatter of Bucks accent," and language functions in the poem as a marker of the man's value to Gurney, his equal in rank. Waterman writes, "The dead soldier is no casual peg for sentiment but a mourned individual...."[49] But this mourning has limitations; as soon as the man goes "over the top," Gurney's sympathy for him ends, and the man becomes "A noble fool, faithful to his stripes" whose qualities of faith and nobility lead only to his death. This man when alive was a source of comfort to Gurney which he memorializes in other poems and his letters, but the private must be practical with his emotions. Gurney is showing the danger of keeping such affection alive for such a man after he is gone. As in "To His Love," Gurney recreates the psychological strategy of dealing with loss by establishing his emotional limits. But while that poem showed the need to forget without the exploration of how best to carry on, Gurney now reconstructs his own means for physical and psychological perseverance.

The description of the "silent one" ends in line six of the poem when the phrase "But I" introduces the speaker's situation, but his role continues implicitly. The speaker survives only because of the example of the man that went before him, and in the reconstruction of the experience as a poem, the survival of the "I" depends upon Gurney's establishing his difference from this "silent one" who no longer chatters in his Bucks accent. Language, which has been symbolic of the men's equality and sympathy, and thus symbolic of the value of the man to the speaker, has been silenced by the war. Death removes all distinctions of class and rank, and the only characteristic the speaker assigns to the soldier in the present is one of lack, his silence, the absence of language. The italicized words and phrases in the poem show the sustained pattern of repetition and contrast which establish the difference between the men of equal rank. To represent an identity of a soldier who will not die "A noble fool," Gurney relates the experience in memory of his own actions in the face of gunfire that emphasize his desire for self-preservation. Their situations as privates cause both men to confront the "unbroken wires," the barriers to their assault upon the enemy. Facing these wires has led to the death of the silent one; assuming the passive role of lying before these wires guarantees not only survival but survival unshaken. The speaker of the poem displays here the priorities of the foot soldier: he might admire the accent of a friend, but too much admiration and sympathy for him is ultimately hazardous to his own health. The death of a friend in effect becomes the means by which Gurney learns how to face a similar experience and survive. He willingly sacrifices the values of "[faith] to his stripes" and nobility if it guarantees that he continue on.

The relationship between the living and dead privates is the first of the human contrasts Gurney draws within the poem. Just as striking is the difference established between the speaker and his commanding officer through the same device of verbal echoes and repetition. The speaker's attitude toward his commander is clear through his description of his "finicking accent," unlike the Bucks accent of the late private. The authority of the "politest voice" is challenged by the very facts of the battlefield that Gurney reveals. The officer points the speaker towards a hole in the wires for him to climb through, but Gurney himself becomes the voice of authority and reason in this situation: "There was no hole no way to be seen / Nothing but chance of death." Gurney, the private, turns the language of the officer upon him to undermine his command, as soldier and officer play out this struggle for authority in absurdly civilized terms. The officer's apologetic request that Gurney attack ("Do you think that you might ...") is followed by an equally polite denial ("I'm afraid not, Sir"). Geoffrey Hill observes, "The perfect good manners of the episode are simultaneously a tone-poem of the class-system, and a parody of what it is that brings two men, through the exercise of traditional discipline and reason, into a situation of unpremeditated terror and absurdity."[50] This politeness is then taken up in the speaker's private curses, "polite to God," when under fire. Such a refusal by a private threatens the structure of authority within the trenches, where officers purportedly command their men for the good of the group, and where the private's duty is to obey. But more important, Gurney argues through the poem, is the private's duty to himself. He commands himself by using the experience of the death of "the silent one" in order to govern his response to imminent danger.

Gurney's deliberate disobeying of the command saves him as much as following the order has led his counterpart to death. One imagines that this would be a poem of strikingly different tone and effect if told from the officer's perspective. While the private, responsible only for self, battles between obeying orders and saving himself, opting for the latter, the officer, responsible for the men he commands, carries the moral weight of the decisions he makes and the deaths, if inadvertent, that these decisions cause.[51] This lack of responsibility enables Gurney's speaker to abandon emotionally "the silent one" on the wires; in the mind of the private bent on surviving, the man is reduced in memory to a voice and in reality to silence. Jacqueline Banerjee writes of the speaker's strategy when in danger, "[H]e homes in on his own situation ... and concentrates on particulars, tingeing his account of them with a sense of the ridiculous which keeps the poem

closely in touch with the actual business of soldiering."⁵² And while he cer-
tainly must attend to the perils that the moment presents, the moment offers
as well a less realistic but equally valuable opportunity. Gurney's remaining
prone in the face of the assault provides him with the means for psycholog-
ical escape from the reality of the moment. He recreates the memory of the
experience of the private by describing his "retreat" in effect to the private
experience of the mind. Hearing the bullets, the speaker responds with
"thought of music." Gurney writes on several occasions of the "music" of
the battlefield, as he transposes the sounds of machine guns and whizz-bangs
to the musical score. He wonders in 1917 "whether any up to date fool will
try to depict a strafe in music. The shattering crash of heavy shrapnel. The
belly-disturbing crunch of 5.9 Crumps and trench mortars. The shrill clat-
ter of rifle grenades and the wail of nosecaps flying loose" (*Letters* 134). In
the poem, he seems able to shut out completely the noise of the battlefield
and imagine music altogether apart from this racket. Indeed, much as the
speaker momentarily escapes from the violence through these thoughts of
music before the closing lines return him to this violence and the chaotic
action of assault and retreat, Gurney himself, in retrospect, recreates this
imagination of music through the patterning of repetition he constructs into
the poem. When he "thought of music" during the barrage of bullets and
shells, the speaker achieved momentary peace. When he recreates a typical
war experience in a poem in the war's aftermath, he strives for a similar
music and psychological peace, constructed within the context of its noises,
explosions, and conflicting voices. Nevertheless, the poem ends upon the note
of the war's ultimate drowning out of the imaginative construct of musical
thought. Gray writes, "as the last line suggests, however often you pull back
there is still the overriding ultimate command to go forward — 'and a sec-
ond time faced the screen.'"⁵³

But much as "The Silent One" ends upon the actual confrontation with
battle when the speaker "faced the screen," and much as the second "First
Time In" revised the experience established in the first to reveal the limits
of the imagined "home," Gurney exposes the ultimate shortcomings of his
imaginative line of defense against the war. One of the two "Near Vermand"
poems presents a familiar scene of the soldier in battle searching the stars
for solace, but the poem reveals an undercurrent that suggests a weakening
of this soldier's belief that imagination can provide any lasting relief from
the physical reality of battle and, likewise, the weakening of the poet's con-
viction that imagination can save him from "the strife / With self."

> Lying flat on my belly shivering in clutch-frost
> There was time to watch the stars, we had dug in:

Looking eastward over the low ridge; March scurried its blast
At our senses, no use either dying or struggling.
Low woods to left — (Cotswold her spinnies if ever)
Showed through snow flurries and the clearer star weather,
And *nothing* but chill and wonder lived in mind; *nothing*
But *loathing* and fine beauty, and wet *loathed clothing*.
Here were thoughts. Cold *smothering* and *fire-desiring*,
A day to follow like this or in the digging or *wiring*.

Worry in snow *flurry* and lying flat, flesh the earth *loathing*.
I was the forward sentry and would be relieved
In a quarter or so, but *nothing* more better than to crouch
Low in the scraped holes and to have frozen and rocky couch —
To be by desperate home thoughts clutched at, and heart-grieved.
Was I ever there — a lit warm room and Bach, to search out sacred
Meaning; and to find no luck; and to take love as believed?
                              [*Collected Poems* 87; italics added].

Whereas the stars have previously functioned as objects for the poet's gaze which remained untouched by war and thus offered some relief, this glance heavenward offers little comfort. Looking next at the landscape, the speaker attempts to hearken back to the untouched memory of the landscape of Gloucester — "(Cotswold her spinnies if ever)" — as an emotional anchor and resource, but this gesture too is short-lived. Gurney, as he has in the conflicting versions of his "First Time In" poems, shows both his reliance upon imagination when other means of psychological self-preservation are removed and his recognition that such imaginative leaps have their ultimate limitations in some facts of experience which refuse to be transformed.

But imagination, however limited it has appeared in the past, now fails utterly in the face of the actual experience; Gurney's private thoughts cannot explain away certain facts of the private's life. The speaker avers that "nothing but chill and wonder lived in mind; nothing / But loathing and fine beauty, and wet loathed clothing." The mind is the site both of the perception of his immediate surroundings and of the imagination that seeks an alternative to these perceptions. For the soldier to hope to use imagination to contend with war's reality, he must ask his mind to sustain two opposing ideas at the same time — "chill *and* wonder;" "loathing *and* fine beauty." The pattern of internal rhymes, italicized above, suggests that in this experience, the perceptions of his immediate surroundings will overwhelm his imaginative resources. The clothing becomes a source of loathing, as does three lines later the earth itself. The speaker projects his own worry upon the flurry of snow. His desire for fire and warmth is immediately undercut by his duty of wiring. And the repetition of "nothing" suggests that this is what truly lies at the core of the experience. Unlike "First Time In," where the speaker's description of the experience in the womblike shelter allowed the layers of physical protection to stand for Gurney's emotional security within the moment, here the soldier is exposed, emotionally and physically, "crouch[ing] / Low in the scraped holes and [having] frozen and rocky couch." Try as he might, he cannot use the stars, the thoughts of Gloucester, or the facts of his surroundings as means of replacing the predominant images and sensations of this solitary dimension of warfare.

The song and companionship had created an imaginative home for the speaker, with value that lasted as long as memory was able to retrieve it, but here the closing lines indicate any home, real or imagined, is a long way off. This war poem is notable for its absence of any of the signifiers of war, other than the trench digging and wiring that tomorrow promises the speaker. The experience offers the body nothing better than the rocky couch and the mind nothing better than these desperate thoughts of home which leave him "heart-grieved." The enemy here is the cold and exposure; the psychological danger comes from the refusal of his surroundings to yield anything for the imagination to transform into something more than itself. It seems as if a Frost speaker has been transported to somewhere "near Vermand" to confront a landscape "[w]ith no expression, nothing to express." And as in Frost, Gurney's speaker has it in him "so nearer home / To scare [himself] with his own desert places" when he questions the memories that constitute his conception of self brought to the trenches.[54] The common trope of contrasting home and the Western front has allowed poets of the First World War to expose what appears "unreal" about warfare to privilege the reality of the simpler, more peaceful days. But Gurney's contrast in the closing lines questions the validity of any prior memory now that war has become part of experience and even questions the very place of imagination within any world at all.

Physically, of course, he has been in the "lit warm room" listening to Bach, but the comfort such a setting has offered is viewed in retrospect as illusory. The memory is reinterpreted, tinged with what he now knows. Bach's music, or art in general, has been the catalyst for the speaker to "search out sacred / Meaning." Such a search yields "no luck," and the speaker is left to conclude that love, and in fact all emotion, is only "believed," therefore subjective, and no more authentically comforting than the nothingness that is his "frozen and rocky couch." This poem seems one to which Gurney's "ars poetica" expressed in the earlier letter both applies and does not. On the one hand, the passage of time between the war and the poem's conception has been necessary for the experience to be "crystallized and glorified" by Gurney into a poetic form. Though the war's immediacy made his prior life seem out of reach except through memory and imagination, it seems unlikely that he would have questioned the validity of these memories without the deterioration of selfhood that ensued in the war's aftermath. On the other hand, though, the poem does not support Gurney's claim in the letter of artistic conviction from 1917 to use poetry in order to learn "by the denial how full and wide a thing Joy may be." The poem presents a situation which denies anything of beauty in its entirety, but the result is not a greater appreciation of beauty, but an expression of skepticism that anything could have ever been beautiful at all. Seen in the context of the poem's conception in 1919, as sanity began to slip, the poem's closing lines become Gurney's desperate plea not for a world untouched by war but for a consciousness free from his continual "strife / With self."

The Asylum Years and the Failure of Self-Therapy

During the span of time which produced the poems from *Rewards of Wonder* and the dozens of uncollected poems, Gurney's mood and degree of mental stability fluctuated — both at home with family and after 1922 in the asylum — in much the same way as the spirit of his poetry. Upon discharge from the hospital in 1919, he returned to Gloucester where his brother Ronald had assumed the role of head of household, Gurney's father David having taken ill and then succumbing to cancer. Hurd depicts Ronald as resentful about his duty to take over the tailoring business which was in disarray.[55] The proposition that Ivor, in his mental state, take part in the family business was ludicrous, and when his scholarship to the music school was reinstated after the war, Gurney decided to commit himself to the study of music he had abandoned when war was declared.[56]

Nineteen nineteen was a year of stability and productivity for him, and though he remained a prolific poet and composer in the subsequent year, the final onslaught of mental illness was beginning. According to Hurd, "He thought nothing of walking from London to Gloucester, sleeping out in bars or under hedgerows when the weather was good, earning a few pence by singing folksongs in country inns."[57] In other words, Gurney's actions reveal a desire to resume his previous life, however odd that life had been, as if the war had not intervened.

But at the same time, his experiences in France were lodged in permanent memory and were a constant reminder that he could not return to his days of youth. In 1921, he failed out of the Royal College of music and survived on a meager war pension and wages from odd jobs. Hurd claims that Gurney began to feel that the country that he served had betrayed him in the war's aftermath: "Were the sufferings of a war poet to count as nothing? Were wounds, and gas, and a lifetime of bad dreams to be assuaged by a 12 / — pension? Was there to be no reward for all the pain he had endured?"[58] A poem written soon before his committal, "Strange Hells," extends the meditation on the powers of imagination in warfare to include the psychological wreckage that, for Gurney, accompanied the aftermath:

> There are strange hells within the minds war made
> Not so often, not so humiliatingly afraid
> As one would have expected — the racket and fear guns made.
> One hell the Gloucester soldiers they quite put out:
> Their first bombardment, when in combined black shout
> Of fury, guns aligned, they ducked lower their heads
> And sang with diaphragms fixed beyond all dreads,
> That tin and stretched-wire tinkle, that blither of tune:
> "Apres la guerre fini," till hell all had come down,
> Twelve-inch, six-inch, and eighteen pounders hammering
>   hell's thunders [*Collected Poems* 140–41].

The title and the first line suggest that the poem will address the "strange hells" of the mind caused by the trauma of battle, a different scene than this first stanza delivers and different as well as the statement of the entire poem. Gurney acknowledges that there are these hells, but they result "not so often" as "one would have suspected." The remainder of this first stanza goes on to create a scene Gurney has drawn many times before: the war is depicted as a battle between the sounds of war —"the racket and fear guns made"— and the songs of the Gloucester soldiers. The singing wins this battle. Gurney represents the power of the song by describing the voices as weapons: "combined black shout / Of fury," "diaphragms fixed beyond all dreads," and "tin and stretched-wire tinkle." The real power of the song's capacity to win this psychological battle is revealed in its title, in English, "After the war is over." Imagining the war's completion enables the Gloucesters to put forth against the "hammering hell's thunders" the strength of their collective song with such conviction. The idea that the war will end and that they will see it through persists in the mind longer than any "strange hells" of the mind that the war might create.

In the revised "First Time In," Gurney has extended the idealized moment from the first version to supply the reality of the next day's battle and the speaker's less ideal imagination and perceptions when under fire. In the "coda" of that poem, either the speaker imagines the "inn evenings of meetings in warm glows" that await him after the war, or perhaps Gurney has experienced some of this comfort during his attempts to reassimilate into the postwar world, the perspective from which he recreates the memory of war experience in 1919. In either case, both of which the poem's conclusion makes possible, Gurney attempts to connect by means of the poem his vision of the postwar future with the idealized memory of the trench experience. The warmth of inn has value, either as imagined by the soldier under fire or recollected by the poet after the war, because of its resemblance to the comfort and song of Gurney's first night in the trenches. While the ending of this earlier poem seriously questions the capacity of the imagination to be a lasting comfort, it does not eliminate the possibility altogether but merely tempers the role of imagination with a dose of the truth. The ending which Gurney, in 1921, provides to "Strange Hells" bears no resemblance to the memory that precedes it:

> Where are they now, on state-doles, or showing shop-patterns
> Or walking town to town sore in borrowed tatterns
> Or begged. Some civic routine one never learns.
> The heart burns — but has to keep out of face how heart burns
> [ll. 11–14].

This conclusion demonstrates that the strength of Gurney's imaginary reconstructions of war, and the function of imagination within the imagined experience, have reached their limits of value in the postwar world to which Gurney returned. Unlike the vision of the warm inns, where veterans of the war were united in common memories, this scene carries through none of the imagery of the war, particularly of the collective experience which has been the source of strength, into the poet's depiction of the postwar present. In his presentation of this concluding stanza on the page, Gurney stresses the isolation of this experience. Gurney draws a self-portrait in this conclusion: on "state-dole," "walking town to town in borrowed tatterns." The true "hell" of the speaker's war experience has not been incurred in battle but arrives in the poem's final line. Confronting a nation which he perceived as ungrateful for or incapable of understanding the sufferings of individuals such as himself, Gurney experienced another wave of the isolation that had, in varying degrees, marked his experience before and during the war as well, and kept the resentment buried within, "out of face how heart burns."

But while his prior isolation — before, during, and for the first three years after the war — provided Gurney with the opportunity to produce such a vast range of poetry and music, the year of 1922 marked the effective end of a life of freedom. In the summer of 1922, his suppression of the symptoms of the disease was no longer possible; he imagined that he was being controlled by electrical impulses emanating from the wireless radio and threatened suicide, even calling the police department demanding a revolver. His brother Ronald finally had Ivor committed to "a country house near

Bristol (a neurasthenic Convalescent Home)" during September 1922, claim-
ing in a letter to Ivor's best friend Marion Scott, "They [the Pensions office,
who was controlling Ivor's military disability pension] think it best he should
not be certified insane for the present."[59]

Acting against any possible improvement in Gurney's condition were
the limited financial resources of his family and friends. The family had lit-
tle to offer in this regard, and Ronald, Ivor's primary caretaker when his con-
dition began to deteriorate prior to his committal, was unable and unwilling,
it seems, to offer much support.[60] Ronald believed that discipline and a
stronger will such as his own would guide Ivor to a productive and func-
tioning life. He grew exasperated at trying to impose such order to a mind
he called "a huge unwieldy mess" and committed his brother, believing at
first that he would convalesce within the year.[61] When Ivor did not improve
and funds for sustaining his stay dried up, friends, such as noted literary
figures Edward Marsh and Walter de la Mare who had recognized Gurney's
talents in his two slender volumes of poetry, intervened and sought to act
on Gurney's behalf in his time of need in late 1922. Family and friends con-
sidered the City of London Mental Hospital, where Gurney eventually landed
when his short stay near Gloucester caused too many complications because
of its proximity to home, better than the other options near Gloucester
which were "public institutions, and by comparison, places of genuine local
horror.... The others were the 'looney bins' and thus the terminus of all
hope."[62] The City of London Hospital, on the other hand, was by all accounts
kind in its treatment of Gurney but still did not have the time, resources,
knowledge, or personnel available to do much more than to provide its
patients with the basic necessities. Gurney was observed, categorized, and
made as comfortable as possible, but was given little careful analysis or treat-
ment.[63]

His doctor, a man named Steen, took the approach toward Gurney's
mental illness that focused on assessing and monitoring his state, rather than
taking measures to intervene and alleviate the suffering. Steen categorized
his condition as "Delusional Insanity (Systematized)," or paranoid schizo-
phrenia in contemporary terms, a diagnosis that Blevins and others have
recently contested. Gurney continued to believe that he was being subjected
to "electrical tortures." Hurd continues:

> The recorded details of his condition do not change much over the
> years. At times (for example, in July 1924) he became aggressive; in
> 1927 he believed there were machines under the floor that were tor
> turing him; in 1929 he claimed to be the author of Shakespeare's plays,
> and the composer of Beethoven and Haydn's works.... He is often
> described as "apathetic and dejected," "withdrawn" and "solitary."[64]

Psychotherapies, such as psychoanalysis, suggestion therapy, or hypnosis, all of which were used extensively to treat and alleviate the symptoms of sufferers of shell-shock and mild neuroses, were not attempted on Gurney, nor is there any reason to suppose they would have done much good because of the nature and severity of his condition. W. H. Trethowan inquires about treatments available to such a patient had he lived today: "Although modern drug therapy might well have controlled his difficult behaviour and perhaps his more distressing symptoms, even to the point of allowing him to live outside hospital in his beloved Gloucestershire, it is doubtful whether any treatment would have restored to him the creative genius lost in the morass of his mental illness."[65] Bipolar disorder — even as extreme and delusional a form of it as Gurney seems to have exhibited — does respond favorably to contemporary drug therapies unavailable in Gurney's time, so the recent studies of Gurney's illness counter Trethowan's claim that all hope would have been lost for Gurney as an artist, even had he lived today.

Gurney continued to write memorable verse during the first few years of his imprisonment within the hospital walls, and Kavanagh has collected seventy of these poems, many of which revisit the war with definite clarity of vision. Gurney recognized, however, that these war years were receding even further into the recesses of memory, within a mind increasingly unable to retrieve them. Many poems from the "asylum years" display Gurney's heightened self-awareness that he has now been certified as the "mad poet" of the war. He asks in one poem, "It is near Toussaints, the living and dead will say: / 'Have they ended it? What has happened to Gurney?" (*Collected Poems* 171). Gurney, in effect both living and dead, is left without a satisfactory explanation for what has reduced him to this state. Has the war ended for him if peacetime has brought him no psychological peace? He directs a similar question "To God" in a poem of the same name:

> Why have you made life so intolerable
> And set me between four walls, where I am able
> Not to escape meals without prayer, for that is possible
> Only by annoying an attendant...? [*Collected Poems* 156].

Much of the verse from the late asylum period is confessional poetry of this sort, a medium for Gurney to voice his torment and frustration, but lacking the quality seen in previous poems that reconstructs and arranges the chaos of his mind into forms providing him reassurance. Like the long autobiographical pieces "The Retreat" or "Chance to Work," "To God" is prose broken into lines of equal length, a poem only to the degree that poetry is defined as any form of self-expression.

Though not by any means his final poetic utterance, "War Books," written probably in 1925, functions as Gurney's most complete retrospective effort to assess the difficult odyssey that has been his life and the final poem in Kavanagh's collection which looks to the years in France as a source of psychological stability. From the asylum, Gurney sums up his career as a war poet, a title he was quite proud of. He acknowledges his weaknesses and tells his largely nonexistent readership of the inspiration for his verse:

> What did they expect of our toil and extreme
> Hunger — the perfect drawing of a heart's dream?
> Did they look for a book of wrought art's perfection,
> Who promised no reading, nor praise, nor publication?
> Out of the heart's sickness the spirit wrote
> For delight, or to escape hunger, or of war's worst anger,
> When the guns died to silence and men would gather sense
> Somehow together, and find this was life indeed,
> And praise another's nobleness, or to Cotswold get hence
> [*Collected Poems* 196].

Silkin writes, "What was wanted, it seemed, was a perfectly 'wrought' art impossible under the circumstances and inappropriate for the experience."[66] Gurney's poetry, particularly that of *Rewards of Wonder*, was not "a book of wrought art's perfection," but Gurney suggests in the poem that in the end, he sees his poetry as having served personal purposes — the "drawing of a heart's dream," perfect or not. The dream of this heart has been to heal himself of the same "heart's sickness." He states the relationship to the war of himself and other survivors as "gather[ing] sense / Somehow together, and find[ing] this was life indeed." Gurney's postwar poetry has sought and has succeeded in gathering sense out of the war experience. The difficulty for him has arrived in the inevitability that this was his life indeed, a life which decreed that he be toppled by the heart's sickness against which his poetry had fought.

Gurney differentiates himself in the poem's closing lines from his fellow poets who became casualties of the war:

> There we wrote — Corbie Ridge — or in Gonnehem at rest —
> Or Fauquissart — our world's death songs, ever the best.
> One made sorrows' praise passing the church where silence
> Opened for the long quivering strokes of the bell —
> Another wrote all soldiers' praise, and of France and of night's stars,
> Served his guns, got immortality, and died well.
> But Ypres played another trick with its danger on me,
> Kept still the needing and loving-of-action body,
> Gave no candles, and nearly killed me twice as well,
> And no souvenirs, though I risked my life in the stuck tanks.

> Yet there was praise of Ypres, love came sweet in hospital,
> And old Flanders went under to long ages of plays' thought in
>   my pages [ll. 10–21].

The poet who "made sorrows' praise" would seem to be Wilfred Owen, as these lines echo the sonnet "Anthem for Doomed Youth," a poem Gurney became familiar with after Owen's death. The poet who "wrote all soldiers' praise" is Brooke, the golden boy who, particularly through "The Soldier," came to represent the lost generation of youth to the British consciousness during the war. By the 1920s, the deaths of these poets had come to be seen as two of England's most lamentable losses, but to Gurney these men at least had received immortality from their country through their living memory and verse. Gurney, a sick man and getting worse, perceives the war as having "played another trick" on him by having kept him alive and in anonymity. Gurney puns on the word "still" describing his "loving-of-action body;" "still" captures his immobility in the trenches but means alive as well. Ypres, or the war itself, has spared Gurney the fate it dealt many of his companions. Ypres gave Gurney no candles or souvenirs, artefacts of his war experience; he possesses the war only in memory.

But despite this treatment by the war, his stance as a war poet has been to praise the war as his "love came sweet" in his retrospective look at his past at Ypres. Gurney, in this final line clings to his belief in art's capacity to transform his past: "old Flanders went under" as the "long ages of plays' thought in [his] pages" during these intervening years have turned the decimated landscape of France into the emotional anchor that it has been for the debilitated poet after the war. Gurney persists in his conviction that art can, if not heal altogether, at least offer relief. However, lost in thought as a child and young man, often alienated from the potential comfort to be found in his comrades in the trenches, alone in his wanderings after the war, he came to be — by the time his life ended — the only one capable of holding such a conviction when facing the reality of his situation. His poetry all but stopped in the late 1920s, and he kept silent vigil over himself as he continued to deteriorate in body and mind within for much of another decade. Gurney was finally granted the release from his torment which he had sought since entering Barnwood House and then the City of London Hospital fifteen years before. On December 26, 1937, Gurney died, succumbing at last to "the strife / With self" that, in the final paradox of his life, had both sustained him and had been his most formidable enemy.

CHAPTER FOUR

"Are they not still your brothers through our blood?" Siegfried Sassoon, Shell Shock, and Living through the Dead

Siegfried Sassoon in his 1935 memoir *Sherston's Progress*, looking back upon the months of July to November 1917 spent at Craiglockhart War Hospital in Edinburgh, recovering from shell shock, explains the means by which he was able to return to fighting the war against which he had lodged his famous protest. Although while hospitalized, Sassoon had the appearance of a fit and balanced officer capable of serving, his reminiscence illustrates the amount of psychological work needed for recuperation. In his memoir, Sassoon describes his talisman, a "lump of fire-opal clasped on a fine gold chain" which he carried with him in the trenches and which he came to call his "pocket sunset":

> I had derived consolation from its marvellous colours during the worst episodes of my war experiences. In its small way it had done its best to mitigate much squalor and despondency. My companions in dismal dugouts had held it in their hands and admired it.
> ... it brought back the past in which I had made it an emblem of successful endurance, and set up a mood of reverie about the old Front Line, which really did feel as if it had been a better place than this where I now sat in bitter safety surrounded by the wreckage and defeat of those who had once been brave.[1]

As he remembers the talisman, Sassoon imagines it as an object with almost magical powers, capable of redeeming an otherwise horrible experience. The "marvellous colors" somehow had made the "worst episodes of [his] war experiences" bearable. Despite its size, Sassoon describes it as "mitigat[ing] much squalor and despondency" that had characterized his perceptions of the entire landscape of battle. The stone even brings men of disparate ranks together in mutual admiration of it, displaying a potential for unification that Sassoon's poetry will represent as a desire at the heart of his anxiety about his role in warfare. Its most significant power, however, occurs within the hospital when the stone grants Sassoon the ability to return to the past and reconstruct the experiences he finds in memory. In retrospect, the experiences in the trenches are seen as better than his situation in the hospital, where the comfort of his feelings of personal safety is tempered by "wreckage and defeat" of shell shocked soldiers around him. He goes on to explain the stone's part in his own healing from shell shock:

> ... It seems to amount to this, ... that I'm exiled from the troops as a whole rather than from my former fellow officers and men. And I visualized an endless column of marching soldiers, singing "Tipperary" on their way up from the back areas; I saw them filing silently along ruined roads, and lugging their bad boots through mud.... The idea of going back there was indeed like death.
>   By these rather peculiar methods I argued it out with myself in the twilight. And when the windows were dark and I could see the stars, I still sat there with my golf bag between my knees, along with what now seemed an irrefutable assurance that going back to the War as soon as possible was my only chance of peace.[2]

Sassoon returns from his reverie of the past to the present of his self-imposed exile at Craiglockhart and extends the import of his protest against the war beyond his own localized situation. His protest had sought to speak for all soldiers; indeed he claimed in his famous declaration to know the thoughts of all the silent sufferers of the war, but he sees now that, though the antiwar statement may have been shared by most soldiers, the gesture of rebellion was only for himself. He imagines "the endless column of marching soldiers," an image of collective male solidarity that excludes him. The talisman crystallizes the conflict for Sassoon by establishing the alternatives as either continued personal suffering in isolation in the hospital, where "the windows were dark and [he] could see the stars," or a return to the idealized body of men in France, a return which "was indeed like death" with all its danger but which "was [his] only chance of peace."

The pocket sunset works as a metaphor for the personal methods enacted by Sassoon through his poetry written around the time of his stay at Craiglockhart, collected in *Counter-Attack and Other Poems* (1918), to allow him to resolve his crisis of protest and to rejoin his men in France. Poems which return and reshape the past or examine the poet's state of mind at present force Sassoon's confrontation with the nature and efficacy of his formal protest waged against the war effort and force an acknowledgment of the sense of loss and of personal responsibility for such loss that is at the heart of his shell shock. Poetry written at the mental hospital functions alongside the psychotherapy utilized by his doctor, W. H. R. Rivers, both of which enabled Sassoon to examine the political strategies of his protest and to conclude that although the *basis* for the declaration — that the war was unjust and by 1917 unnecessary — was defensible, the *means* of protest — the willed removal of himself from the trenches — created a psychological conflict that the political urgency of the protest could not address. Although the war should end, it would not, and a Second Lieutenant could not make it stop with mere words, however grounded in morally sound argument they were. The protest in fact exacerbated Sassoon's psychological problem at the root of his trauma. As his diaries and reminiscences show, the cause of the psychological disturbance that, at least in part, led to his hospitalization was his anxiety about his role and responsibility for the sufferings of those he commanded. The protest served only to keep him at a greater distance from this suffering and more helpless than ever to alleviate it. The poems which lead to his return to active duty, written from a position of distance in time and place from the fighting, do not create a newfound belief in the military aims of the war, but do enable a strengthening of his conviction that a return to his men, even if it promises death, is preferable to his exile and is in effect his only option. This discussion will chart the representations of varying degrees of distance between Sassoon and the suffering victims within his poetry. His healing from shell shock and the resolution of the protest are reflected through a reduction of physical and emotional distance between himself and his charges in his poetic representations of the war experience, representations which enable the poet to transcend the barriers of class that separate the officer and his enlisted men.

The first of Sassoon's lifelong attempts to "get the war right" in writing comes within the poems that comprised his earliest volume, *The Old Huntsman* (1917), published before his arrival at Craiglockhart. A nervous Wilfred Owen approached Sassoon in his room at Craiglockhart in Edinburgh where both were recovering from shell shock in 1917 and asked the older poet to inscribe five copies of the volume that Owen felt had captured the experience of the trenches better than any other.[3] This volume seeks to depict the war in all its stark reality by means of techniques that have come to be seen as trademarks of Sassoon's style. Although a few of its early poems exhibit patriotic sentiments and belief in the righteousness of the national cause, most — especially those written after the Somme in July 1916 in which Sassoon participated and where his raids into No Man's Land earned him the nickname "Mad Jack" and the Military Cross for valor — display his characteristic methods of satire, colloquial language, and irony through which he put forth his anti-war stance, arguing that the ignorance of proponents of the war across the Channel and in Parliament were greater enemies than the Germans. The ironic method that Sassoon employs in these poems privileges their political statements over any chance for personal or emotional exploration that they may offer for the poet. For instance, in "In the Pink," Sassoon's juxtaposition of the words of a soldier's love letter home with the soldier's imminent death functions as implicit commentary from the poet that the war is unjust, but this commentary limits the degree of sympathy the poet can convey for the man.[4] Owen learned this technique of juxtaposition for ironic effect from his conversations with Sassoon while both recovered in the hospital, and he put them to use in his early war poems, such as "The Letter."[5] The conclusion of Sassoon's "A Working Party" implies the author's feelings of despair for the wasted lives by simply providing the depiction of such a death: "And as he dropped his head the instant split / His startled life with lead, and all went out" (*Collected Poems* 20). The poet need not editorialize about what he has presented in poems such as these; the realistic portrayal of warfare is enough to educate and influence the readership of the actualities experienced by the nation's men, messages that for his earliest war poetry function as the poet's primary aims.

Numerous critics have approached the war poetry of Sassoon by focusing upon its satiric and ironic strategies.[6] "They," a frequently anthologized poem, employs the juxtaposition of the reality of the Western front and the ignorance of those in England for similar ironic effect, and the extensive critical attention paid to these techniques make much detailed discussion of them unnecessary (*Collected Poems* 23). Characteristic of many of Sassoon's war satires in *The Old Huntsman* is the poet's removal of himself to relate the experience from an omniscient perspective, a tactic which seeks to elicit an emotional response from the reader rather to reveal the perspective of the poet. When Sassoon does involve a first person speaker, he does so to provide a lens through which an experience is viewed, rather than to investigate or uncover the speaker's response to the experience. In these closing lines of "Died of Wounds," the speaker describes a wounded soldier in the next bed in a hospital:

> ... [I] heard him shout,
> "They snipe like hell! O Dickie, don't go out" ...
> I fell asleep ... Next morning he was dead;
> And some Slight Wound lay smiling on the bed
> [*Collected Poems* 28].

Even though the speaker provides a first-hand account of the event, he sleeps through the soldier's actual death and avoids emotional involvement with the soldier or the fact of his passing. The speaker does not interpret the cries of the man as appeals for sympathy or comfort; they are annoyances that prevent him from falling asleep. He keeps the next patient at an emotional distance by means of the label "Slight Wound" which relieves him of the burden of representing him in any human terms. Any disgust or pity the poet might have for the experience about which he writes, the solitary death of the wounded soldier, is evoked only through the eliciting of such an emotion from the reader who takes in Sassoon's representation of the event. Irony functions in the poems of *The Old Huntsman* in provoking responses of pity or disgust from the reader by the deliberate elimination or sublimation of those emotions by both the speaker and the poet.

But there is a danger in believing that poems displaying this detachment from the experience comprise the totality of Sassoon's poetic response to the war. Certainly, Sassoon's stark representation from a perspective of emotional distance is his most frequent mode of expression, and it is not to misunderstand the poet to emphasize this predominance. But detachment, irony, and satire are not the only strategies employed, and educating his readership to a reality from which they were shielded is not the only purpose for his poetry. Sassoon's subsequent volume *Counter-Attack* (1918) shows, in addition to poems in the "conventional" Sassoon mode, an increasing degree of overt personal involvement in the episodes and the speakers' treatments of them. As a Lieutenant, overseeing about thirty five enlisted men, Sassoon experienced the complex combination of command and responsibility for his men, and admiration and sympathy for those who were his inferiors in rank. Bonds formed for these men were quickly severed by sniper fire or shelling, as the war has done to a private O'Brien in this entry in Sassoon's diary:

> But he was a dead man when at last we lowered him over the parapet on to a stretcher: and one of the stretcher-bearers examined his wounds and felt for the life that wasn't there, and then took off his round helmet with a sort of reverence — or it may have been only a chance gesture. I would have given a lot if he could have been alive, but it was a hopeless case — a bomb had given him its full explosion. But when I go out on patrols his ghost will surely be with me; he'll catch his breath and grip his bomb just as he used to do.[7]

The amount of time the soldiers spend lingering over the dead body, searching for life, is only the beginning of the psychological impact of O'Brien's death on Sassoon. He both imagines his ghost on the battlefield and gives the dead man another immortality through his written record of him. The death in March 1916 of his fellow Lieutenant David Thomas, commanding a nearby platoon, hit Sassoon particularly hard, and Moeyes speculates that Sassoon deliberately flirted with death because of such emotional losses he himself had experienced, taking unnecessary but often heroic risks in battle for his men.[8] Quinn describes Sassoon's actions after Thomas' death as those "of a distraught lover" in the days following the loss.[9] Sassoon writes:

> Now he comes back to me in memories, like an angel, with the light in his yellow hair, and I think of him at Cambridge last August when we lived together four weeks in Pembroke College in rooms where the previous occupant's name, Paradise, was written above the door.... I lay there under the smooth bole of a beech-tree, wondering, and longing for the bodily presence that was so fair.... So I wrote his name in chalk on the beech-tree stem, and left a rough garland of ivy there, and a yellow primrose for his yellow hair and kind grey eyes, my dear, dear.... So Tommy left us, a gentle soldier, perfect and without stain. And so he will always remain in my heart, fresh and happy and brave [*Diaries* 45].

Significant within this reverie is Sassoon's sublimation of his feelings for Thomas into the chance occurrence of the word "Paradise" inscribed upon the doorway of the room they shared when both were on leave in 1915. Someone else had already provided a written description of their relationship for them, a word capturing the ideal time together which consisted of only the two men. In order to keep such memories of this ideal time alive, Sassoon enacts a similar process of writing once Thomas' "bodily presence that was so fair" is no longer present, resurrecting through imagination the body of Thomas through his "textual" representation created by inscribing his name on the tree. Only through this process of recreation can Thomas "remain in [his] heart, fresh and happy and brave."

Sassoon's feelings for Thomas appear to have been so strong that they surfaced in this overt form in the diary entry. Sassoon eulogizes his boyhood friend Gordon Harbord in his poem "Together" by keeping the memory of this man "fresh and happy and brave" in a vision of a postwar return to their fox-hunting days in the Kent countryside:

> He's jumped each stile along the glistening lanes;
> His hand will be upon the mud-soaked reins;
> Hearing the saddle creak,
> He'll wonder if the frost will come next week.
> I shall forget him in the morning light;
> And while we gallop on he will not speak:
> But at the stable-door he'll say good-night
> [*Collected Poems* 95–96].

As in the diary entry describing Thomas, Sassoon creates an imaginary world of two in the wake of Harbord's death; the fallen soldier accompanies Sassoon on his solitary excursions and mimics his actions. A common thread uniting all these writings about fallen soldiers is the absence of the war from impacting the memory or imagination of the experience between the two men — an interesting omission since the war was responsible for severing Sassoon's emotional connection with each. Sassoon uses, in both the spontaneous diary entry and the poem, textual forms as a means of creating a world free from the war's influence. Another dimension of these relationships that made them so ideal and worthy of returning to in memory was the equality of rank between Sassoon, Thomas, and Harbord, all of the upper class and all Lieutenants. Emotional representations of the relationships are thus free from any of the markers of class that necessarily distinguish and distance Sassoon from his men. The poems of *Counter-Attack* will demonstrate Sassoon's attempts in reconstructing his experience of warfare in poetry to negotiate between the levels of personal involvement with the many facets of his experience as soldier and commander. Elevated in class and rank, Sassoon felt a degree of detachment from the sufferings of others that surfaces in his frequently detached tone. But such detachment is as well ironic, veils Sassoon's desire to connect and sympathize with suffering that is not his own, and simultaneously reveals his inability to put such a desire into a form other than an ironic one. Many poems of *Counter Attack* remove this barrier of irony between Sassoon and his reader and introduce into the poet's means for representing the war the potentially curative technique of confession and autobiography. These poems reveal Sassoon's desire for survival and removal of himself from the dangers of the experience while exposing at the same time his guilt for having survived when many under his watch had not. By means of the memories of these fallen soldiers Sassoon will enact a symbolic reunion with those who have survived. Through the course of the volume and other poems written during his recuperation from shell shock, Sassoon constructs a method of diminishing the emotional distance between himself and the men to whom he will return.

The Politics and Psychology of Sassoon's Shell Shock

Siegfried Sassoon's hospitalization for shell shock between July and November 1917 makes for a complicated story, and one must look back upon the months preceding his famous protest against the war to sort out the political and psychological factors precipitating his stay at Craiglockhart War Hospital in Edinburgh.[10] Sassoon's own writings and the impressions he made on others during these months provide evidence that a near psychological breakdown did contribute to his hospitalization. The process toward potential incapacitation from battle fatigue had begun months before his arrival at Craiglockhart as the year and half of exposure in the trenches took its inevitable toll. He had suffered through the deaths of those close to him in spirit — Lieutenant Thomas and Hamo, his brother, killed at Gallipoli in November 1915 — and had witnessed the deaths of those living in close proximity to him, under his command, men such as Private O'Brien. Sassoon's personal reflections from the months before his formal protest show the cumulative impact of watching men die, helpless to save them. On February 22, 1917, after a short leave, he confesses to his diary:

> The silence and the clean air did me good. It seemed easier to think clearly, a sore need now. My brain is so pitifully confused by the war and my own single part in it....
> And while I lie awake staring at the darkness of the tent my own terrors get hold of me and I long only for life and comfort, and the weeks before me seem horrible and agonizing. I haven't the physical health to face the hardship and nerve-strain. Nothing seems to matter but a speedy release from the hell that awaits me.
> Yet I should loathe the very idea of returning to England without having been scarred and tortured once more. I suppose all this "emotional experience" (futile phrase) is of value. But it leads nowhere now (but to madness). There is little tenderness left in me: only bitter resentment and a morbid desire to measure the whole ignominy which men are brought to by these fearful times of "sanguinary imbecility" (as Conrad calls it).
> For the soldier is no longer a noble figure; he is merely a writhing insect among this ghastly folly of destruction [*Diaries* 133–34].

This entry reflects the stresses which the conflicting roles that the war asked Sassoon to play had upon his psychological constitution. The difficulty for Sassoon comes in reconciling his "own single part" with the war's complexities. When thinking of himself alone, nothing matters but self-preservation — his desires for "life and comfort" and the "speedy release from the hell that awaits." But he is well aware of the pull upon him in the opposite direction. A return to England without being "scarred and tortured once more" is, in his mind, the equivalent of cowardice. He suggests that the total effect of these competing impulses results in his movement toward madness and the deadening of "tenderness" or compassion he might feel for his men. The choice for Sassoon comes down to either security, with its drawback of cowardice; or further personal risk and suffering, alleviated by the knowledge that he has acted responsibly in continuing to lead his men but which might bring him closer to breakdown. The protest months later will become the means by which he tries to keep the code of honor intact while avoiding the complete collapse that seems, in February 1917, imminent.

Similar anxieties about his conflicted relationship to the war would begin to surface in his poetry written that spring. Months later, after Sassoon arrived at Craiglockhart in July 1917 and he and Wilfred Owen became friends, Owen asked Sassoon whether he would submit any of his work to Craiglockhart's newspaper *The Hydra*, which Owen edited as part of his "work-cure" prescribed by his doctor Arthur Brock.[11] Sassoon offered him a draft of "The Rear Guard," a poem written in April 1917, before the protest and before his arrival at Craiglockhart, which would later be included in *Counter-Attack*:

> *(Hindenburg Line, April 1917)*
>
> Groping along the tunnel, step by step,
> He winked his prying torch with patching glare
> From side to side, and sniffed the unwholesome air....
>
> Savage, he kicked a soft, unanswering heap,
> And flashed his beam across the livid face
> Terribly glaring up, whose eyes yet wore
> Agony dying hard ten days before;
> And fists of fingers clutched a blackening wound.
>
> Alone he staggered on until he found
> Dawn's ghost that filtered down a shafted stair
> To the dazed, muttering creature underground
> Who heard the boom of shells in muffled sound.
> At last, with sweat of horror in his hair,
> He climbed through darkness to the twilight air,
> Unloading hell behind him step by step
>   [*Collected Poems* 69–70].

Perhaps Owen's position as editor of the newspaper that published the poem allowed him to internalize its setting and situate his poem, "Strange Meeting," written in January 1918, in a similar underground locale:

> It seemed that out of battle I escaped
> Down some profound tunnel, long since scooped
> Through granites which titanic wars had groined.[12]

Owen uses the underground setting as a site for psychological exploration after having completed his recovery from shell shock. As the previous chapter has discussed, Owen gives the dead soldier, who is both friend and enemy to the speaker, a voice, and the dead man's monologue establishes this character as a "double" for the speaker, revealing Owen's prior psychological struggles at Craiglockhart with his role as poet and soldier. Although Sassoon's poem shares its setting, it lacks this psychological and autobiographical depth, in part because of the time of its conception. He keeps the experience at an emotional distance by narrating the confrontation between the living and the dead through an omniscient, third-person voice. In both poems, the protagonist confronts a dead soldier, but in "The Rear Guard," the sight of the corpse is a horror from which the soldier flees, while Owen's speaker in "Strange Meeting" remains and yields his control over the experience to the voice of the dead. Sassoon's poem strives for realism, rather than the dream state that characterizes "Strange Meeting" and enables the supernatural conversation.

Sassoon's poem was composed before the overt action of protest and before Craiglockhart, around the time he was hospitalized for a shoulder wound in April, 1917, suffered during his fighting near the Somme River, against the German's Hindenburg Line; nevertheless, it displays his anxiety in a repressed form to return to the fighting, an anxiety which surfaces within the protagonist's symbolic journey towards his surfacing in the "twilight air" of warfare. This anxiety to return will prove to be at the heart of Sassoon's version of shell shock, so this representation of a soldier's brief journey away from the war underground that ends with his speedy return to the surface world of fighting sheds light upon the psychological stresses which would intensify throughout his ordeal of 1917. The omniscient speaker of the poem regards the dead soldier that the protagonist encounters as a "soft, unanswering heap," represented through a catalogue of body parts — a face, eyes, a fist of fingers. The underground world, despite the realism of the poem's depiction of it, is the place of nightmare visions. It is the horror of this man's death that prompts the protagonist's flight, especially the look of agony remaining on the corpse's face and his clutching of the wound, both of which suggest the lingering effects of life upon the dead body. Even though the reaction of fear to such a gruesome sight is understandable, it is significant that the soldier flees toward "the boom of shells in muffled sound" and toward the war which had been responsible for the corpse he had just glimpsed. "Dawn's ghost" which illuminated the stair into the tunnel and "the twilight air" at the top of the stair are the means of escaping the "darkness" underground, and such descriptions give the battlefield an ironic quality of peace. In the hospital recovering from a shoulder wound and recollecting his thoughts into poetic form about the war from this position of distance, Sassoon crafts into the protagonist's experience a structure mirroring his own. As the talisman described in *Sherston's Progress* would later enable him to realize, returning to the war was the only means of achieving inner peace.

The revisions Sassoon made to the poem between this draft in April, which he gave to Owen, and its final form in October of that year, before publication, were for the most part minor.[13] He had no stanza breaks in the draft, and various phrasings were amended in the revision, such as "prying torch" for the original "tiny torch" in line two, and "Terribly" which replaced "Horribly" in the sixth line of the passage. The most significant changes occur in the concluding lines of the poem, which had originally read:

> Gasping, he staggered onward till he found
> Dawn's ghost that filtered down a shafted stair,
> To clammy creatures groping underground,
> Hearing the boom of shells with muffled sound.
> Then with the sweat of horror in his hair,
> He climbed with darkness to the twilight air [*Diaries* 158].

Sassoon sought to emphasize the solitude of the soldier while underground by changing "Gasping" to "Alone." The terror experienced through one-on-one confrontation between the living and the dead can be alleviated by the soldier's return to the companionship of his fellow men in the trenches above the underground passage. The most significant change in these concluding lines is Sassoon's addition of the last line, "Unloading hell behind him step by step," which was absent in the original draft. With this final line, Sassoon provides closure to the poem by completing the rhyme (through repetition) that had been promised by the beginning of the poem. The addition of this last line connects the poem's conclusion with its opening image, "Groping along the tunnel, step by step," and underscores the subtext of the poem as a metaphoric journey to the poet's reconciliation with the war. "Groping" suggests a world of uncertainty and indecision experienced alone, apart from battle, whereas "Unloading hell behind him" connotes the determination to return to it. The revisions to the poem are significant for framing an understanding of the processes by which Sassoon would recover not simply from a physical injury but later, in October when revising the poem into its final form at Craiglockhart, from psychological trauma as well. He would "unload" or relieve himself of the distance between himself and his men by renouncing the protest that had brought his separation from the war upon him.

So, in the spring of 1917, Sassoon's diaries exhibited the mounting conflict within him between his desire for survival and for the fulfillment of his duty, and the poems written during these months begin to display his working through the conflict in artistic forms. The factor that precipitated Sassoon's entry into Craiglockhart War Hospital was his public statement of protest against the war, sent to his commanding officer and to many of Sassoon's friends on June 15, 1917, which read in part:

> I am making this statement as an act of wilful defiance of military
> authority, because I believe that the War is being deliberately
> prolonged by those who have the power to end it. I am a soldier,
> convinced that I am acting on behalf of soldiers....
>
> I have seen and endured the sufferings of the troops, and I can
> no longer be a party to prolonging those sufferings for ends which
> I believe to be evil and unjust....
>
> I am not protesting against the military conduct of the War, but
> against the political errors and insincerities for which the fighting
> men are being sacrificed.
>
> On behalf of those who are suffering now, I make this protest
> against the deception which is being practised on them. Also I
> believe that it may help to destroy the callous complacency with
> which the majority of those at home regard the continuance of
> agonies which they do not share, and which they have not sufficient
> imagination to realize [*Diaries* 173–74].

Sassoon's relationship to his men, as described in the declaration, is telling.
The protest is waged not because of his personal suffering but because he
has "seen and endured" the suffering of his men. The suffering which Sas-
soon experiences and to which he objects is the structure of warfare that he
believes implicates him because of his place in the chain of command. He
is rejecting this power structure that places the burden of responsibility upon
him and, in so doing, creates a double burden of suffering for him to bear —
both his and his men's. Sassoon circulated the statement to enough acquain-
tances for it to make a ripple in the consciousness of several people back home
before it arrived in the hands of military and political figures who were forced
to decide upon a course of action. He writes to his commanding officer, "I
am fully aware of what I am letting myself in for," suggesting that he antic-
ipated a court martial to bring greater publicity to his cause (*Diaries* 177).
Moeyes summarizes the political fallout: "Sassoon's statement was read out
in the House of Commons by the liberal MP for Northampton H. B. Lees-
Smith on 30 July 1917. In his reply the Under-Secretary for War called upon
the Honourable Members not to exploit this action by a gallant officer who
was at present in a disturbed state of mind, thus managing to avoid any fur-
ther discussion on the subject."[14] Although the text of Sassoon's letter ran
the next day in both *The Times* and *The Daily Mail*, the British war machine
was able to avoid any prolonged political damage from the incident. The
public statement had little noticeable impact on the public consciousness
which continued to support the war and to function, according to Sassoon,
as the enemy of "callous complacency" against which his personal war was
in part being directed. Undoubtedly, his pacifist acquaintances Bertrand
Russell and Lady Ottoline Morrell played some part in planting the seeds of

an active protest within his mind, and Morrell wrote Sassoon in a letter after the statement was circulated, "It is *tremendously fine* of you doing it. You will have a hard time of it, and people are sure to say all sorts of foolish things. They always do — but nothing of that sort can really tarnish or dim the value of such a True Act" (*Diaries* 178). But this adulation from such a figure of notoriety was not the motivating factor. For Sassoon, the statement was a political expression based on personal belief acquired through his firsthand knowledge of life in battle, not the result of philosophical conviction about the immorality of warfare. In fact, he neither condemns war in general nor even this war in and of itself within the document; he cries out only against the political system that has prolonged this war needlessly, has implicated him in the suffering of his men, and has thus made it morally suspect.

Weeks later, when Sassoon had waged the protest, the war authorities were attempting to resolve his case quietly. Not wanting to deliver a dishonorable discharge to a decorated officer, the Medical Board considered committing Sassoon into an institution as "proof" of his imbalance. The hospitalization was a political act, as was the protest itself, but the political nature of the actions on both sides of the question of Sassoon's mental state should not obscure the psychological trauma that Sassoon had endured. The poet Robert Graves, whom Sassoon befriended during the war, acted on Sassoon's behalf in testifying before the medical board considering his mental state. Graves recalls his impressions of Sassoon in his memoir of the war, *Goodbye to All That* (1929):

> ...He looked very ill; he told me that he had just been down to the Formby links and thrown his Military Cross into the sea. We discussed the political situation; I took the line that everyone was mad except ourselves and one or two others, and that no good could come of offering common sense to the insane....
>
> At last, unable to deny how ill he was, Siegfried consented to appear before the medical board.
>
> Much against my will, I had to appear in the role of a patriot distressed by the mental collapse of a brother-in-arms — a collapse directly due to his magnificent exploits in the trenches. I mentioned Siegfried's "hallucinations" in the matter of corpses in Piccadilly.... Being in nearly as bad a state of nerves as Siegfried myself, I burst into tears three times during my statement.... I prayed that when Siegfried came into the board-room after me he would not undo my work by appearing too sane.[15]

A number of factors complicate this gesture on the part of Graves, not least of which are the eleven years that elapsed between the event and its retelling. Since Graves wanted to spare his friend from the unpleasantness of a dishonorable discharge for what had become a politically futile gesture, he attempts — or so he claims — to play a role for the medical board, exaggerating the mental anguish of his friend. Within this narrative as well, however, are the admissions that Sassoon was "in a bad state of nerves." Graves says that not only did Sassoon look ill, but that he admitted this illness as well before the board interview. Graves also suggests that his own state of nerves was not that different from his friend's. The war had made both men's grip on sanity tenuous, and Graves, purportedly speaking from a position of authority, claims to be capable of assessing Sassoon's mental state when he appears not altogether far from collapse himself. Graves would return to the fighting, which he considered madness itself, while his friend Sassoon resisted the madness of the war and was hospitalized for an act which both men described as the sanest behavior of anyone involved.

In a diary entry from February 1917, Sassoon had exclaimed, "The best that a brave and thoughtful creature can hope for now is to become a sort of ignoble Hamlet" (*Diaries* 133). Whether the "insanity" existed within Sassoon or solely in the canvas of war surrounding him is the same question which Shakespeare's protagonist dramatized. But the inner thoughts confessed within the diaries provide further evidence that the madness of war had seeped inward to infect Sassoon's own mental functioning. He confirms the occurrence of the "hallucinations of corpses" that Graves employed to sway the medical board towards Sassoon's committal. Recovering from his shoulder wound in April 1917, awaiting his return to France, Sassoon describes his sleepless nights:

> ... the horrors come creeping across the floor: the floor is littered with parcels of dead flesh and bones, faces glaring at the ceiling, faces turned to the floor, hands clutching neck or belly; a livid grinning face with bristly moustache peers at me over the edge of my bed, the hands clutching my sheets. Yet I found no bloodstains this morning.... I don't think they mean any harm to me. They are not here to scare me; they look at me reproachfully, because I am so lucky, with my safe wound.... One boy, an English private in full battle order, crawls to me painfully on hands and knees, and lies gasping at the foot of my bed; he is fumbling in his tunic for a letter; just as he reaches forward to give it me his head lolls sideways and he collapses on the floor; there is a hole in his jaw, and the blood spreads across his white face like ink spilt on blotting-paper. I wish I could sleep [*Diaries* 161–62].

Away from the fighting, with time to reflect on what occurred there as he had by means of the poem "The Rear Guard," written during the same hospital stay, Sassoon displays anxieties which take ghastly forms when the memories of the carnage he observed come to the surface as his conscious control over them relaxes at nighttime. At first the vision is of body parts — "flesh and bones," "faces," "hands clutching at neck or belly," even a "moustache"— similar to the corpse in "The Rear Guard." Only after these parts take a complete human form do they gather moral import. Subconsciously feeling that his "safe wound," his "Blighty," makes him guilty of failing to lead his men and guilty of enjoying a safe reprieve from battle in the hospital, Sassoon judges himself by means of the construction of the images of the dead who return to judge him reproachfully. Lieutenant Sassoon takes care to note the rank of the final ghost in his waking nightmare. This private, presumably a man under Sassoon's command, extends a letter, a symbol of communication between himself and Sassoon. Significantly, in his vision, Sassoon does not extend his arm to accept the gesture, perhaps because of the distinction in rank between them. After this missed connection, the private dies. The imagery of his death emphasizes Sassoon's anxieties about his relationship with these men: the soldier fails to communicate through the letter to his superior; the superior fails to meet his extended hand halfway, and the fact of death becomes another symbolic "text" or expression within the nightmare, as Sassoon describes the blood through the metaphor of "ink spilt on blotting paper." Any communication between the men, written or spoken, is silenced by the death itself. Such a hallucination reveals the concerns characteristic of officers suffering from shell shock, namely the internal struggle waged to resolve the competing desires of personal responsibility for the sufferings and deaths of others and personal safety and survival.

The anxiety which surfaces in the vision hinges upon the distance separating Sassoon from his private. The intervention of the war increases the separation between them and prevents any physical contact which could serve as a symbol of Sassoon's expression of sympathy and comfort for the dying man, an expression which will prove to be a gesture of psychological importance in Sassoon's method of representing his "healing" in later poetry. Interestingly, the "hallucination," which secured Sassoon's place at Craiglockhart through Graves' testimony, while providing evidence of Sassoon's tenuous psychological balance, is actually a revelation of his anxieties about *not* fighting, rather than a display of his reluctance to return which characterized most sufferers of shell shock. The visions of death and carnage, symbolic of the horrors he had witnessed, converge into representations of how he should go about living and commanding his living men, through a "speedy return" not to England but to the front. Sassoon would complete the psychological exploration of the anxieties represented in the hallucination while at Craiglockhart between July and November. The different contexts of his two hospital stays, however, are significant. Sassoon had received his shoulder wound in April through no fault of his own, even though the hallucinations suggest repressed guilt over his "Blighty" wound; rather he had received it on one of his courageous forays into No Man's Land. Though this wounding introduced distance between Sassoon and his men who remained in the trenches, the hospitalization at Craiglockhart two months later, brought on by Sassoon's own conscious and deliberate act of rebellion, increased this physical and psychological distance and prolonged the separation.

On October 17, 1917, a month before Sassoon's release from Craiglockhart, Sassoon included a poem titled "Death's Brotherhood" in a letter to Lady Ottoline Morrell. He reveals his new state of mind about the protest which she had supported, stating, "This poem will show you what I feel like. And it is the truth" (*Diaries* 191). The poem, retitled "Sick Leave" when collected in *Counter-Attack*, crafts the chaotic and irrational world of hallucinations into the order of a poetic form, and this reconstruction establishes the psychological reconciliation, which the diary entry left unresolved in April, between Sassoon, the men who had died on his watch, and the men to whom he would soon return the subsequent month:

> When I'm asleep, dreaming and lulled and warm,—
> They come, the homeless ones, the noiseless dead.
> While the dim charging breakers of the storm
> Bellow and drone and rumble overhead,
> Out of the gloom they gather about my bed.
> They whisper to my heart; their thoughts are mine.
> "Why are you here with all your watches ended?
> From Ypres to Frise we sought you in the Line."
> In bitter safety I awake, unfriended;
> And while the dawn begins with slashing rain
> I think of the Battalion in the mud.
> "When are you going out to them again?
> Are they not still your brothers through our blood?"
> [*Collected Poems* 85].

Sassoon establishes a three-part structure of poem, which moves from the initial image of peace and comfort, to the words of the ghosts, to an articulation of his final dilemma. The first five lines establish Sassoon's conflicted attitude toward his own security: the poem's opening line, taken alone, sets a scene that gives no indication of what awaits the speaker as he sleeps comfortably within his sheltered room, but the subsequent line shows the internal turmoil of the speaker as he perceives "the noiseless dead." At this point of the poem, both the warm speaker and the silent spectres are in contrast to the storm raging outside. Because he has no conscious thought of the war as he sleeps, the war manifests itself in his subconscious, though the world outside the room and the internal conflict remain at a distance.

The central three lines display the speaker's awareness, not fully acknowledged in Sassoon's diary entry of his hallucinations, that the ghosts are projections of the conflict within his consciousness: "They whisper to my heart; their thoughts are mine." But these seem to be thoughts the speaker would be incapable of articulating without the ghosts' appearance and voice to bring such difficult material to the surface. In his description of his hallucination, the ghosts were notably silent; here he has given them voice to articulate his internal crisis that has taken clearer shape by means of its poetic representation and to begin to bridge the psychological distance he perceives between himself and his memories of the fallen conscripts. They "speak to [his] heart," as well, suggesting a degree of emotional connection not previously acknowledged which later poems will intensify through more overtly homoerotic means. These ghosts know the battlefield well, searching for the speaker "From Ypres to Frise," the entire arena of the front line in which Sassoon had fought, and suggesting that duty demands he be nowhere other than the trenches. The closing five lines mirror the opening five by situating the speaker within the safety of the room, as night gives way to daylight, but he now reinterprets this same physical position. His safety has become "bitter," and the solitude experienced as comfort within the hospital is characterized by the word "unfriended," when "friended" by his troops is now seen to be the ideal situation to which he hopes to return, much as the soldier flees the condition of solitude in the underground world of "The Rear Guard" for the companionship to be found in the war itself. The rain outside the hospital room, which had been symbolic early in the poem of the external world from which the speaker was safe, is now the means by which the speaker reconnects psychologically with his "Battalion in the mud" across the English channel.

The struggle to rejoin his men in France is a battle waged within and against his mind; the speaker can interpret safety and solitude only as markers of his own abandonment of responsibility. He cannot bring those who have fallen and who inhabit his nightmares back to life. The best he can do is to accept once again command over those still living whom he had left behind through his gesture of protest. The closing question asked by the phantom shows that the confrontation with the fact of soldiers' deaths and the speaker's place in relation to these deaths is crucial to allow his complete return, in body and in mind, to the men: "Are they not still your brothers through our blood?" Through the blood of the dead the speaker remains connected in the "blood" of brotherhood to the living men, and through the blood of the dead he will become capable of returning in hopes of preventing further loss or shedding blood of his own. The image of blood within the hallucination in the diary was symbolic of the disconnection between Sassoon and his men, living and dead, as the blood spilled like ink and cut short the gesture of communication represented by the private's letter to his officer. Reconstructing the psychological experience of guilt into poetic form, Sassoon writes the means for his own psychological healing by stressing the common "blood" or humanity of all men, regardless of rank. If he is able to remove in his mind the socially constructed impediments to complete sympathy, he can return and lead once again.

The debate has continued over the question of whether Sassoon was actually shell shocked because his version of shell shock was a different variety than that most commonly experienced by officers at Craiglockhart, whose psychological responses were deeply ingrained defense mechanisms produced by the mind to force their exit from the trenches. Most of the shell shock cases were uphill battles for the doctors at Craiglockhart whose task was breaking down the defenses of self-preservation to bring about a quick "healing" and return to the fighting.[16] Sassoon's diaries indicate similar desires to escape the war, but his case is unique for the degree to which he prioritized his responsibility to the troops over self-preservation and to the degree that his belief in a code of duty could outmatch his own individual desire for safety. This is not to say, however, that the pull toward personal security did not exist. The psychological manifestations of Sassoon's feelings of responsibility rely upon symbolic usage of horrible images of battle — the fragmented bodies of the dead and the ghostly beckonings of men whom Sassoon had led — to illustrate that although Sassoon began to speak of his need to return, his subconscious desires to avoid the horrific experiences of warfare still connected his case in part with other more "typical" shell shock victims. Elaine Showalter disagrees: "Sassoon's experience was particularly striking because he was not in fact shell-shocked at all, and class privilege accounted for his categorization as neurasthenic rather than insubordinate."[17] Granted, if a private were to wage a similar protest, he would have been dealt with as a malingerer. However, such a scenario is unlikely because the war did not cause within the typical private the feelings of responsibility for men beneath or around him that Sassoon was articulating. Sassoon's class did not necessarily offer him a position of complete privilege in the war since this social position instilled the notion that he had to speak out for those who could not because of their class. Showalter overlooks the evidence of shell shock within Sassoon's writings to argue the case solely in terms of its politics. Carole Shelton expresses the combination of class, politics, and psychology responsible for the hospitalization more completely: "That he was suffering from shell shock does not invalidate the sincerity of his protest; that his protest was sincere does not prove wrong the diagnosis of shell shock. Rather, his inablility to suppress his instinct for self-preservation allowed his bitterness at the war to surface."[18] The process of reconstructing the hallucination experienced while wounded in the shoulder into a poem, which speaks of his anxieties in attempts to resolve the psychological crisis, provides a model for the processes of poetic creation that continued during this period in 1917 and that would lead to his eventual return.

W. H. R. Rivers and the Irrepressible War Experience

Perhaps complicating the question of the extent of Sassoon's mental anguish is the relative lack of conflict between Sassoon and his doctor, W. H. R. Rivers, who was assigned to his case at Craiglockhart. After initial conversations and assessment, Rivers decided upon a course of treatment which consisted of hour long sessions of analysis in the doctor's office every other evening. Because Rivers did not perceive Sassoon to be a threat to himself or to others, and because his condition was in no way physically debilitating, Sassoon was allowed to make use of much of his time as he saw fit, playing a round a golf almost daily, touring the countryside of the region, dining with visitors from London, such as Lady Morrell and Robbie Ross, writing poetry, and striking up friendships with other patients, most notably Wilfred Owen, whose poetic career Sassoon helped set upon its final direction. By Sassoon's accounts, he found his time at Craiglockhart to be restorative to his nerves, and his major complaint during the initial weeks of his stay was that he did not belong in the company of the other patients. He writes to Robbie Ross, "There are 160 Officers here, most of them half-dotty. No doubt I'll be able to get some splendid details for future use" (*Diaries* 183). And indeed, at no time between his arrival in June until the com position of "Survivors" later that summer, in which he put the "splendid details" of the acute cases of shell shock to use, did Sassoon resemble the typical patient. Campbell observes that the work "is the only Craiglockhart poem to be prompted, not by Sassoon's 'anti-war complex' or his memories of the trenches, but by life among the inmates of 'Dottyville.'"[19] The poem reads:

> No doubt they'll soon get well; the shock and strain
>   Have caused their stammering, disconnected talk.
> Of course they're "longing to go out again," —
>   These boys with old, scared faces, learning to walk.
> They'll soon forget their haunted nights; their cowed
>   Subjection to the ghosts of friends who died, —

> Their dreams that drip with murder; and they'll be proud
>   Of glorious war that shatter'd all their pride ...
> Men who went out to battle, grim and glad;
> Children, with eyes that hate you, broken and mad
>   [*Collected Poems* 90].

Sassoon, like Doctor Rivers, had had a stammer since childhood, but not one caused by the shock of warfare as it did these soldiers.[20] Nor did he suffer from paralysis, tremors, or other breakdowns of motor functioning. But beneath their physical appearances, Sassoon and the men had in common "haunted nights," "subjection to the ghosts of friends who died," and "dreams that drip with murder." These were the symptoms that had in part landed him in the hospital, although despite their horrific content, the nightmares before Craiglockhart in April gave voice to Sassoon's desire to return to the fighting, rather than to flee it. And by the time of his arrival, the nightmares had abated, and he appears to have been more troubled by his inability to sleep because of the screams of fellow patients in the night. So despite the condescension in tone in his descriptions of the other inhabitants of "Dottyville," Sassoon was largely correct to see his psychological situation as distinct from the rest of the men, about whom he is skeptical that they are "longing to go out again." Wilfred Owen's "Mental Cases" describes a similar group of men as Sassoon represents in "Survivors," but Owen does so with considerably greater power and sympathy for them, due to the fact that his experience of shell shock caused a greater resemblance between himself and the acute cases within the poem than Sassoon ever experienced.

Despite the "stiff upper lip" put forth in his letter to Ross, insinuating that he did not belong, further evidence suggests that his appearance and claims for complete stability were masking conflicts which he needed the time at Craiglockhart to resolve. By November, immediately before his release, according to his letters, Sassoon once again was having similar nightmares, expressing his need to rejoin his men, and it is around this time that he wrote "Sick Leave."[21] Unfortunately, Sassoon stopped keeping his diary during the time at Craiglockhart, perhaps feeling that sessions of psychoanalysis with Rivers and the writing of poetry were enough to satisfy the most introspective episode of his life. Rupert Hart-Davis has included the surviving letters from this time period in his edition of the *Diaries* covering the war years to keep the narrative of Sassoon's war experience intact. To reconstruct the actual therapy administered by Rivers and its relationship to Sassoon's eventual release and the ending of his protest, one must look at these letters, his fictionalized reminiscence of the period eighteen years later in *Sherston's Progress*, and Rivers' own writings about his methods of therapy. Caesar describes Sassoon's memoir as "a far more cheerful account of Craiglockhart than is to be found in ... the letters."[22] This noticeable difference in tone is understandable, since when looking back upon the experience, Sassoon had the benefit of knowing that he not only endured his hospital stay but also had survived the war, whereas while hospitalized, the possibility of a court martial, while deferred, was still alive, and the possibility of death in France, should he ever return, appeared at moments an inevitability.

In both his letters and his memoirs, Sassoon reports having a great deal of admiration for Rivers. He writes to Robbie Ross on July 26, "Rivers, the chap who looks after me, is very nice. I am very glad to have the chance of talking to such a fine man" (*Diaries* 183). On July 30, in a letter to Lady Morrell, he appears more guarded in his impressions of him: "My doctor is a sensible man who doesn't say anything silly. His name is Rivers, a notable Cambridge psychologist. But his arguments don't make any impression on me. He doesn't *pretend* that my nerves are wrong, but regards my attitude as abnormal. I don't know how long he will go on trying to persuade me to modify my views" (*Diaries* 183–84). Sassoon's recollections of Rivers in his memoir tend toward adoration of the man in gratitude for the impact the doctor made upon him, both in his assistance in reconciling Sassoon's crisis concerning the war and, in a larger sense, in prompting Sassoon's increased degree of self-knowledge brought about through their contact: "I can only suggest that my definite approach to mental maturity began with my contact with the mind of Rivers."[23] Rivers, for his part, displays the impact Sassoon's anti-war stance had upon his own reflections upon the war through his analysis of his own dream in *Conflict and Dream* (1922), which he interpreted as his own psychological struggles with his position toward the war, "which had been definitely of the 'fight to the finish' kind."[24] He concludes that Sassoon, disguised as "Patient B," had prompted the dream:

> So long as I was an officer of the R. A. M. C., and of this my uniform was the obvious symbol, my discussions with B on his attitude towards the war were prejudiced by my sense that I was not a free agent in discussing the matter, but that there was the danger that my attitude might be influenced by my official position ... and I was fully aware of an element of constraint in my relations with B on this account.[25]

The degree to which Sassoon influenced the doctor's own psychology is evidence of the unique respect each grew to feel for the other, which continued in their friendship after the war. Topics of discussion during their sessions of therapy ranged from Sassoon's personal experiences in battle to more abstract issues such as European politics and economics.

Another frequent topic of conversation was Sassoon's dreams of war, which had ended but were still of interest to Rivers. He mentions in *Conflict and Dream* another influence Sassoon may have had upon his thinking. In his discussion of dreams and psycho-neuroses, Rivers argues for the connection, both in content and in psychological function, between dreams and poetry:

> It is possible to take the images of the manifest content of a poem and discover more or less exactly how each has been suggested by the experience, new or old, of the poet. It is also possible, at any rate in many cases, to show how these images are symbolic expressions of some conflict with is raging in the mind of the poet, and that the real underlying meaning or latent content of the poem is very different from that which the outward imagery would suggest.... There is also a striking resemblance with [dreams] in that the poem may come in a state closely resembling a dissociation from the experience of ordinary life.[26]

Rivers qualifies his argument of the similar functioning of dreams and poetry by acknowledging that the poem "is very rarely the immediate product of the poetic activity, but has been the subject of a lengthy process of a critical kind, comparable with that which Freud has called the secondary elaboration of the dream."[27] The poems discussed thus far support Rivers' hypothesis. The poem "Sick Leave" is Sassoon's "secondary elaboration" of the nightmares he had had months before, in which the poem, written at the end of the stay at Craiglockhart, creates a resolution for the guilt expressed by means of the dream, experienced prior to his arrival at Craiglockhart, in which this resolution had not yet been envisioned. "The Rear Guard," written before his shell shock, while appearing in its "manifest content" to be a narrative in which a soldier encounters a corpse and flees from the sight, reveals as its subtext the author's desire to escape from a position of solitude and to rejoin his men on the battlefield, a subtext which Sassoon's revisions emphasized. Sassoon's processes of composition of these poems, as the dream in April becomes the poem in November in "Sick Leave," and the draft from April becomes the revised version of "The Rear Guard" in October, displays the extent to which the process of poetic representation was involved within the concurrent therapeutic approaches of Rivers during these same months of 1917.

Sassoon's written memories of the time together might lead a reader to infer that he was simply biding his time in the mental wards with the legitimately shell shocked before the opportunity arose for his return to France. In *Siegfried's Journey* (1946), he records his recollection of Rivers' assessment of his mental state: "The patient is a healthy-looking man of good physique.

There are no physical signs of any disorder of the nervous system. He discusses his recent actions and their motives in a perfectly intelligent and rational way, and there is no evidence of any excitement or depression."[28] In his earlier memoir, Sassoon recalls a conversation during one of his tri-weekly sessions with Rivers:

> One evening I asked whether he thought I was suffering from shell-shock.
> "Certainly not," he replied.
> "What *have* I got, then?"
> "Well, you appear to be suffering from an anti-war complex." We both of us laughed at that.[29]

Though establishing that indeed Sassoon did not fit the prototype of shell shock characterizing Craiglockhart's inhabitants, and revealing Rivers' awareness that for all practical purposes, Sassoon was under his care because of his political actions rather than for any visible manifestations of trauma, these descriptions are potentially misleading. Sassoon wrote both memoirs in the war's aftermath, and elsewhere in *Sherston's Progress*, he writes, "I would give a good deal for a few gramophone records of my 'interchanges of ideas' with Rivers ... at the moment of writing I feel very much afraid of reporting our confabulations incorrectly."[30] Sassoon was indeed suffering from an "anti-war complex." He had rejected the war through the intellectual means of his protest, rather than through the unconscious means that characterizes the defense mechanism at the heart of shell shock, but despite Sassoon's efforts in letters and memories of his particular case to present himself as entirely different from the rest, all were united at Craiglockhart for their psychological strategies of removing themselves from the stresses of combat.

And it was the task of Rivers and all the doctors at Craiglockhart to make all shell shock victims once again fit to serve, if at all possible, and the therapeutic approach Rivers took to Sassoon's case indicates that despite the appearance of complete congeniality between doctor and patient, Rivers did consider this "anti-war complex" as an impediment to Sassoon's well-being that therapy must address. Rivers collected his theories about war neuroses, based upon his time at the Magull Military Hospital from July 1915 to September 1916 and at Craiglockhart between October 1916 and November 1917, in his volumes, *Conflict and Dream* (1922) and *Instinct and the Unconscious* (1923), both published after his death in 1922. The titles of these works alone suggest an affinity between Rivers' psychological models for neuroses and Sigmund Freud's, but Rivers discusses in a 1916 article, "Freud's Psychology of the Unconscious" where his thinking diverges from that of the man who was his greatest influence:

It is a wonderful turn of fate that just as Freud's theory of the unconscious and the method of psycho-analysis founded upon it should be hotly discussed, there should have occurred events which have produced on an enormous scale just those traumas of paralysis and contracture, phobia and obsession, which the theory was especially designed to explain. Fate would seem to have presented us at the present with an unexampled opportunity to test the truth of Freud's theory of the unconscious, in so far as it is concerned with the production of mental and functional nervous disorder.[31]

Rivers came to believe, based upon his observations, in many of Freud's notions about the causes of such neuroses, as he states, "According to Freud, forgetting — and especially the forgetting of unpleasant experience — is not a passive but an active process, one in which such experience is thrust out of consciousness and kept under control by a mechanism which by a metaphorical simile Freud has termed the censor."[32] He diverges from his mentor in his thinking about the role that Freud's theories upon the formation of sexual identity played in the phenomena of war trauma:

> The point is that while we have over and over again abundant evidence that pathological nervous and mental states are due, it would seem directly, to the shocks and strains of warfare, there is, in my experience, singularly little evidence to show that, even indirectly and as a subsidiary factor, any part has been taken in the process of causation by conflicts arising out of the activity of repressed sexual conflicts.[33]

The timing of the war, in retrospect, does appear to have brought psycho-analytic strategies of therapy a great deal of currency in offering so many cases of neuroses to treat by means of its tenets. Rivers utilized the Freudian conception that the source of the manifestation of the neurosis could be traced to experiences which the sufferer repressed because of the trauma that they brought to his conscious mind, but he stopped short of applying Freudian methods completely in his treatment of his patients because of his skepticism that psycho-sexual issues contributed to their immediate situations. He did not rule out the possibility that such conflicts contributed to personality formation or to other neuroses not associated with the hardships of warfare, but given a job to do by the military in which he served as both doctor and captain, he could afford to take a more practical approach in restoring psychological balance to his patients, rather than to work to excavate these psycho-sexual concerns from their unconscious.

Though Rivers' sessions with Sassoon did not dwell upon Freudian notions such as Oedipal complexes and the like, Sassoon's increasing acknowledgment of his own repressed homosexual feelings while under the guidance of Rivers suggests that the self-inspection brought about through both psychoanalysis and the writing of poetry led to Sassoon's confrontation with this dimension of selfhood as well. Quinn relates an event on November 9, near the end of Sassoon's stay, in which Lady Ottoline Morrell visited him at Craiglockhart. According to Morrell's memoirs, "Sassoon apparently opened himself up fully to Lady Ottoline, confessed his homosexuality, and admitted that 'women were antipathetic to him.'"[34] Quinn goes on to argue for the significance of this acknowledgment to Sassoon's healing from his psychological conflict: "[T]he discussion clarifies that at least a part of his motivation to return was due to homosexual guilt. Sassoon was transforming his suppressed homoerotic interest for Owen, Graves (who had just announced to him his decision to marry Nancy) ... and others into a more generalized and acceptable form of love: a loyalty to those men who served with him."[35] His homosexuality was a facet of his identity to which Sassoon could never fully reconcile himself: he married in 1933 and had a son, and as late as 1962, he referred to his homosexuality as his "tortured inward self."[36] His admission of homosexual desire at Craiglockhart led not only to his return to his men as a means of displacing this desire into a socially acceptable role of officer above them, but led also to poetic representations of his relationship to the men that stressed the removal of emotional and physical distance between them.

For his part in enabling Sassoon's return, Rivers took a three-pronged approach. In his therapy for shell shock he sought to bring forth from its repressed state through relaxed conversation the experience of warfare responsible for the shell shock, to confront the experience "resolutely" with his patient, since the experience can never be "thrust wholly out of his life," and to construct methods by which the patient could come to terms with the experience and his part within it. He advises fellow therapists of shell shock victims on these methods:

> [The patient's] experience should be talked over in all its bearings. Its good side should be emphasized, for it is characteristic of the painful experience of warfare that it usually has a good or even a noble side.... By such a conversation an emotional experience, which is perhaps tending to become dissociated, may be intellectualised and brought into harmony with the rest of the mental life.... As a matter of practical experience the relief afforded to a patient by the process of talking over his painful experience, and by the discussion how he can readjust his life to the new conditions usually gives immediate relief and may be followed by great improvement or even rapid disappearance of his chief symptoms.[37]

Sassoon's familiarity with the theoretical approaches of his doctor is evident in his poem written in the August of 1917, "Repression of War Experience," which was also the title of a talk given by Rivers earlier that summer. The poem takes the form of a dramatic monologue, spoken by a shell shock sufferer either to himself, about his mental state, or to another patient, in a state similar to his own. The speaker displays the processes by which the mind attempts to repress unpleasant memories of the war but the impossibility that these experiences are ever to be forgotten. Interestingly, as Campbell notes, Sassoon was also awaiting word of the military's response to his formal protest, suggesting that the political and psychological complications involved in that episode were as well in need of "repression."[38] The poem begins:

> Now light the candles; one; two; there's a moth;
> What silly beggars they are to blunder in
> And scorch their wings with glory, liquid flame —
> No, no, not that, — it's bad to think of war,
> When thoughts you've gagged all day come back to scare you;
> And it's been proved that soldiers don't go mad
> Unless they lose control of ugly thoughts
> That drive them out to jabber among the trees
> > [*Collected Poems* 89–90].

The speaker in the poem is still subjected to traumatic memories of the war because he has not yet learned to "control [his] ugly thoughts." Within the consciousness of the shell shocked soldier, his memories of war were regarded as nothing but ugly; there was, as far as he was concerned, no "good" or "noble side" to redeem the horrors. The mind's defense mechanism seeks to repress the horrific memories, but they never fully disappear. The war comes to manifest itself for this sufferer in the seemingly innocent image of the moth, attracted to candlelight. The moth's unwitting flight into death by fire brings forth the soldier's comparison of the moth to his own helpless situation in warfare.[39] But this is a line of thought that leads to the surfacing of the painful memories, which the soldier seeks to repress once again. Rivers' thinking seeks to avoid such patterns of repression and expression of tormenting thoughts, as resonate in the poem's conclusion:

> You're quiet and peaceful, summering safe at home;
> You'd never think there was a bloody war on! ...
> O yes, you would ... why, you can hear the guns.
> Hark! Thud, thud, thud, — quite soft ... they never cease —
> Those whispering guns — O Christ, I want to go out
> And screech at them to stop — I'm going crazy;
> I'm going stark, staring mad because of the guns
> > [*Collected Poems* 89–90].

Sassoon blurs the distinction between the actual guns in France, which the speaker hears from across the English channel, and the guns which continue to fire in his mind, in order to emphasize that the attempts to alleviate the suffering through repression in effect reduce the sufferer to a state wherein he lacks all control over perception. Reality and hallucination seem indistinguishable; the past experiences in war merge with his present inability to manage the torment.

As in the poem, "Survivors," Sassoon does not overtly tell his own story in "Repression of War Experience." However, Rivers applied strategies in therapy to understand what conflict Sassoon was repressing by means of his protest and by what means the experiences of warfare could be expressed, reconsidered, and "brought into harmony with the rest of the mental life." Since the event that landed Sassoon in the mental hospital was political in nature, Rivers raised the topics of Britain's political actions in the war, European politics at large, and Sassoon's obvious effectiveness as a leader of his men. According to Showalter, "This talking cure was intended to make Sassoon feel uneasy about the gaps in his information and to emphasize the contrast between his emotional, and thus feminine, attitude toward the war and Rivers' rational, masculine, Cambridge don's view of it."[40] Whether or not one believes that gender expectations were at the heart of Rivers' approach to Sassoon's case, it is certain that he was committed to seeing his patient recover and return to active service, and for Sassoon this recovery hinged upon his rejection of the basis of his protest. Sassoon was reluctant to back down, however, as he indicates in a letter to Lady Morrell: "I have told Rivers that I will not withdraw anything that I have said or written, and that my views are the same, but that I will go back to France if the War Office will give me a guarantee that they really will send me there" (*Diaries* 190). Resistant to conceding to the doctor, though eager to remove himself from what he now called "intolerable surroundings" at Craiglockhart (*Diaries* 191), Sassoon rationalized a compromise of sorts in his mind by means of Rivers' subtle strategies to enable the patient to focus upon the "good" or "noble side" of the war experience. For Sassoon that good side was the companionship of his men back in France. He writes to Morrell, "After all I made my protest on behalf of my fellow-fighters, and (if it is a question of being treated as an imbecile for the rest of the war) the fitting thing for me to do is to go back and share their ills" (*Diaries* 190). Rivers approach to Sassoon's case has been able to elicit his feelings toward this noble dimension of the war, Sassoon's relationship to the men he leads, and through suggesting that Sassoon realize the value that is to be gained through this contact, the return to the trenches has come to outweigh the competing desire for personal safety. Rivers' psychotherapy contributed to Sassoon's healing from his version of shell shock by enabling the poet to reinterpret the experience of warfare and to adjust his emphasis away from solitary suffering toward emotional connection between soldiers. While this process of psychological adjustment was occurring, Sassoon was constructing poetic representation of his relationship to his men reflecting this new emphasis.

Reducing the Distance through Emotional Representation: Sassoon's Counter-Attack *Against Shell Shock*

Wilfred Owen has been shown to have developed a language for addressing and representing the dead in a poem like "Strange Meeting," and the formal means for articulating the seemingly ineffable nature of combat in the poems of the last year of his life, most notably "Spring Offensive," a development that began in part through Sassoon's instruction and guidance during their brief friendship begun at Craiglockhart. Likewise, Sassoon's poems of *Counter-Attack* exhibit an increasing willingness to engage in subjective expression. The technique of satire proves incapable of providing a full voice to the necessity of using poetic forms as sites of emotional confrontation with his situation, although many of the poems of *Counter-Attack* display similar strategies for articulating his protest against the war which had landed him in the mental hospital. Even the title of one poem, "Editorial Impressions," which mocks the press' efforts to provide reports from the front that are both realistic and optimistic, suggests that the satiric mode is alive and well. Silkin argues that because of the predominantly satiric method of his verse, "Sassoon achieves neither compassion nor pity. Hardly, at any rate."[41] Thorpe goes on to fault the "subjective" poems of *Counter-Attack* for their "rawness of emotion and the undisciplined expression of it."[42] Moeyes takes issue with claims such as these, saying that pity and compassion were not the poet's primary intentions but that he achieves an implicit pity for others' sufferings through devices that seem to eliminate the place for emotion within the poem. He states, "the driving force behind Sassoon's satires *is* an overwhelming emotion," and that the pity within the poem comes by means of the reader's involvement with the subject matter, even when the speaker seems apart from its emotional impact.[43] One can take this notion a step further; the poetry, which had never been divorced from Sassoon's personal experiences and observations in the trenches despite its detachment in tone, now gives evidence of even greater personal motivation for its composition that is inextricably linked to the psychological battles the poet was waging during the conception of the poems. And poems that strive for seeming objectivity through irony reveal the subjectivity of the poet grappling with his own personal crisis.

A satiric poem like "Lamentations" can represent his own psychological situation only obliquely, obscuring his own loss in a narrative which stresses the speaker's, and by implication the poet's, detachment and irony. Upon inspection, however, the poem gives evidence of entering into intensely personal terrain for the poet.

> I found him in the guard-room at the Base.
> From the blind darkness I had heard his crying
> And blundered in. With puzzled, patient face
> A sergeant watched him; it was no good trying
> To stop it; for he howled and beat his chest.
> And, all because his brother had gone west,
> Raved at the bleeding war; his rampant grief
> Moaned, shouted, sobbed, and choked, while he was kneeling
> Half-naked on the floor. In my belief
> Such men have lost all patriotic feeling [*Collected Poems* 76].

The irony is clear, though complex: if there ever were a man in need of consolation, this is the man, but it is difficult to conceive of a more callous response from the speaker. Complicating the understanding of the poem is the relationship between the event, as Sassoon recalls it in autobiography, and the shaping of the experience into the poem. Lane connects the poem to Sassoon's narrative of the same episode in *Memoirs of an Infantry Officer* (1929) in which the author recalls asking about the sobbing man's well-being and "still hear[ing] the uncouth howlings" as he leaves the guard-room.[44] Sassoon's narrative of the episode also includes the detail that he had learned of his reassignment to a new battalion before coming across the grieving soldier: "...I wanted to go where I was already known, and the prospect of joining a strange battalion made me feel more homeless than ever."[45] Having felt detached from his previous battalion and having anticipated the bonds that he would be forced to establish with his new men, Sassoon occupies a position of isolation from his fellow soldiers that makes his detachment from the scene he is about to witness understandable.

The description of the man that Sassoon observes grieving is much the same as in the poem, but the author includes in the autobiography the words of the sergeant: "[T]he man's been under detention for assaulting the military police, and now 'e's just 'ad news of his brother being killed. Seems to take it to 'eart more than most would. 'Arf crazy, 'e's been, tearing 'is clothes off and cursing the War and the Fritzes. Almost like a shell-shock case" (397). Sassoon responds to the entire episode by retiring to a canvas shed within the Base Depot, munching on a bit of chocolate, and commenting, "Well,

well; this is a damned depressing spot to arrive at!" (397). The similarities and differences between the two versions of the story are instructive. In neither case does Sassoon describe any gesture of comfort toward the suffering man; after all, he did not know him, and the man was not under his command. And in both cases, the tone of emotional detachment dominates the speaker's perspective. But, in the autobiography, written after the passage of twelve years and written in a form that permits further elaboration, Sassoon includes telling details, most notably the amateur assessment of "shell shock" from the sergeant, and is sure to represent himself as unmoved by the entire event, even though he has been moved enough as an author to reconstruct the experience twice in writing.

These complicating factors invite an analysis of the relationship that Sassoon has constructed psychologically between himself and the suffering soldier. In the poem the relationship between the speaker and the soldier is marked by distance, which is evoked through the inability of any of the characters within the poem to find an adequate language for grief. The opening clause, "I found him," suggests the relationship between the speaker and the soldier that will be the poem's focus, but the speaker and the reader do not find the man until the fourth line of the poem. The speaker is impeded by the "blind darkness" and his own "blunder[ing]" in his approach to the soldier, details which predict his own ineffectiveness in comforting him. The sergeant functions as an intermediary between the speaker and this man, and his "puzzled, patient face" suggests that even a man closer to the sufferer in rank lacks the words of consolation. The grieving man, as well, seems incapable of finding the language to convey his grief: he "howled and beat his chest. / ... Moaned, shouted, sobbed, and choked." The first five lines of the poem establish the pathos of the moment: a man grieves with sadness beyond words, and two other men observe the grief, helpless to intervene. The soldier is never identified as a private, and the autobiography establishes that he was not a man under Sassoon's command and was instead someone he stumbled upon by chance. But the presence of the sergeant within the scene and Sassoon's rank of Lieutenant imply the increasing distance between the man, the sergeant, and the speaker. So although facts of his experience do not make Sassoon responsible in any way for the man's suffering, the stratification of rank crafted into the ten line poem creates an emotional situation that calls out for the speaker to sympathize with a man beneath him.

The poem goes out of its way to avoid such sympathy because of the poet's use of irony as a mechanism for self-defense. That is, if the poem were to stop and leave the reader with such an image of grief, or to continue with the creation of this pathos, Sassoon would have used the poetic vehicle as a means of confronting his memory of this dimension of warfare and of exposing his inefficacy in responding to an emotional situation. The "turn" of the poem arrives in the sixth line when the speaker's attitude toward the pathetic sight before him constructs a barrier for the speaker preventing him from experiencing the pain of the man he observes. He relies upon the class distinction between them to establish this distance within the poem. The private "howled and beat his chest" because words could not convey the loss, but these actions, as recorded by an officer, suggest as well an animalistic quality to the man, separate from the decorum of the upper class, a brutish sexuality which the speaker finds repugnant. The reason the speaker provides for the howls and chest-beating is "because his brother had gone west," cloaking the fact of death in euphemism. The speaker suggests that the soldier's response is inappropriate; the truth that Sassoon and the reader recognize is that the response is the only one appropriate for the gravity of his loss. By presenting the soldier as both somehow dehumanized by the loss of his brother and uncivilized in his response, the speaker utilizes the distinctions in class separating them to sustain the emotional distance between them. We cannot, therefore, find the speaker guilty of insensitivity because of these many levels of difference.

The irony by which the poem operates, of course, is that the accusation of insensitivity is exactly what the poem seeks to elicit from the reader. This irony intensifies as the contrast between the soldier and his officer is crystallized in the last three lines, when the man

> Moaned, shouted, sobbed, and choked, while he was kneeling
> Half-naked on the floor. In my belief
> Such men have lost all patriotic feeling.

The speaker's response to the man is conflicted: on the one hand, he cannot take his eyes off the soldier's display, extending the line of description beyond the iambic pentameter of the other lines of the poem, but his reaction to this image yields the biting irony that is the poem's final statement. The irony functions much as it had four lines earlier in the more subtle jab that "his brother had [merely] gone west." But while "going west" employs jargon which identifies the speaker as part of the army, the closing line echoes the sentiment of the military propaganda machine, far removed from the day to day trials of the war's participants, which were echoed by the civilian world, where any act not in accordance with abstract notions of heroism might be branded as cowardice or a lack of patriotism. The closing line approximates "the old Lie" of patriotic self-sacrifice in battle that Wilfred Owen railed against in "Dulce et Decorum Est," which Owen was drafting at Craiglockhart at almost the same time as Sassoon's writing of this poem.[46] By echoing the words of the ignorant commanders of the war and the civilian populace, the speaker creates an even greater emotional remove between himself and the soldier.

Perhaps the most effective irony of the concluding line is the fact that it is indeed true — the man has lost all patriotic feeling. But the reader is not asked to question the soldier's patriotism because of this line, nor is he asked to believe in it either since patriotism is not the issue in the poem. What then is the reader supposed to feel when reading this conclusion? What is the poet's emotion that has led him to such an expression? Lane assesses the poem in terms of his perception of its limitations in emotional revelation, stating that "Sassoon, by adopting a persona, allows the poem to make its own point without his editorial intrusion."[47] He notes that the poem's last line establishes the speaker's need to shut out the emotional import of the event, while the prose account displays Sassoon's desire for emotional connection to the suffering, making it "the more moving account of despair...." Lane, however, finds the poem false to its subject matter: "By subordinating the inherent pathos of the situation to his satiric intention, Sassoon makes his point — but misses a much larger one."[48] But the poem is a success as an emotional statement of sympathy for the man because of its honesty in expressing Sassoon's capability to confront and convey the emotion at the moment of writing. When he had the benefit of the distance of twelve years, he could dwell upon the memory more fully, but when the experience is fresh — four months old, between the event in February 1917 and the poem's conception in July, according to the chronology given in Sassoon's autobiography — he erects emotional barriers preventing full disclosure when reconstructing the experience at Craiglockhart. Rather than seeing the poem's speaker as a "persona," a voice at a remove from the revelation of selfhood and feeling to be found in the autobiography, one can see "Lamentations" as the expression of selfhood at a psychological moment that insists upon this emotional detachment and removal.

Sassoon's experiences of war preceding both the event and the creation of the poem shed further light upon the poet's emotion. The scene itself seems one that would occur frequently in the trenches — a soldier learns of the death of a friend or family member, and he exhibits an appropriate display of grief. What makes the subject matter so important that Sassoon would both write the poem and revisit it in autobiography is its similarity to his own experience of a brother who had "gone west." His brother Hamo died at Gallipoli in November of 1915, an event which left Sassoon feeling not only the loss of a sibling but a debt to him, as he relates in his diary on December 3, 1915: "I don't want to go back to the old inane life which always seemed like a prison. I want freedom, not comfort.... I have lived well and truly since the war began, and have made my sacrifices; now I ask that the price be required of me. I must pay my debt. Hamo went: I must follow him" (*Diaries* 22). He must follow Hamo into battle, and possibly into death as well. The loss of Hamo led to the elegy "To My Brother" from *The Old Huntsman*, which concludes:

> Your lot is with the ghosts of soldiers dead,
> And I am in the field where men must fight.
> But in the gloom I see your laurell'd head
> And through your victory I shall win the light
> [*Collected Poems* 12].

Writing the poem in late 1915, Sassoon still clings to a belief in the patriotic purpose for his brother's loss, a belief which would soon change in his representations of other casualties and human responses to such losses, as in "Lamentations." At this early stage of the fighting, before the Battle of the Somme in July 1916, the poet believes that the death has purpose in contributing to what the poet is sure will be an ultimate victory. Though his brother is dead, the parallel structures Sassoon constructs in these lines between the living and the dead underscore the connection remaining through the common belief in the moral righteousness of the cause, even though this belief has led to the separation of the two brothers. This insistence on maintaining connection between the living and the dead in "To My Brother" is in stark contrast to the speaker's insistence upon distance between the living participants of "Lamentations." This early war poem is notable as well for the involvement of the first person speaker who overtly reveals the personal emotion without the irony that marks the later poem. By the time of "Lamentations" both Sassoon and the grieving soldier have "lost all patriotic feeling," and because the poem suggests that patriotism is not the proper response to such a loss, Sassoon is in effect correcting the sentiment of "To My Brother." One does not deal with the aftermath of grief through jingoistic utterance, he suggests. Rather the man who grieves must struggle to find an adequate language for grief, as does the soldier. "Lamentations," though it seems to be another poem "in Sassoon's style,"[49] is as well a poem of personal revelation, however guarded that revelation may be.

The anger of the grieving man in "Lamentations" is understandable, as is the nihilism of the speaker which generates such a callous response to the man's display, but anger and bitterness are only stages in the emotional response to loss along the way to his complete acceptance of it. One might say that the patriotism espoused in "To My Brother" is Sassoon's form of rationalization to convince himself that the death had meaning and purpose. The discussion in the earlier chapter of Owen has argued that the emotional note of "Dulce et Decorum Est" is one of anger at its close, and that this anger which dominates the second half of the poem, directed outward towards an ignorant readership or civilian populace, is not an entirely satisfying response to the subjective experience of the speaker who witnesses the horrible image of the man drowning in gas. The emotional confusion inherent within "Lamentations" demonstrates a similar inability to address the source of the trauma completely. Lane is correct to see a limitation in "Lamentations," but his assessment of what that limitation is seems off the mark. Rather than Sassoon's missed opportunity to explore "the inherent pathos of the situation" in favor of "his satiric intention," the poem is instead an exploration of a situation that has lodged in memory because of its resemblance to loss he had himself endured, and the resulting representation of the loss denotes the desire for self-protection from such a potential outpouring of emotion that marks the stage of Sassoon's grief upon the poem's composition.

He begins to imagine a closer relationship to his men in subsequent poems of the Craiglockhart period that forego the irony of a poem like "Lamentations." The closing line of "Sick Leave" has provided an indication of Sassoon's focus that will enable him to recuperate from his psychological trauma, with its political manifestations, and return to his Battalion, able to lead once again. The ghost of the dead soldier, silent within his record of his hallucination but with a voice in the poem, asks the speaker about his "Battalion in the mud" in France, "Are they not still your brothers through our blood?" In one sense, it is "through" the blood spilled by the dead that Sassoon has felt compelled to wage his protest, acting — he believed — out of a sense of brotherhood on their behalf. But seeing as well that such a protest has removed him from a position of responsibility over them and potential for able leadership of them, he desires a return. "Through" the blood of those who have died (that is, by means of an acceptance of this death) will he be able to return. A similar psychological struggle is played out, once again with the metaphor of a storm used in "Sick Leave," in the poem, "Autumn," written in October 1917, soon before his release from the mental hospital. Sassoon had enjoyed the countryside (not to mention the golf courses) of Edinburgh while hospitalized, but the poem questions the degree to which such a landscape can establish peace within the poet:

> October's bellowing anger breaks and cleaves
> The bronzed battalions of the stricken wood
> In whose lament I hear a voice that grieves
> For battle's fruitless harvest, and the feud
> Of outraged men. Their lives are like the leaves
> Scattered in flocks of ruin, tossed and blown
> Along the westering furnace flaring red.
> O martyred youth and manhood overthrown,
> The burden of your wrongs is on my head
> [*Collected Poems* 88].

The poet reinterprets images of landscape and peace as irrevocably tinged with the markers of war. The natural world in autumn, perhaps because of the season's associations with death, functions as a canvas onto which Sassoon projects his guilt. Ivor Gurney employs a similar strategy of imaginative projection of emotion onto an otherwise neutral background of nature in several of his poems, but for a different purpose. Writing about the war in retrospect, Gurney turns to nature as a means of achieving psychological disconnection from the facts and memories of battle. Sassoon's poem, however, suggests that for him, such an escape was not a possibility. The trees become "battalions;" the sound of their breaking branches in an autumn storm is imagined as both the sound of grieving and "the feud / Of outraged men."

The metaphors of the poem are not especially complex in replicating the inescapable connections in the poet's mind between the war and everything that is not the war. However, a memory recalled in *Sherston's Progress* about what seems to be the same storm in autumn sheds further light on the poem's method of self-incrimination: "Autumn was asserting itself, and a gale got up that night. I lay awake listening to its melancholy surgings and rumblings as it buffeted the big building. The longer I lay awake the more I was reminded of the troops in the line. There they were, stoically enduring their roofless discomfort while I was safe and warm."[50] Sassoon finds himself guilty for his situation of physical comfort, where he has the luxury of turning the storm into a metaphor for the war from his warm bed, unlike his men to whom the storm means nothing more than more of the endless mud. The poem's closing line suggests the scope of this responsibility through a double meaning. As an apology for having abandoned the men, Sassoon takes on the burden both for how the men have been wronged by war and also for their "wrongs" or mistakes made while fighting. The poet, apart from the actions, takes responsibility not only for their suffering but for the actions of his inferiors which he cannot control. And through his establishing that separation carries with it such a double burden, the prospect of returning begins to appear as more of a relief.

"Autumn" closes upon the note of responsibility that has been implicitly shirked in "Lamentations," where the speaker keeps his emotional distance. "Banishment," while arguing out in more straightforward terms the psychological conflict between the officer and the dead and living men beneath his command that had been represented as a dreamlike vision in "Sick Leave," marks the development in Sassoon's poetry of a new emotional expression that will effect his reconciliation with the men of his Battalion. "Banishment" was written almost concurrently with the poem "Sick Leave," in the closing weeks of Sassoon's stay at Craiglockhart. He establishes the psychological situation in the sonnet's octave:

> I am banished from the patient men who fight.
> They smote my heart to pity, built my pride.
> Shoulder to aching shoulder, side by side,
> They trudged away from life's broad wealds of light.
> Their wrongs were mine; and ever in my sight
> They went arrayed in honour. But they died,—
> Not one by one: and mutinous I cried
> To those who sent them out into the night
>   [*Collected Poems* 86].

Thorpe has called "Banishment" "a public apologia for his public protest against the War" in which the poet "strains after a consciously poetic dignity ... with a disfiguring rhetoric."[51] And while clichés such "smote my heart to pity" and "life's broad weald of light" do not show the innovative technique of colloquial usage in poetry that characterizes Sassoon's most memorable work, autobiographical, confessional poetry is a terrain that Sassoon has not traveled in war verse since his first idealistic efforts at capturing the experience. The sonnet form, through its counterpoint of octave and sestet, provides the poem with a means of organizing the conflict into a structure that enables the poet to posit the resolution of the conflict. The octave establishes the complicated relationship between Sassoon the officer and his men.

His proximity to the men while fighting has led to both Sassoon's pity and pride for them, responses that hinge upon a degree of difference existing between their experiences. And Sassoon suggests that in some way the men were responsible for him by creating these feelings: "They smote my heart to pity, built my pride." At the same time, although pity suggests that Sassoon feels a part of their pain, and pride that he feels a part of their success, these emotional responses keep him apart from them, in a state of elevation and thus detachment. To feel pity and pride necessitates that the experience eliciting the emotion be not that of the speaker. The "men who fight," as opposed to the officer who writes from a position of incapacitation, march "shoulder to shoulder," on an equal level with one another. Sassoon continues to complicate this relationship, calling their wrongs his own but their punishment — death — theirs alone, as they "trudge away from life's broad wealds of light / ... arrayed in honour," and thus trudge away from the living poet. The question that the poem seeks to resolve is where to locate blame for the deaths of these "patient men." The opening clause of the poem, "I am banished," is a curious use of the passive voice, since Sassoon realizes now that he in effect had banished himself through the protest. He calls himself "mutinous," an adjective that alludes to his rejection of his assigned duty but also connotes an unlawful abandonment of this role. But in the closing lines of the octave, he locates responsibility on others, not himself, for sending "them out into the night" to death.

The sestet functions as Sassoon's willed belief that he has been absolved for his actions. He uses the metaphor of the night that the octave's last line constructed for the dead soldiers as a transition to his conviction to act now on behalf of the living.

> The darkness tells how vainly I have striven
> To free them from the pit where they must dwell
> In outcast gloom convulsed and jagged and riven
> By grappling guns. Love drove me to rebel.
> Love drives me back to grope with them through hell;
> And in their tortured eyes I stand forgiven.

The darkness is at once symbolic of nothingness, representative of the futility of his protest in alleviating any suffering, and symbolic of the dead men who have marched into the night, sent out by a force beyond the control of Sassoon. This assignation of blame to the war itself, or to the political powers that keep the war going, is a crucial development in Sassoon's belief in responsibility for his men. He admits that he himself is up against a "darkness" in his efforts to offer salvation for his men, subject to the same forces that send the men out into the night. The poem significantly offers no single human figure upon which to affix responsibility — the enemy of War in the abstract has replaced more specific enemies, such as women in "The Glory of Women," the press in "Editorial Impressions," members of Parliament in "Fight to the Finish," all of whom Sassoon lampoons for their ignorance of war's reality elsewhere in *Counter-Attack*. In "Banishment," war in the abstract is not depicted as an enemy to be defeated; war is "the pit where they must dwell" without him, and he will "grope with them through hell" if he returns. The significance is that the war will remain unchanged with or without him.

The change that the poem signifies is an emotional one — the development, understanding, and articulation of love. Quinn calls the love expressed in the poem for his men an emotion more generalized and acceptable to contemporary society than were his feelings of homosexual love which he began to acknowledge at Craiglockhart.[52] This is certainly true, but the declaration of love within the poem offers Sassoon not only a means by which to sublimate his homosexuality but a means of expressing an emotion for his men, beneath him in rank and class, which could transcend the boundaries of class that kept him at a distance, capable of expressions of only pity or pride. According to Stephen, Sassoon writes "love poems about the soldiers with whom they served and who they saw slaughtered, love poems where the overwhelming emotion of love totally demotes any need to talk of physical consummation."[53] The gesture by which his love for the men is in effect "consummated" is Sassoon's return to the fighting to eliminate the physical and emotional distance between them. Only through that return will the balance of power shift to a state of mutual sympathy and equality; while the commanding officer leads the men, they in turn possess the power to judge and forgive their commander for having left. The men, Sassoon now included, "grope ... through hell," where men are "convulsed and jagged and riven / By grappling guns." "Banishment" is a poem unique to Sassoon's body of work because of its degree of abstraction in its meditation about the war. That is, rather than providing the reader with the portrait of an individual sufferer characterized through a colloquial idiom marked by jargon of the trenches, Sassoon stands back from the particulars of war to show how this stage of his emotional response has emerged out of his reflection about the war's entire canvas. Seen from this distance, the war unites both officer and enlisted man in a common human struggle, where the political voice of an individual poet and officer who railed against the "callous complacency" of everyone apart from the war itself is silenced and the most powerful weapon imagined by which to fight the battle is the love uniting the participants.

On November 26, 1917, Sassoon was recommended for a return to general service by Rivers and was promptly passed fit by the medical board at Craiglockhart. He was sent first to Limerick for re-training, and then to Kantara, Palestine in March 1918 where he joined the Twenty-Fifth Battalion of the Royal Welsh Fusiliers who would soon return to France.[54] In Palestine, Sassoon was afforded the opportunity to take a reflective stance upon the war, like the perspective displayed in "Banishment," as he states in his diary in April 1918: "When I compare my agony of last year with the present, I am glad to find a wider view of things. I am slowly getting outside it all. Getting nearer the secret places of the heart also, and recognising its piteous limitations" (*Diaries* 238). But his platoon would soon return to France, and when considering the immediate prospect of the return he had so desired, he displays the very next day a resurgence of the anxieties that forced his prior removal from the fighting: "[H]ere I am after nearly four year of this business, faced with the same old haggard aspect of soldier-life — a very small chance of complete escape unblemished, a big chance of being killed outright — ditto of being intolerably injured — a certainty of mental agony and physical discomfort — prolonged and exasperating — a possibility of going mad or breaking down badly..." (*Diaries* 239). Arriving at Marseilles in early May, Sassoon reassures himself: "I must never forget Rivers. He is the only man who can save me if I break down again. If I am able to keep going it will be through him" (*Diaries* 246).

Specifically, he remembers Rivers' therapeutic approach that enabled Sassoon to focus upon the "good" and "noble side" of the war as a means of understanding and accepting his own role within it. His poem "The Dug-Out," collected in his subsequent volume *Picture Show* (1918), was inspired by a sight of one of his men as they moved by train toward the trenches. He writes in his diary on May 10, "The other three — Morgan, Phillips, and Jowett — are asleep in various ungainly attitudes. J. looks as if he were dead" (*Diaries* 247). The poem takes as its focus the speaker's perspective upon one of these sleeping soldiers:

> Why do you lie with your legs ungainly huddled
> And one arm bent across your sullen, cold,
> Exhausted face? It hurts my heart to watch you,
> Deep-shadow'd from the candle's guttering gold;
> And you wonder why I shake you by the shoulder;
> Drowsy, you mumble and sigh and turn your head ...
> *You are too young to fall asleep for ever;*
> *And when you sleep you remind me of the dead*
> [*Collected Poems* 102].

Without Sassoon's revelation in the diary that the poem emerged from his experience on a train heading toward the front, one would assume that it were a trench sketch like many others that Sassoon had written. Looking at the poem, however, the reader notices that none of the details within it identify the setting as a train, a trench, or anywhere else connected to the war. According to Stephen, "The poem's strength lies in its sensuality and the total absorption of the poet with his subject, an absorption that reduces the world to one man gazing at another."[55] The gaze still suggests a degree of separation between the two inhabitants of this world, however, as the speaker indicates by telling the sleeping form, "It hurts my heart to watch you." Sassoon includes the speaker's gesture of shaking the sleeping soldier, which is a simple touch, but which possesses symbolic significance. The details upon which the speaker focuses throughout the poem are once again a catalogue of the man's body parts — his legs, arm, face, shoulder, and head — much like the fragmentation of the body which Sassoon had suggested in "The Rear-Guard" or in his record of his hallucinations in the hospital. The speaker of the poem creates this "world of two" not simply by limiting his perspective to perceive this other man while blocking out the rest of the war, but by in effect creating an image of a whole man out of the parts that he focuses upon individually. The speaker touches the other man to show the means by which the appearance of death becomes evidence of life.

Unlike "Banishment," a poem that utilized a much wider lens for viewing the war as a whole in order to comment upon the relationship of the men within it, "The Dug-Out" characterizes this relationship by means of eliminating evidence of the context of war that has brought the feelings of the speaker for the man into being. This quality of the poem is significant for a number of reasons. This creation of an emotional world containing only the two men in "The Dug-Out" is in stark contrast to a similar setting in "Lamentations" were the scope of the war's impact is reduced to its few participants. In the earlier poem, irony served as the speaker's means of keeping the grieving man apart and alone in his grief— the half-naked body was the site where the effects of the war were made most visible in the poem, where the poet makes manifest the result of the brother's death in battle in the emotional expression of the person whom the death most affected. Irony functioned as a protective device for Sassoon in "Lamentations" for the reason provided by the conclusion of "The Dug-Out." That is, the soldier grieving for his brother has reminded Sassoon himself of the dead — his brother Hamo, but the speaker and poet choose to deflect the grief, rather than to confront it. In "The Dug-Out," Sassoon's rejects the use of irony within the poem in one of his most sincere expressions of compassion for another man. This soldier is not suffering in any overt way, but his suffering is implicit within the poem since he is identified as having existed within the same experience of war as had the speaker. Both men, having seen time in the trenches, know the posture that a dead body takes.

Secondly, the creation of this "world of two" suggests a relationship between the speaker and the object of his affection that resembles many of Sassoon's other attempts to represent his proximity or distance from other soldiers. In the early "To My Brother," he sought to keep a connection alive between himself and his dead brother Hamo by envisioning only the patriotic ideals for which they both fought. His diary entry after Lieutenant Thomas' death recalled their shared experience at Cambridge when they in effect created a "Paradise" capable of shutting out the rest of the world, and the elegy "Together" accentuated this notion of a world of two. Likewise, "The Dug-Out" removes all details which would identify either the speaker or the soldier by rank. The diary tells us that an officer looked at a private and saw him in an attitude resembling death, but in the poem, Sassoon imagines a scene without this stratification of class in order to emphasize the common humanity of all men involved. It was by means of this focus upon the "noble side" of the war that Rivers and Sassoon were able to construct a means by which he could return in body and in spirit. The war is only the implied enemy of the poem which chooses to foreground instead the relationship of two men where all distance — in class, in degrees of suffering, in physical space — separating them has been eliminated. Moeyes sees Sassoon's relationship to the war, rather than to his own sexuality, as motivating a poem such as "The Dug-Out": "Though [homosexuality] is certainly likely to have played a part, the main inspirational source for Sassoon's war poetry is not to be found in the beauty of some of the young soldiers, but in a his sense of responsibility for the men directly under his command."[56] This is true, but it is by representing the beauty of the young soldier asleep, and by displaying the physical contact between officer and private that has the emotion of love and sympathy as its impetus, that Sassoon is able to transcend the barriers of class to craft an expression of love free from the class demarcations inhibiting other emotional responses.

When he writes "The Dug-Out" in July 1918, Sassoon comes upon a method for representing the war that seems ages removed from the anger and bitterness that inspired his fierce satires against the "callous complacency" back home. But there is no less outrage against the war in this poem, even though it chooses to show an experience of emotional connection that appears to transcend for a moment the horrors of war itself. Yet, it is the war itself that has taught the speaker what death looks like and frightens the speaker because the soldier looks so much like it. Sassoon himself had one final brush with death around the time of the poem's composition. On July 13, 1918, he received a wound in the head that would end his service in the war for good, but even during his evacuation to the hospital, his thoughts were for his men. He writes two days later, "I am amputated from the Battalion. When I was hit it seemed an unspeakable thing to leave my men in the lurch, to go away into safety. 'I won't say goodbye; I'm coming back,' I said to the little Company Sergeant-Major" (Diaries 274). He regards his wounding as an "amputation," a removal of a part of the body of men which, without him, is no longer whole. "The Dug-Out" has shown the bonds between men which create such a whole, and the poem is testimony to the "good" side that has emerged from the war. Sassoon would have never come to acknowledge this perspective upon the fighting without his four years of experience, which have shown his responses to the war change from patriotism, to disillusionment, to breakdown, to his return to the fighting — this time fighting for a nobler cause.

EPILOGUE

War and Modern Poetry

This study of the poetry of the Great War began with a discussion of T. S. Eliot's *The Waste Land*, arguing that uniquely personal circumstances on the part of the poet — in this case, Eliot's own nervous breakdown and marital difficulty — could contribute to the processes of poetical composition and subsequently, to the processes of psychological healing. Eliot's epic is notable for, among other things, its seeming lack of a central and unified consciousness; he prefers instead to distribute fragments of this consciousness to the poem's numerous speakers. Nevertheless, his gestures toward unification at the poem's end and his desire to shore fragments against his own ruins predict the more sustained belief in the edifying powers of faith and consciousness to be enacted years later in *The Four Quartets*. Despite its appearance of objectivity and fragmentation, *The Waste Land* springs from the same personal need as does most poetry, modernist or not. Said another way, Eliot's personal perceptions of the cultural wasteland around him led to the creation of the poem, and further, his need for the personal expression of his own psychological difficulties at that time led to his creation of a poetic expression that served a specific personal need through the creation of such apparent objectivity. For the modernist writers in Europe during the war years — Eliot, Pound, Yeats, among others — the Great War seemed a symptom of tendencies within Western culture that had been in effect for at least a decade. The war was the first wholly Modern military conflict, the first time Europe would be forced to reckon with such a slaughter of its populace effected by the technologies of "total war" which were the by-products of the Victorian Age's forces of industrialization and its faith in progress. And across the Atlantic,

191

men such as Stevens and Frost — who was living in England during the war's first year and befriended the poet Edward Thomas, a casualty in 1917 — envisioned a psychological landscape which was distinctively Modern, even though the war did not impinge upon it directly. The war did not create these new movements in poetry in the manner that it clearly marked the change for men like Owen, Gurney, and Sassoon. But this examination of shell shock, psychological breakdown, and healing through poetic composition enables a re-envisioning of the critical divide that seems to dominate discourse about literature of the time period of the First World War — the perception of a division between those who were there and those who were not. The poets Wilfred Owen, Ivor Gurney, and Siegfried Sassoon were not simply Georgian poets in the trenches, forced to create a new idiom when their inherited Georgian pastoralism proved an inadequate idiom for the ruined landscape that became their home in France. Nor were they strictly Modern in the sense of Eliot, Yeats, Frost, or Stevens, inheriting a literary tradition that they would both co-opt and reconstruct to reflect their contemporary concerns. But the personal function that the composition of war poetry served for Owen, Gurney, and Sassoon has much in common with the poetics of these high modernists. Understanding the personal need to craft their war poems allows an understanding of the connection between these contemporaries, even though their experience within or without the war keeps them apart.

Such connections between the War Poets and the modernists can be envisioned only in retrospect; soldiers voiced hostility toward the ignorance at home, and those in England were likewise unable to approach the extent of the suffering endured by the war's survivors. During the war, Owen and Sassoon spoke for the majority of soldiers who perceived an unbridgeable psychological division between those in France and those who remained back in England, avant-garde artists included. And after the war, Eliot's relative silence about the value of the verse created and Yeats' outright hostility towards this type of poetry reflected the perception that the poetics of modernism had no room for the thinking that spawned this poetry of war which, according to Yeats, was limited in its impact to this historical moment that, in the twenties and thirties, was receding into history. Yeats infamously excluded Owen from his 1936 edition of *The Oxford Book of Modern Verse*. He excluded Gurney — nearing death in the asylum at this point — in all likelihood because he had made no lasting impact on the poetic world, and his volume where he both found his voice and recorded the beginnings of that voice's disintegration, *Rewards of Wonder*, was never published during his lifetime. Yeats did select four of Sassoon's poems for the anthology, including "On Passing the New Menin Gate," Sassoon's 1928 poem of commemoration for the men fallen during the war.[1]

According to Yeats, a poem such as this one demonstrates the proper treatment of war in poetry — to monumentalize the dead, to make their deaths symbolic and timeless, rather than to recreate the experience of such deaths in all their horror and immediacy. In a letter discussing the critical reception of his anthology, Yeats pulls no punches in his assessment of Owen:

> My anthology continues to sell and the critics get more and more angry. When I excluded Wilfred Owen, whom I consider unworthy of the poets' corner of a county newspaper, I did not know I was excluding a revered sandwich-board man of the revolution, and that somebody has put his worst and most famous poem in a glass-case in the British Museum — however, if I had known it, I would have excluded him just the same. He is all blood, dirt, and sucked sugar stick (…he calls poets "bards," a girl "a maid" and talks about "Titanic wars"). There is every excuse for him but not for those who like him.[2]

This passage reveals Yeats' belief that the poetry of war is of limited value to an audience in 1936 because the poems are confined to the context that produced them. To call Owen a "sandwich-board man of the revolution" suggests that the poems served a purpose for only that political moment and to only those who passed by the "sandwich-board" man and knew the context to which he was referring. The poem in the British Museum, "Dulce et Decorum Est," is no less propaganda than the propaganda against which Owen wrote the poem, according to such thinking. There is every reason that the war would generate such voices, but none that the poetry should continue to be read and its message applied to a context beyond itself. One can question the aesthetic judgment that would exclude such poetry that "dates itself" and confines itself to the political moment, and numerous critics have questioned Yeats for this charge he levied.

But one must admit also that Yeats is consistent in upholding and articulating his standards and that, according to his reading, the work of Owen and his fellow soldier-poets falls short. In the Introduction to his Anthology, Yeats writes about Owen and Sassoon, without mentioning them by name, in a tone less rancorous than in the letter:

> The writers of these poems were invariably officers of exceptional courage and capacity, one [Sassoon] a man constantly selected for dangerous work; all, I think, had the Military Cross; their letters are vivid and humorous, they were not without joy — for all skill is joyful — but felt bound, in the words of the best known [Owen], to plead the suffering of their men. In poems that had for a time considerable fame, written in the first person, they made that suffering

> their own. I have rejected these poems for the same reason that made
> Arnold withdraw his *Empedocles on Etna* from circulation; passive
> suffering is not a theme for poetry.... If war is necessary, or necessary
> in our time and place, it is best to forget its suffering as we do the
> discomfort of fever, remembering our comfort at midnight when our
> temperature fell, or as we forget the worst moments of more painful
> disease.[3]

Having seen the specific psychological context of shell shock and mental ill-
ness that generated the considerable work of composition for Owen, Gur-
ney, and Sassoon allows readers to question whether Yeats was informed
enough about their poetry to make such a blanket dismissal. When he says
that "passive suffering is not a theme for poetry," he seems to have misread
the impetus that brought their poetry into being and has lumped all war
poems into the category of photographic representation of battle or of the
subjective recollection of suffering. Interestingly, Gurney's ability to construct
poems around the genuinely happy memories that redeem the horror seems
to fit Yeats' criteria; of course, the failure of Gurney's third volume to be
published kept such work from the critical eye. Granted, the Great War
forced all three poets and all its participants into extended periods of pas-
sivity, and as the discussion of the conditions of trench life earlier indicated,
such passive suffering produced not the poetry itself but the psychological
breakdown. If the poems are to be at all true to the experience of the trenches,
they must in part represent such "passive suffering." But what Yeats seems
to ignore or to be unwilling to consider is that such poetry of war came about
only through the active endeavor of attempting to reverse the process of dis-
integration that the war brought about. Sassoon's precise focus upon the
sleeping soldier in "The Dug-Out" in order to exclude the rest of the war,
Gurney's ability to reconstruct and sustain a redemptive vision of solidarity
in his "First Time In" poems, and Owen's redefinition of heroism in "Spring
Offensive" are each crucial poems to allow readers to understand the processes
of poetic composition for each and the poetic principles and intentions that
went into such composition. For Owen and Sassoon in particular, these
poems mark the climax of processes which reveal a faith in the imagination
to function as a force that can resist or stave off the reality of war — a real-
ity present in every dimension of the soldier's experience but moved to the
periphery or out of the poem altogether in the poet's efforts to re-envision
the memory. Such exclusion or reinterpretation of the dangers and physical
realities of battle into either silence or into a relief surrounding the poet's
creation and assertion of something redemptive is itself an active pursuit. It
is an active assertion of will at which these men could not have arrived with-
out first having undergone a breakdown in their poetic identity, a frag-

mentation that the poetic trajectory worked by degrees to put back together again.

Eliot writes in his 1921 essay, "The Metaphysical Poets," of one of the central tenets of his modernist technique of pastiche, which he was currently employing in his composition of *The Waste Land*:

> When a poet's mind is perfectly equipped for its work, it is constantly amalgamating disparate experience; the ordinary man's experience is chaotic, irregular, fragmentary. The latter falls in love, or reads Spinosa, and these two experiences have nothing to do with each other, or with the noise of the typewriter or the smell of cooking; in the mind of the poet these experiences are always forming new wholes.[4]

The poet appears passive, too, in this description — a filter through which the experience of modern or everyday experience is processed. But for Eliot, the assembly of a poem like *The Waste Land* is an inclusionary act — (an exclusionary one, as well, as Pound's radical excisions to the original manuscript would attest). The poet who is "perfectly equipped" for the work of poetry must work to choose which fragments of modern life to include to create the modernist poem, which despite (in Eliot's case) its appearance of passivity and formlessness is actively "forming new wholes." The war poets operated from a similar desire to form such wholes; however, for them the poetry was part of the project of forming the new "whole" of a psychological coherence and poetic identity. These central poems by Sassoon, Owen, and Gurney — taking the sleeping soldier out of the trenches through the poet's imaginative and loving gaze; turning German gunfire into the sky's fury against humanity to unburden the poet from the crisis of personal responsibility and guilt; hearing the songs of Welsh soldiers against the backdrop of shelling, so that the soldiers and the war "are the music while the music lasts" — create new wholes and emerge from the personal desire to tap into imaginative resources with greater urgency, necessity, and — finally — activity.[5] And theirs was an activity perhaps beyond that which the civilian context and stance of the artist demanded of men like Yeats or Eliot.

When one re-envisions the poetry of these soldier-poets as emerging not simply out of the political context that Yeats found so limiting aesthetically but out of the personal need to confront and resolve the crisis of psychology that manifested itself as shell shock, one can see the motivating principle behind composition for Owen, Sassoon, and Gurney as resembling the search for anchoring systems operating in the universe, chronicled in such astonishing length and complexity in Yeats' *A Vision*. Yeats' famous seances, which operated under the presumption that he acted as the passive recipient of these apparently objective truths to explain the universe, demanded instead that he embrace the role of the active and imaginative artist who reconstructed them linguistically and symbolically. Yeats the man may have believed that he was a vehicle into which flowed the evidence of the system of gyres and cones, but Yeats the poet was the active agent who reconstructed glimpses of this imaged or perceived world into poems which achieve their value for the poet in becoming microcosms of that imagined order and testament to the mind's capacity to form and sustain such constructions.

On the other side of the Atlantic, Robert Frost, though without such faith in elaborate mysticisms, espoused a similar belief in the redemptive potential of poetic form and structure to counter the chaos of the cosmos. The political climate of Europe in the early months of the war forced Frost to cut short his stay in England, but not before forming one of his few lasting and genuine friendships with the British poet, Edward Thomas, who enlisted after Frost departed and was gruesomely killed by a direct hit of a shell in 1917.[6] Like Eliot and Yeats, Frost was not oblivious to the war which caused him personal suffering over Thomas' loss, even though his personal experience of the war years afforded him the opportunity to keep the war itself from any detectable impact on his verse. Yet Frost's faith in the value of poetic form connects his thinking with the function of poetry for Owen, Sassoon, and Gurney. He writes in his 1935 "Letter to 'The Amherst Student'" of his theories of formalism that apply just as readily to the poetry he composed before and during these war years:

> There is at least so much good in the world that it admits of form and the making of form. And not only admits of it, but calls for it. We people are thrust forward out of the suggestions of form in the rolling clouds of nature. In us nature reaches its height of form and through us exceeds itself. When in doubt there is always form for us to go on with. Anyone who has achieved the least form to be sure of it, is lost to the larger excruciations. I think it must stroke faith the right way. The artist, the poet might be expected to be the most aware of such assurance. But it is really everybody's sanity to feel it and live by it. Fortunately, too, no forms are more engrossing, gratifying, comforting, staying than those lesser ones we throw off, like vortex rings of smoke, all our individual enterprise and needing nobody's cooperation; a basket, a letter, a garden, a room, and idea, a picture, a poem. For these we haven't to get a team together before we can play. The background is hugeness and confusion shading away from where we stand into black and utter chaos; and against the background any small man-made figure of order and concentration. What pleasanter than that this should be so? ... To me

any little form I assert upon it is velvet, as the saying is, and to be considered for how much more it is than nothing.[7]

And in this excerpt from his 1946 essay, "The Constant Symbol," he strikes a similar chord:

> Every single poem written regular is a symbol small or great of the way the will has to pitch into commitments deeper and deeper to a rounded conclusion and then be judged for whether any original intention it had has been strongly spent or weakly lost; be it in art, politics, school, church, business, love or marriage — in a piece of work or in a career. Strongly spent is synonymous with kept.[8]

Any form, according to Frost, as momentary as a smoke-ring or as seemingly minor as a sonnet, is a symbol of the will and is as valuable as velvet. The resulting poetic form, which emerges out of the will's desire that there be forms in a universe moving toward decay and disorder, is an expression of an individual poised on the edge between isolated despair and imaginative reprieve. The form is what saves Frost — and saves humanity, he suggests — from the chaos without and the threat of insanity within. The creation of poetic and musical forms is what even in December 1916, before he had seen the most intense fighting he would witness and before had begun to lapse into psychosis, Ivor Gurney recognized would offer his best hope of psychological salvation. He writes in his letters:

> After all, my friend, it is better to live a grey life in mud and danger, so long as one uses it — as I trust I am now doing — as a means to an end. Someday all this experience may be crystallized and glorified in me; and men shall learn by chance fragments in a string quartett or a symphony, what thoughts haunted the minds of men who watched the darkness grimly in desolate places.[9]

For Gurney, to crystallize the "grey life in mud and danger" is to glorify it by transforming it into an expression of imagination and faith. The resource by which such a transformation occurs is what gives the individual, in Gurney's estimation, his "nobility," and this source is a fount from within, pressing out against the world around him to "form dreams of noble lives," to resurrect "the memory of their home and friends to strengthen them," and imaginatively "to walk in pleasant places in faithfull dreams."

Frost creates forms not to contend with the trenches but to contend with his own "desert places" within the mind and within the desolate landscape. He admires the form for how much more it is than nothing, and Gurney, who finds himself "Near Vermand," confronts both gunfire and — perhaps more terrifying — nothing more than a "frozen and rocky couch."[10]

Gurney — like Frost, and also, by extension, like Owen and Sassoon — transforms the expression of dejection and terror into the emotional form that is the poem, written in 1921 not as a salvation from gunfire but to stave off schizophrenia, the formless dissociation of consciousness occurring within the mind. The more chaotic that these external and internal realities become for Gurney and for all the war poets, the more remarkable the urge and the ability become to resist the chaos and to assert visions of heroism, or tenderness, or fleeting beauty against the darkness.

The poetry of the First World War — especially that which was written by those who suffered the greatest psychological damage — if envisioned as forming a part of the therapeutic endeavors to heal from such disintegration, enables critics to connect this subset of early Twentieth-Century poetry with concurrent trends of modernism, which has come to be regarded as the main current of literature produced in the decade before and the decades after the Great War. These men entered the trenches Georgians and came out of the fighting deeply changed but unable, yet, to express the nature of that change. Many soldiers who survived would remain inarticulate. In expressing and constructing a vision of that process of change, and in reconstructing a version of the identity that the war disrupted, Wilfred Owen, Ivor Gurney, and Siegfried Sassoon became their own sort of modernist assemblers and architects of order. That they did so for personal reasons and out of desperate necessity in no way diminishes the value of the poetic endeavor — quite the contrary. That they found themselves in a war that would debilitate them in a manner that called for such imaginative potential to be tapped is itself a testament to the extent of their suffering and to the lasting value of their verse as a window into this Modern moment. When Pound exhorted his fellow members of the artistic avant-garde to "make it new," he was not speaking to the men in the trenches. Owen, Gurney, and Sassoon came upon this principle on their own. What they were making "new" and "whole" again was in fact the versions of themselves necessary if they and their voices were to endure.

Chapter Notes

Introduction

1. Peter Ackroyd, *T.S. Eliot: A Life* (New York: Simon and Schuster, 1984), 110.
2. Ackroyd, *T.S. Eliot,* 115.
3. Ackroyd, *T.S. Eliot,* 116.
4. T. S. Eliot, *The Waste Land, Collected Poems of T.S. Eliot* (New York: Harcourt, Brace, and Company. 1991), 76. Eliot translates this line from Dante's *Purgatorio* as: "he hid himself in the fire which refines them."
5. From the "Vigil of Venus": "When shall I be as the swallow?"
6. From Gerard de Nerval, Sonnet "El Desdichado": "The Prince of Aquitaine in the ruined tower."
7. From Kyd's "Spanish Tragedy": Hieronymo, avenging the murder of his son, says to the players, "Why then I'll find a part for you" so that the murderers of his son are also killed.
8. From the *Upanishads*: "Give. Sympathize. Control."
9. The formal ending to the *Upanishads*, translated by Eliot as: "The peace which passeth understanding."
10. *Army Report of the War Office Committee Enquiry into "Shell Shock"* (London: His Majesty's Stationery Office, 1922), 92.
11. Anthony Babington, *Shell-Shock: A History of the Changing Attitudes to War Neurosis* (London: Leo Cooper, 1997), 168.
12. See Fussell's chapter, "Adversary Proceedings" in *The Great War and Modern Memory* (New York: Oxford University Press, 1975), 74–113.
13. Quoted in Frank Field, *British and French Writers of the First World War* (London: Cambridge University Press, 1991), 74.
14. Eric Leed, *No Man's Land: Combat and Identity in World War I* (London: Cambridge University Press, 1979), x.
15. Paul Moeyes, *Siegfried Sassoon: Scorched Glory* (London: Macmillan, 1997), 29.
16. Siegfried Sassoon, *Siegfried Sassoon's Diaries: 1914–1918,* ed. Rupert Hart-Davis (London: Faber and Faber, 1983), 26.
17. Siegfried Sassoon, "The rank stench of those bodies haunts me still." *The Penguin Book of First World War Poetry,* ed. Jon Silkin (New York: Penguin, 1979), 124–26.

Chapter One

1. Babington, *Shell Shock,* 43.
2. G. Elliot Smith and T. H. Pear, *Shell Shock and Its Lessons* (London: Manchester University Press, 1918), 1.
3. *War Office,* 91.
4. John T. MacCurdy, *War Neuroses* (London: Cambridge University Press, 1918), 1.
5. Charles S. Myers, *Shell Shock in France* (London: Cambridge University Press, 1940), 66.
6. E. E. Southard, *Shell-Shock and Other Neuropsychiatric Problems, Presented in Five*

Hundred and Eighty-Nine Case Histories (Boston: W. M. Leonard, 1919), 405.

7. War Office, 92.

8. War Office, 96.

9. M. D. Eder, *War-Shock: The Psycho-Neuroses in War Psychology and Treatment* (London: William Heinemann, 1917), 8.

10. Thomas Salmon, *The Care and Treatment of War Neuroses ("Shell Shock") in the British Army* (New York: National Committee for Mental Hygiene, 1917), 30.

11. John T. MacCurdy, *War Neuroses* (London: Cambridge University Press, 1918), 22.

12. MacCurdy, *War Neuroses*, 26.

13. Abram Kardiner, *The Traumatic Neuroses of War* (New York: Paul B. Hoeber, 1941), 92–96.

14. Ernst Simmel in Sigmund Freud, et al., *Psycho-Analysis and the War Neuroses* (London: The International Psycho-Analytical Press, 1921), 36.

15. Leed, *No Man's Land*, 189.

16. Hamilton Marr, *Psychoses of the War, Including Neurasthenia and Shell Shock* (London: Oxford University Press, 1919), 168, 179–80. Recent studies of the life of Gurney call into question the conventional diagnosis of schizophrenia, contending that his patterns of productivity followed by depression indicate bipolar disorder as a more accurate diagnosis. See the discussion of Gurney in the third chapter, as well as Arnold Rattenbury, "The Sanity of Ivor Gurney," *Ivor Gurney Society Journal* 6 (2000): 5–22 and Pamela Blevins, "New Perspectives on Ivor Gurney's Mental Illness," *Ivor Gurney Society Journal* 6 (2000): 29–58.

17. War Office 144.

18. Wilfred Owen, "Mental Cases," *The Poems of Wilfred Owen*, ed. Jon Stallworthy (New York: Norton, 1986), 146.

19. Babington, *Shell Shock*, 121

20. Babington, *Shell Shock*, 121

21. Salmon, *Care and Treatment*, 14.

22. Smith and Pear, *Shell Shock and Its Lessons*, 9.

23. MacCurdy, *War Neuroses*, 14.

24. MacCurdy, *War Neuroses*, 15.

25. Smith and Pear, *Shell Shock and Its Lessons*, 6.

26. Babington, *Shell Shock*, 86.

27. Stephen Kern, *The Culture of Time and Space: 1890–1930* (Cambridge: Harvard University Press, 1983), 308.

28. Henri Barbusse, *Under Fire* (London: J. M. Dent, 1916), 17–18.

29. Quoted in Malcolm Brown, *The Im-perial War Museum Book of the Somme* (London: Sidgwick and Jackson, 1996), 124.

30. Leed, *No Man's Land*, 181.

31. Smith and Pear, *Shell Shock and Its Lessons*, 64.

32. Smith and Pear, *Shell Shock and Its Lessons*, 8.

33. Norman Fenton, *Shell Shock and Its Aftermath* (St. Louis: C. V. Mosby Co., 1926), 22–30.

34. For an interesting instance of how Freud's controversial ideas became even more so during the war because of these "war neuroses," see K. R. Eissler, *Freud as an Expert Witness: The Discussion of War Neuroses Between Freud and Wagner-Jauregg*, trans. by Christine Trollope (Madison, CT: International University Press, 1986). In 1920 Freud was called by Austrian authorities to testify about the nature of war neuroses in the trial of the Austrian therapist Karl Wagner-Jauregg who was accused of inhumane treatments of sufferers of shell shock. Wagner-Jauregg employed electro-shock treatments, like those of the British doctor Lewis Yealland discussed in the following section, in an effort to rid the patient of his incapacitating symptoms. Prosecutors called upon Freud, whose ideas by this time had been responded to with respect, admiration, as well as hostility from various practitioners of psychotherapies, to show that more humane and more effective treatments had been available to Wagner-Jauregg which he had ignored. Eissler has retrieved the transcripts of the two days of testimony, during which Freud was repeatedly slandered by supporters of Wagner-Jauregg and depicted as a charlatan. Freud mysteriously did not mount counterattacks to the character assassination, beyond steadfastly endorsing his own approach. Wagner-Jauregg was acquitted, and his psychiatric career continued with little ill effect from the trial.

35. Leed, *No Man's Land*, 164.

36. Karl Abraham, *Psycho-Analysis and the War Neuroses*, 32.

37. MacCurdy, *War Neuroses*, 15.

38. Ferenczi, *Psycho-Analysis and the War Neuroses*, 15.

39. Ferenczi, *Psycho-Analysis and the War Neuroses*, 10.

40. Freud, *Psycho-Analysis and the War Neuroses*, 2.

41. MacCurdy, *War Neuroses*, 23.

42. Fenton, *Shell Shock and Its Aftermath*, 149.

43. Rivers, in "Preface" to MacCurdy, *War Neuroses*, viii.

44. MacCurdy, *War Neuroses*, 9.

45. Fenton, *Shell Shock and Its Aftermath*, 37.

46. MacCurdy, *War Neuroses*, 122–23.

47. MacCurdy, *War Neuroses*, 123.

48. Leed, *No Man's Land*, 167.

49. MacCurdy, *War Neuroses*, 126.

50. War Office, 97–98.

51. Ivor Gurney, *Collected Letters*, ed. R. K. R. Thornton (London: Carcanet, 1991), 115.

52. Salmon, *Care and Treatment*, 40–41.

53. W. H. R. Rivers, *Instinct and the Unconscious* (London: Cambridge University Press, 1922), 192–93.

54. Babington, *Shell Shock*, 56.

55. Babington, *Shell Shock*, 119.

56. Lewis R. Yealland, *Hysterical Disorders of Warfare* (London: Macmillan and Co., 1918), 25.

57. Yealland, *Hysterical Disorders*, 144.

58. Yealland, *Hysterical Disorders*, 138.

59. Yealland, *Hysterical Disorders*, 22.

60. Yealland, *Hysterical Disorders*, 195.

61. Eissler, *Freud as an Expert Witness*, 27.

62. Yealland, *Hysterical Disorders*, 111.

63. Babington, *Shell Shock*, 66.

64. Smith and Pear, *Shell Shock and Its Lessons*, 99

65. Eder, *War-Shock*, 145.

66. Kardiner, *Traumatic Neuroses*, 142.

67. Smith and Pear, *Shell Shock and Its Lessons*, 38.

68. Leed, *No Man's Land*, 175.

69. MacCurdy, *War Neuroses*, 83.

70. Marr, *Psychoses of the War*, 122.

71. Salmon, *Care and Treatment*, 39, 52.

72. Smith and Pear, *Shell Shock and Its Lessons*, 50.

73. Myers, *Shell Shock in France*, 55.

74. Eder, *War-Shock*, 133.

75. Leed, *No Man's Land*, 176.

76. Sigmund Freud, *Beyond the Pleasure Principle*, ed. James Strachey (New York: Norton, 1961), 16.

77. Freud, *Beyond the Pleasure Principle*, 38.

78. Marr, *Psychoses of the War*, 123–24.

79. Rivers, *Instinct and the Unconscious*, 190–91.

80. Marr, *Psychoses of the War*, 60–62.

81. Marr, *Psychoses of the War*, 51.

82. Rivers, *Conflict and Dream*, 148–49.

83. Rivers, *Conflict and Dream*, 149.

Chapter Two

1. Wilfred Owen, *Collected Letters*, eds. Harold Owen and John Bell (London: Oxford University Press, 1967), 273. Hereafter *Letters*.

2. Dominic Hibberd, *Wilfred Owen: A New Biography*, (Chicago: Ivan R. Dee, 2002), 214.

3. Wilfred Owen, "The Sentry," *The Poems of Wilfred Owen*, ed. Jon Stallworthy (New York: Norton, 1985), 165–66, ll. 1–10. Hereafter *Poems*.

4. Douglas Kerr, *Wilfred Owen's Voices: Language and Community* (Oxford: Clarendon Press, 1993), 225.

5. Kerr, 226.

6. Hibberd, *Wilfred Owen: A New Biography*, 226.

7. The most thorough discussion of Owen's months in combat can be found in Dominic Hibberd's recent biography *Wilfred Owen: A New Biography*, 203–42.

8. Hibberd, *Wilfred Owen: A New Biography*, 246–47.

9. See, in particular, Hibberd's chapter-length treatment of the relationship in *Wilfred Owen: A New Biography*, 264–83, and Jean Moorcroft-Wilson's chapter "Strange Meeting" in the biography *Siegfried Sassoon: The Making of a War Poet* (New York: Routledge, 1998), 387–425.

10. Siegfried Sassoon, *Siegfried's Journey*, (New York: Viking, 1945), 86.

11. Sassoon, *Siegfried's Journey*, 90–91.

12. Paul Norgate, "Shell Shock and Poetry: Wilfred Owen at Craiglockhart Hospital," *English* 36(1987): 1–35.

13. Norgate, "Shell Shock and Poetry," 11.

14. Norgate, "Shell Shock and Poetry," 6.

15. Dominic Hibberd, "A Sociological Cure for Shell Shock: Dr. Brock and Wilfred Owen," *Sociological Review* 25(1977): 378.

16. Hibberd, "A Sociological Cure," 378.

17. Sassoon, *Siegfried's Journey*, 96.

18. Kerr, *Wilfred Owen's Voices*, 201.

19. Dominic Hibberd, *Wilfred Owen: The Last Year* (London: Constable and Company, 1992), 22.

20. Norgate, "Shell Shock and Poetry," 5.

21. Hibberd, "A Sociological Cure," 380.

22. Hibberd, *The Last Year*, 24.

23. Arthur Brock, *Health and Conduct* (London: Williams and Norgate, 1923), 172.

24. Hibberd, *The Last Year*, 87.

25. Hibberd, *The Last Year*, 87.

26. Dominic Hibberd, *Owen the Poet*

(Athens: University of Georgia Press, 1986), 88.

27. Hibberd discusses the poem as steeped in the language of Romanticism, Owen's greatest influence. See Hibberd, *Owen the Poet*, 110–11. Silkin goes so far as to brand the sonnet as a falling back into Owen's youthful idiom in an effort to deal with the topic of war for which Owen lacked an appropriate language. See Jon Silkin, *Out of Battle: The Poetry of the Great War* (Oxford: Oxford University Press, 1972), 210–11. Kerr and Lane both stress the language of the church pervading the octave as the speaker struggles to find adequate prayers for the fallen. See Kerr, *Wilfred Owen's Voices*, 82–83; and Arthur Lane, *An Adequate Response: The War Poetry of Wilfred Owen and Siegfried Sassoon* (Detroit: Wayne State University Press, 1972), 127–30.

28. Hibberd, *Owen the Poet*, 111.

29. Hibberd, *Owen the Poet*, 111.

30. T. S. Eliot, *The Waste Land*, 76. Eliot translates the line, *"Poi s-ascose nel foco che gli affina,"* from Dante's *Purgatorio* as, "He hid himself in the fire which refines them."

31. Mark Sinfield, "Wilfred Owen's 'Mental Cases': Source and Structure," *Notes and Queries* 227(1982): 340.

32. Echevarria, Berta Cano, "Victims and Victimizers in Wilfred Owen's Poetry," *Focus on Robert Graves and His Contemporaries* 2(1995): 22.

33. E. D. H. Johnston, *English Poetry of the First World War: A Study in the Evolution of Lyric and Narrative Form* (Princeton: Princeton University Press, 1964), 174.

34. Hibberd, *The Last Year*, 52. Silkin observes within the poem the use of colloquialism and approximations of soldiers' speech that Owen grew to appreciate from Sassoon's poems and from conversations with him. See Silkin, *Out of Battle*, 220.

35. Johnston, *English Poetry*, 174–75.

36. Lane, *An Adequate Response*, 134.

37. See Stallworthy's notes to the poem, 166.

38. Hibberd, *Owen the Poet*, 114.

39. See Hibberd, *Wilfred Owen: A New Biography*, 235, who raises the possibility that Owen's platoon was gassed in early April, 1917, an experience forming the basis for the poem.

40. Hibberd, *Owen the Poet*, 115.

41. Lane, *An Adequate Response*, 134.

42. Horace, *The Odes and Epodes*, trans. C. E. Bennet (Cambridge: Harvard University Press, 1934), 174–5.

43. Paul Fussell, *The Great War and Modern Memory* (London: Oxford University Press, 1975), 292.

44. Caesar, *Taking It Like a Man*, 157.

45. See Stallworthy's notes to the poem, 123.

46. Hibberd, *The Last Year*, 85–90.

47. Caesar, *Taking It Like a Man*, 85.

48. Kerr, *Wilfred Owen's Voices*, 165. See also Stallworthy's notes to the poem, 124. He observes that Owen is ironically alluding to Shelley's discussion of poetic "sensibility" through the poem's title.

49. Silkin, *Out of Battle*, 246.

50. Backman, *Tradition Transformed*, 82.

51. Welland, *Wilfred Owen: A Critical Study*, 67–68. See Stallworthy's notes to the poem for the text of Graves' "Two Fusiliers," 102. The allusion to Graves' poem, and its subject matter of soldiers "closely bound / ... by the wet bond of blood," offers another means of entry into Owen's psychology. Owen, like Graves and Sassoon, was homosexual, and like these older poets, the homoerotic quality of his war poetry became a means of both revealing and concealing this dimension of personality, socially unaccepted during the war. See the subsequent discussion of Owen's "Greater Love" and the later chapter on Sassoon for further exploration of the connections between psychology, sexuality, and poetry.

52. Johnston, *English Poetry of the First World War*, 181.

53. See Stallworthy's notes to the poem, 143.

54. Johnston, *English Poetry of the First World War*, 92.

55. Hibberd, *Owen the Poet*, 57.

56. See Hibberd, *Owen the Poet*, 150–53; 197–201, Hibberd, *The Last Year*, passim, and more recently, Hibberd, *Wilfred Owen: A New Biography* for more detail about Owen's sexuality and its impact upon his life and work than can be examined here. In these studies, Hibberd provides a clear narrative of Owen's increasing awareness and acceptance of his sexual orientation during his short adult life, an acceptance which Hibberd depicts as having been brought about in significant part through his relationship with Sassoon.

57. Hibberd, *Owen the Poet*, 199–200.

58. For further discussion of the impact of Owen's sexuality upon his verse, including poems not written about the war, see especially Caesar, *Taking It Like a Man*,

115–68; Joseph Cohen, "Owen Agonistes," *English Literature in Transition* 8(1965): 253–68; Philip Larkin, "The Real Wilfred: Owen's Life and Legends," *Encounter* (1975): 73–81; and Fussell's exploration of the homoerotic tradition in British poetry in relation to the war, 273–89.

59. Martin Stephen, *The Price of Pity: Poetry, History, and Myth in the Great War* (London: Leo Cooper, 1996), 190.

60. In 1921, John Middleton Murry discussed the poet's use of assonance or half-rhyme: "The tone is single, low, muffled, subterranean.... These assonant endings are indeed the discovery of a genius; but in a truer sense the poet's emotion discovered them for itself. They are a dark and natural flowering of this, and only this, emotion." Quoted in Dennis Welland, *Wilfred Owen: A Critical Study* (London: Chatto and Windus, 1978), 108. Welland provides a sophisticated discussion of the thematic import of this device, particularly as the falling vowel sounds (escaped / scooped; years / yours) contribute to the tone of "hopelessness" which is the phantom's topic of discussion. See Welland, 118–20. Hibberd analyzes the message within this spectral character's speech in terms of the influence of Sassoon's and Bertrand Russell's ideas of pacifism. See Hibberd, *Owen the Poet,* 132–33. And almost all critics have focused upon, in one way or another, the highly allusive quality of the poem, particularly as it draws from Romantic and contemporary texts formative to Owen's poetic development: Shelley's *The Revolt of Islam,* Keats' "The Fall of Hyperion," Wordsworth's "Intimations" Ode, Wilde's "The Ballad of Reading Gaol," Harold Monro's *Strange Meetings,* and Sassoon's "The Rear Guard." See Welland, 100–03; Sven Backman, *Tradition Transformed: Studies in the Poetry of Wilfred Owen* (Lund: Liber Laromedel, 1979), 99; Kerr, 233, 249).

61. See Stallworthy's notes to the poem, 126.

62. Silkin, *Out of Battle,* 237–38.

63. Hibberd, *The Last Year,* 101–04.

64. Hibberd, *Wilfred Owen: A New Biography,* 311.

65. See Backman, *Tradition Transformed,* 97.

66. Hibberd, *Owen the Poet,* 172.

67. Denis Winter, *Death's Men: Soldiers of the Great War* (London: Penguin, 1982), 80–81.

68. Fussell, *The Great War and Modern Memory,* 41.

69. Welland, *Wilfred Owen: A Critical Study,* 110.

70. Welland, *Wilfred Owen: A Critical Study,* 130.

71. Sassoon's poem, "The Rear-Guard," written six months before "Strange Meeting," and which Sassoon submitted to *The Hydra* when Owen was its editor at Craiglockhart, occurs in a similar underground setting and describes a soldier's confrontation with a dead soldier in a darkened tunnel. Interestingly, in Sassoon's poem, it is the sound of gunfire which enables the soldier to return to the hellish vision and return to the "safety" of the war occurring above him. See the subsequent chapter on Sassoon for further discussion of the relationship between the two poems.

72. Hibberd, *Owen the Poet,* 181.

73. See Stallworthy's notes to the poem, 192.

74. Hibberd, *Owen the Poet,* 184.

75. Kenneth Simcox, *Wilfred Owen: Anthem for a Doomed Youth* (London: Woburn, 1987), 64.

76. Welland, *Wilfred Owen: A Critical Study,* 80.

77. See Fussell, *Great War and Modern Memory,* 52–56.

78. Hibberd, *Owen the Poet,* 191.

79. Welland, *Wilfred Owen: A Critical Study,* 81.

80. Lane, *An Adequate Response,* 139.

81. Lane, *An Adequate Response,* 141.

82. Lane, 141.

Chapter Three

1. From Charles Tomlinson's "To a Christian Concerning Ivor Gurney," *Jubilation* (New York: Oxford University Press, 1995), 60.

2. For a lengthy discussion of the formal strategies of Gurney's verse, see Mark William Brown. *The Poetry of Ivor Gurney: A Study of Influences,* (Doctoral Dissertation, Vanderbilt University, 1989). Brown sees the influence of Gloucester's unique geographic and architectural qualities as providing an avenue for understanding the formal innovations within Gurney's poetry about the city and its people.

3. Michael Hurd, *The Ordeal of Ivor Gurney* (New York: Oxford University Press,

1978), 123. This discussion, and indeed all discussions, of Gurney's life and work, are indebted to Hurd's definitive biography of the poet and musician. Hurd has succeeded in establishing a clear narrative of the life of Gurney out of his often fragmentary and undated letters, personal reminiscences, and medical records.

4. See *The Ivor Gurney Society Journal* 6(2000), which contains articles debating the nature of Gurney's illness: Arnold Rattenbury, "The Sanity of Ivor Gurney," 5–22; Anthony Boden, "Ivor Gurney: Schizophrenic?" 23–28; and Pamela Blevins, "New Perspectives on Ivor Gurney's Mental Illness," 29–58.

5. Hurd, *Ordeal*, 1–3.

6. Ivor Gurney, *The Collected Poems of Ivor Gurney*, ed. P. J. Kavanagh (Oxford: Oxford University Press, 1982), 261–65. Hereafter *Collected Poems*.

7. Samuel Hynes, "The Squaring of Human Sorrow," *Times Literary Supplement,* 13 October 1978, 1137.

8. Hurd, *Ordeal*, 7.

9. W. H. Trethowan, "Ivor Gurney's Mental Illness," *Music and Letters* 62 (1981): 307–08. Trethowan challenges the thinking under which many early discussions of Gurney's work have operated — that his mental illness was brought on by trauma experienced in the trenches. The author acknowledges that the war may have precipitated the recurrence of mental instability which Gurney had exhibited previously and contributed to the severity of this relapse, but he believes a version of the malady would have resulted with or without the events of 1914–1918.

10. Hurd, *Ordeal*, 11.

11. Hurd, *Ordeal*, 25.

12. Hurd, *Ordeal*, 26.

13. Hurd, *Ordeal*, 35.

14. Hurd, *Ordeal*, 36.

15. Ivor Gurney, *Collected Letters*, ed. R. K. R. Thornton (London: Carcanet, 1991), 2. Hereafter *Letters*. Thornton's edition expands upon his prior volume, *Ivor Gurney: War Letters*, ed. Thornton (London: Carcanet, 1983). While the earlier volume contains over three hundred letters written during the period of Gurney's service in the war, the *Collected Letters* expands this time frame to include his years of musical study before the war and the years afterwards (1919–1922) before being institutionalized. Thornton provides the reader with a sense of the letters produced when in the mental hospital, but hundreds more exist and remained uncollected because of their length, incoherence, and redundancy.

16. Hurd, *Ordeal*, 53.

17. Denis Winter, *Death's Men: Soldiers of the Great War* (London: Penguin, 1982), 82. Winter gives an invaluable history of the day to day life of British officers and enlisted men during the war, based largely upon surviving memoirs of the participants.

18. Blevins, "New Perspectives," 45.

19. Boden, "Ivor Gurney: Schizophrenic?" 25.

20. Richard Hoffpauir, "The War Poetry of Blunden and Gurney," *Poetry Nation Review* 12(1985): 46.

21. P. Joy King's article "'Honour', 'Heroics' and 'Bullshit': Ivor Gurney's Private Vision," *Critical Survey* 2(1990): 144–50, made first notice of the connection between Gurney's military rank and his unique vision. King's analysis takes a slightly different approach than this study, in investigating this vision as that of the skeptical serviceman's attitudes towards the absurdity of military order and protocol.

22. Leed, *No Man's Land*, 81.

23. Winter, *Death's Men*, 53.

24. Donald Davie, "Ivor Gurney Recovered," *Under Briggflats* (Chicago: University of Chicago Press, 1989), 199.

25. Andrew Waterman, "The Poetic Achievement of Ivor Gurney," *Critical Quarterly* 25(1983): 12.

26. Winter, *Death's Men*, 54.

27. Owen, "Anthem for Doomed Youth," *Collected Poems*, 76

28. Owen, "Apologia Pro Poemate Meo," *Collected Poems*, 102–03.

29. R. K. R. Thornton has combined the two books of poetry published during his lifetime into a single volume: Ivor Gurney, *Severn and Somme and War's Embers*, ed. R. K. R. Thornton (London: Carcanet, 1987). This edition fills in holes that Kavanagh's edition created through its selections from these two war books.

30. Silkin, *Out of Battle*, 123.

31. Silkin, *Out of Battle*, 124.

32. Hurd, *Ordeal*, 158.

33. Trethowan, "Ivor Gurney's Mental Illness," 304.

34. See Blevins' section "Distinguishing between manic-depressive illness and schizophrenia" in her article, "New Perspectives on Ivor Gurney's Mental Illness," 31–34.

35. Hurd, *Ordeal*, 123.

36. Donald Davie, operating under the premise that this volume was the one that Gurney attempted to publish, writes of this collection, "The publishers were right to reject it.... . *Rewards of Wonder* seems to represent a violent mutilation by this erstwhile lyrical poet of his lyric voice. There is one exercise after another in headlong, mostly couplet, rhyme, much of the time intolerably strained and grotesque, looping up extremely heterogeneous matter into six-foot or even seven-foot accentual lines," 197. Kavanagh, who likewise argues that this volume was the rejected one in his introduction to the *Collected Poems*, agrees that the rejection was understandable, but sees a value in Gurney's stylistic, syntactic, and metrical oddities: "Gurney begins to sound original, pressing music out of ordinary speech. With signs of the pressure too, queer contortions and omissions which became part of his manner. They are intentional, as changes in his notebooks show, and are part of his homage to his beloved Elizabethans, especially Shakespeare...." *Collected Poems*, 11.

37. Lucas, *Ivor Gurney*, 35.

38. See the introduction to Ivor Gurney, *80 Poems or So*, ed. George Walter and R. K. R. Thornton (Manchester: Carcanet, 1997).

39. Alfred Lord Tennyson, "The Lotos-Eaters," *Norton Anthology of English Literature*, volume Two, Fifth ed., ed. M. H. Abrams (New York: Norton, 1986), 1104–08. Gurney knew Tennyson's work well. In July 1916, he writes Marion Scott requesting that his copy of Tennyson's collected poems be sent to him in France (*Letters* 124). Elsewhere he praises the work of Tennyson, along with George Eliot and Meredith, as "the striving of an original mind to be more original" (*Letters* 41) and later says, "Let us leave perfection to Tennyson ..." (*Letters* 67).

40. Winter, *Death's Men*, 56.

41. Jeremy Hooker, "Honouring Ivor Gurney," *Poetry Nation Review* 17(1980): 17.

42. John Lucas, *Ivor Gurney* (London: Northcote House, 2001), 99.

43. Winter, *Death's Men*, 55–56.

44. Waterman, "Poetic Achievement," 15

45. See Paul Fussell's chapter "The Troglodyte World" in *The Great War and Modern Memory*, 36–74. In addition to giving the reader a graphic depiction of the daily life of the entrenched soldier, with anecdotes of cat-eating rats and rum rations, Fussell discusses the recurrent imagery of sunrises and sunsets in poetry and memoirs of the war.

These were the tensest moments of the day for the common soldier, the hour of the ritualized "stand-to" in preparation for mounting an attack or defending against an enemy's.

46. Fussell, *Great War and Modern Memory*, 55.

47. Rattenbury and Blevins each give a date of composition for "The Silent One" as 1926, or as Rattenbury puts it, "deep into the asylum years" (10; Blevins, 50). But because the period is marked by great lucidity as shown in the letters, only punctuated by odd moments such as the Beethoven letter, the entire period of his career represents, in this argument, the struggle to sustain this clarity through the creation of these poems.

48. Bernard Bergonzi, *Heroes' Twilight* (London: Carcanet, 1965), 87.

49. Waterman, "Poetic Achievement," 13.

50. Geoffrey Hill, "Gurney's 'Hobby,'" *Essays in Criticism* 34(1984): 112

51. See the prior chapter's discussions of Wilfred Owen's "Dulce Et Decorum Est" and "The Sentry" in particular for just such psychological situations. Owen's speakers in those poems, officers like himself, expose the guilt that accompanied life and death decisions made in battle within precisely the same dynamic as seen in "The Silent One." There the speakers, officers who have survived, reveal similar distinctions in the survivor's mind between the living and the dead, which contribute to the shell shock of the poet for which the poetic representations seek to provide relief.

52. Jacqueline Banerjee, "Ivor Gurney's 'Dark March': Is It Really Over?" *English Studies* 70(1989): 124.

53. Piers Gray, *Marginal Men: Edward Thomas; Ivor Gurney; J. R. Ackerley* (London: Macmillan, 1991), 85.

54. Robert Frost, "Desert Places," *Robert Frost: Collected Poems, Prose, and Plays* (New York: Library of America, 1995), 269.

55. Hurd, *Ordeal*, 127.

56. Hurd, *Ordeal*, 142–44.

57. Hurd, *Ordeal*, 139.

58. Hurd, *Ordeal*, 145.

59. Hurd, *Ordeal*, 153.

60. Hurd, *Ordeal*, 152–53.

61. Hurd, *Ordeal*, 154.

62. Hurd, *Ordeal*, 155.

63. Hurd, *Ordeal*, 159. See also Blevins, "New Perspectives on Ivor Gurney's Mental Illness" for a discussion of his treatment in the asylum, who argues that Gurney was the sad

victim of an unsympathetic and cruel brother
and a psychiatric community incapable of
recognizing the exact nature of his illness and
how best to treat it.

64. Hurd, *Ordeal*, 158–59.

65. Trethowan, "Ivor Gurney's Mental Ill-
ness," 308.

66. Silkin, *Out of Battle*, 127.

Chapter Four

1. Siegfried Sassoon, *Sherston's Progress*,
The Complete Memoirs of George Sherston
(London: Faber and Faber, 1937), 538–539.

2. Sassoon, *Sherston's Progress*, 540–41.

3. See Sassoon's chapter of reminiscences
about Owen in *Siegfried's Journey* (New York:
Viking, 1946), 86–102.

4. Siegfried Sassoon, *Collected Poems:
1908–1956* (London: Faber and Faber, 1984),
18. Hereafter *Collected Poems*.

5. Owen, *The Poems of Wilfred Owen*,
114.

6. See especially Jon Silkin, *Out of Battle*
(Oxford: Oxford University Press, 1972);
E. D. H. Johnston, *English Poetry of the First
World War* (Princeton: Princeton University
Press, 1964); Patrick J. Quinn, *The Great War
and the Missing Muse* (Selinsgrove: Susque-
hanna University Press, 1994); and Patrick
Campbell, *Siegfried Sassoon: A Study of the War
Poetry* (Jefferson, North Carolina: McFarland,
1999). These critics, and many others, pro-
vide careful analysis of Sassoon's satiric tech-
niques in his early war poetry, discussing
matters of irony, realism, and tone, all of
which contribute to the anti-war message they
envision at the heart of the poet's vision.

7. Siegfried Sassoon, *Siegfried Sassoon's
Diaries: 1914–1918*, ed. Rupert Hart-Davis
(London: Faber and Faber, 1983), 68. Here-
after *Diaries*.

8. Paul Moeyes, *Siegfried Sassoon: Scorched
Glory* (London: Macmillan, 1997), 36.

9. Quinn, *The Great War and the Miss-
ing Muse*, 172–73.

10. Clearly, the most detailed and author-
itative account of the years of Sassoon's war
experience can be found in Jean Moorcroft
Wilson's recent biography *Siegfried Sassoon:
The Making of a War Poet* (New York: Rout-
ledge, 1999). While this study relies upon
biographical details primarily relevant to Sas-
soon's psychological condition, Wilson offers
a much more thorough treatment of Sassoon's
war years in all their varied dimensions.

11. Hibberd, *Owen the Poet*, 173. Wilson
also narrates this developing friendship in her
chapter "Strange Meeting," 387–425.

12. Owen, *The Poems of Wilfred Owen*,
125–27.

13. Jean Moorcroft Wilson discusses the
composition and subsequent revisions to the
poem which occurred on the same day in
April in *Siegfried Sassoon: The Making of a
War Poet*, 352–53.

14. Moeyes, *Scorched Glory*, 46.

15. Robert Graves, *Goodbye to All That*
(New York: Doubleday, 1985), 262–63.

16. As the earlier chapter has argued,
Owen was one of these more difficult cases at
Craiglockhart, and his doctor, Arthur Brock,
created a method of treatment called "ergo-
therapy" to overcome the shell shock at the
heart of his patients' incapacitation. For
vivid, albeit fictional, representations of
processes of recovering attempted at Craig-
lockhart, see Pat Barker's trilogy about the
First World War, especially *Regeneration*
(New York: Penguin, 1991).

17. Elaine Showalter, "Male Hysteria: W.
H. R. Rivers and the Lessons of Shell Shock,"
*The Female Malady: Women, Madness, and
English Culture 1830–1980* (New York: Pan-
theon, 1985), 178. Though Showalter sees
Sassoon's particular case as a political rather
than psychological battle, her analysis of
Rivers' use of Freudian psychoanalytic tech-
niques offers a persuasive discussion of shell
shock as the result of conflicted gender expec-
tations. Soldiers, and particularly officers,
were expected to act in accordance with mas-
culine ideals of warfare, but the facts of bat-
tle reduced them to passive, "feminized"
victims, roles which the men were incapable
of accepting.

18. Carole Shelton, "War Protest, Hero-
ism, and Shellshock: Siegfried Sassoon, a
Case Study," *Focus on Robert Graves and His
Contemporaries* 1(1992): 49.

19. Campbell, *Siegfried Sassoon: A Study of
the War Poetry*, 165.

20. Richard Slobodin, *W. H. R. Rivers*
(New York: Columbia University Press,
1978), 63.

21. Caesar, *Taking It Like a Man*, 90.

22. Caesar, *Taking It like a Man*, 89.

23. Sassoon, *Sherston's Progress*, 534.

24. W. H. R. Rivers, *Conflict and Dream*
(New York: Harcourt, Brace, and Co, 1923),
170.

25. Rivers, *Conflict and Dream*, 171. The
conflict which Rivers articulates in this dis-

cussion is brought to fictional life in the third installment of Pat Barker's trilogy of the war, *The Ghost Road* (New York: Penguin, 1995). In this novel, set in 1918, Rivers grows less and less certain that he is acting in the best interest of either the soldiers whom he treats or the nation which he serves in enabling the men's recovery from shell shock.

26. Rivers, *Conflict and Dream*,148–49.

27. Rivers, *Conflict and Dream*, 149

28. Sassoon, *Siegfried's Journey*, 95.

29. Sassoon, *Sherston's Progress*, 518.

30. Sassoon, *Sherston's Progress*, 534.

31. W. H. R. Rivers, "Freud's Psychology of the Unconscious," *The Lancet* 16 June 1917: 912.

32. Rivers, "Freud's Psychology," 913.

33. Rivers, "Freud's Psychology," 913.

34. Quinn, *The Great War and the Missing Muse*, 193.

35. Quinn, *The Great War and the Missing Muse*, 193.

36. Moeyes, *Scorched Glory*, 260.

37. Rivers, "Freud's Psychology," 914.

38. Campbell, *Siegfried Sassoon: A Study of the War Poetry*, 152.

39. Silkin finds the poem flawed because the potential power of metaphors, such as the moth, are sacrificed within the poem in order to strive for truthfulness in capturing the psychological functioning of a traumatized soldier: "The connection Sassoon makes between glory (a kind of incandescence) and fire is tragically apt, and yet in this instance not full or felt enough…. it is though he had censored a metaphoric insight for the sake of verisimilitude; since, for instance, the man in the poem is not a poet and would not be as articulate as the metaphor would seem to make him had it been denser and more allusively complex." *Out of Battle*, 164–65.

40. Elaine Showalter, "Rivers and Sassoon: The Inscription of Male Gender Anxieties," *Behind the Lines: Gender and the Two World Wars*, eds. Margaret Randolph Higonnet et al, (New Haven: Yale University Press, 1987), 66.

41. Jon Silkin, Introduction to *The Penguin Book of First World War Poetry* (New York: Penguin, 1981), 32. Silkin sees Sassoon as representative of what he calls the "second stage of consciousness" demonstrated by poets of the First World War. The first stage is poetic support for "the prevailing patriotic ideas," as in the work of Brooke. Sassoon's embodies the role of protest, inferior according to Silkin's hierarchy to a poet like Owen

embodying the "stage of consciousness" characterized by compassion. See Silkin, 29–34.

42. Michael Thorpe, *Siegfried Sassoon: A Critical Study* (London: Oxford University Press, 1966), 30.

43. Moeyes, 61–62.

44. Lane, *An Adequate Response*, 112.

45. Siegfried Sassoon, *Memoirs of an Infantry Officer, The Complete Memoirs of George Sherston* (London: Faber and Faber, 1964), 396.

46. Owen, "Dulce et Decorum Est," 117–18. The poem closes with the Horatian adage: "Dulce et decorum est / Pro patria mori," or "It is sweet and fitting to die for one's country."

47. Lane, *An Adequate Response*, 111.

48. Lane, *An Adequate Response*, 112.

49. See Wilfred Owen's letter from Craiglockhart to his mother of August 22, 1917 in which he tells of his attempts to write "something in Sassoon's style." Wilfred Owen, *Collected Letters*, eds. Harold Owen and John Bell (London: Oxford University Press, 1967), 485–87. Many of Owen's earliest poems of war employ Sassoon's techniques of colloquial language and irony, stylistic strategies that provided the younger poet with a foundation for all later efforts to represent the experience in poetry.

50. Sassoon, *Sherston's Progress*, 527.

51. Thorpe, *Siegfried Sassoon: A Critical Study*, 29.

52. Quinn, *The Great War and the Missing Muse*, 193.

53. Martin Stephen, *The Price of Pity: Poetry, History and Myth in the Great War* (London: Leo Cooper, 1996), 190.

54. Sanford Sternlicht, *Siegfried Sassoon* (New York: Twayne, 1993), 12.

55. Stephen, *The Price of Pity*, 190.

56. Moeyes, *Scorched Glory*, 55.

Epilogue

1. Siegfried Sassoon, "On Passing the New Menin Gate," *The Oxford Book of Modern Poetry*, ed. W. B. Yeats (New York: Oxford University Press, 1936), 259.

2. W. B. Yeats, *The Letters of W. B. Yeats*, ed. Allan Wade (London: Rupert Hart-Davis, 1954), 874–75. See, among others, Jahin Ramazani, *Yeats and the Poetry of Death* (New Haven: Yale University Press, 1990); John Sparrow, "Mr. Yeats Selects the Modern Poets," *Times Literary Supplement* 21

November, 1936; D. N. G. Carter, "W. B. Yeats and the Poetry of the First World War," Focus *on Robert Graves and His Contemporaries* 1(1989): 13–22; Hermann Peschmann, "Yeats and the Poetry of War," *English* 15(1965): 181–84; and T. R. Henn, *W. B. Yeats and the Poetry of War* (London: Oxford University Press, 1967).

3. Yeats, "Introduction" to *The Oxford Book of Modern Poetry*, xxxiv–xxxv.

4. T. S. Eliot, "The Metaphysical Poets," *Selected Prose of T. S. Eliot*, ed. Frank Kermode (New York: Farrar, Straus, and Giroux), 64.

5. T. S. Eliot, "The Dry Salvages," Collected Poems: 1909–1962 (New York: Harcourt, Brace and Company, 1991), 126–133.

6. See John Evangelist Walsh's biography of these years of Frost's life, *Into My Own: The English Years of Robert Frost* (New York: Grove, 1988). For a discussion of the relationship between Frost and Edward Thomas, see Robert Richman, "In Search of Edward Thomas," *The New Criterion* 1(1982): 1–16.

7. Robert Frost, "Letter to 'The Amherst Student,'" *Robert Frost: Collected Poems, Prose, & Plays*, ed. Richard Poirier and Mark Richardson (New York: Library of America, 1995), 740.

8. Frost, "The Constant Symbol," 786.

9. Ivor Gurney, *Collected Letters*, ed. R. K. R. Thornton (London: Carcanet, 1993), 171.

10. Gurney, 171.

Bibliography

Ackroyd, Peter. *T. S. Eliot: A Life*. New York: Simon and Schuster, 1984.
Army Report of the War Office Committee Enquiry into "Shell Shock." London: H. M. Stationery Office, 1922.
Babington, Anthony. *Shell-Shock: A History of the Changing Attitudes to War Neurosis*. London: Leo Cooper, 1997.
Backman, Sven. *Tradition Transformed: Studies in the Poetry of Wilfred Owen*. Lund: Liber Laromedel, 1979.
Banjeree, Jacqueline. "Ivor Gurney's 'Dark March': Is It Really Over?" *English Studies* 70(1989): 115–31.
Barbusse, Henri. *Under Fire*. Trans. W. Fitzwater Wray. London: J. M. Dent, 1974.
Barker, Pat. *The Eye in the Door*. New York: Penguin, 1993.
_____. *The Ghost Road*. New York: Penguin, 1995.
_____. *Regeneration*. New York: Penguin, 1991.
Bergonzi, Bernard. *Heroes' Twilight*. London: Carcanet, 1965.
Blevins, Pamela. "New Perspectives of Ivor Gurney's Mental Illness." *The Ivor Gurney Society Journal* 6(2000): 29–58.
Boden, Anthony. "Ivor Gurney: Schizophrenic?" *The Ivor Gurney Society Journal* 6(2000): 23–28.
Breen, Jennifer. "Wilfred Owen: 'Greater Love' and Late Romanticism." *English Literature in Transition* 17(1974): 173–83.
_____. "Wilfred Owen (1893–1918): His Recovery from 'Shell-Shock'." *Notes and Queries* 23(1976): 301–5.
Brock, Arthur. *Health and Conduct*. London: Williams and Norgate, 1923.
Brooke, Rupert. *The Collected Poems of Wilfred Owen*. Ed. George Edward Woodberry. New York: Dodd, Mead, and Company, 1930.
Brown, Malcolm. *The Imperial War Museum Book of the Somme*. London: Sidgwick and Johnson, 1996.
Brown, Mark William. *The Poetry of Ivor Gurney: A Study of Influences*. Doctoral Dissertation. Vanderbilt University, 1989.
Caesar, Adrian. "The 'Human Problem' in Wilfred Owen's Poetry." *Crtical Quarterly* 29(1987): 67–84.

_____. *Taking It Like a Man: Suffering, Sexuality, and the War Poets.* Manchester: Manchester University Press, 1993.

Campbell, James. "Combat Gnosticism: The Ideology of First World War Poetry Criticism." *New Literary History* 30(1999): 203–15.

_____. "'For You May Touch Them Not': Misogyny, Homosexuality, and the Ethics of Passivity in First World War Poetry." *ELH* 64(1997): 823–42.

Campbell, Patrick. *Siegfried Sassoon: A Study of the War Poetry.* Jefferson, NC: McFarland, 1999.

Carter, D. N. G. "W. B. Yeats and the Poetry of the First World War." *Focus on Robert Graves and His Contemporaries* 1(1989): 13–22.

Cohen, Joseph. "Owen Agonistes." *English Literature in Transition* 8(1965): 253–68.

_____. "Wilfred Owen: Fresher Fields than Flanders." *English Literature in Transition* 7(1964): 1–7.

Cole, Sarah. *Modernism, Male Friendship, and the First World War.* Cambridge: Cambridge University Press, 2003.

Corrigan, Dame Felicitas. *Siegfried Sassoon: Poet's Pilgrimage.* London: Victor Gollancz, 1973.

Davie, Donald. "Gurney's Flood." *London Review of Books* 3–16 February 1983. 7.

_____. "Ivor Gurney Reconsidered." *Under Briggflatts.* Chicago: University of Chicago Press, 1989. 194–203.

Echevaria, Berta Cano. "Victims and Victimizers in Wilfred Owen's Poetry." *Focus on Robert Graves and His Contemporaries* 2(1995): 21–24.

Eder, M. D. *War-Shock: The Psycho-Neuroses in War Psychology and Treatment.* London: William Heinemann, 1917.

Eissler, K. R. *Freud as an Expert Witness: The Discussion of War Neuroses between Freud and Wagner-Jauregg.* Trans. Christine Trollope. Madison, CT: International University Press, 1986.

Eksteins, Modris. *Rites of Spring: The Great War and the Birth of the Modern Age.* New York: Doubleday, 1989.

Eliot, T. S. *Collected Poems: 1909–1962.* New York: Harcourt, Brace, and Company, 1991. 51–76.

_____. *Selected Prose of T. S. Eliot.* Ed. Frank Kermode (New York: Farrar, Straus and Giroux, 1990.

Elliot Smith, G., and T. H. Pear. *Shell Shock and Its Lessons.* London: Longmans, Green, and Co., 1918.

Fenton, Norman. *Shell Shock and Its Aftermath.* St. Louis: C. V. Mosby Co., 1926.

Frost, Robert. *Robert Frost: Collected Poems, Prose, and Plays.* New York: Library of America, 1995.

Freud, Sigmund. *Beyond the Pleasure Principle.* Ed. James Strachey. New York: Norton, 1961.

_____, S. Ferenczi, Karl Abraham, Ernst Simmel, and Ernest Jones. *Psycho-Analysis and the War Neuroses.* London: The International Psycho-Analytical Press, 1921.

Fussell, Paul. *The Great War and Modern Memory.* London: Oxford University Press, 1975.

Graves, Robert. *Goodbye to All That.* New York: Doubleday, 1985.

Gray, Piers. *Marginal Men: Edward Thomas, Ivor Gurney, and J. R. Ackerley.* London: Macmillan, 1991.

Gurney, Ivor. *Best Poems and The Book of Five Makings.* Ed. R. K. R. Thornton and George Walter. London: Carcanet, 1995.

_____. *Collected Letters.* Ed. R. K. R. Thornton. London: Carcanet, 1991.

_____. *Collected Poems.* Ed. P. J. Kavanagh. Oxford: Oxford University Press, 1982.

_____. *Eighty Poems or So.* Ed. George Walter and R. K. R. Thornton. London: Carcanet, 1997.

_____. *Ivor Gurney: War Letters.* Ed. R. K. R. Thornton. London: Carcanet, 1983.

_____. *Poems of Ivor Gurney.* Ed. Edmund Blunden. London: Chatto and Windus, 1973.

_____. *Severn and Somme and War's Embers.* Ed. R. K. R. Thornton. London: Carcanet, 1987.

_____. "The Springs of Music." *Musical Quarterly* 8(1922): 319–23.

Henn, T. R. *W. B. Yeats and the Poetry of War.* London: Oxford University Press, 1967.

Hepburn, James. "Wilfred Owen's Poetic Development." *Modern British Literature* 4(1979): 97–108.

Hibberd, Dominic. *Owen the Poet.* Athens: University of Georgia Press, 1986.

_____. "A Sociological Cure for Shell Shock: Dr. Brock and Wilfred Owen." *Sociological Review* 25(1977): 377–86.

_____. "Some Notes on Sassoon's Counter-Attack and Other Poems." *Notes and Queries* 227(1982): 341–42.

_____. *Wilfred Owen: A New Biography.* Chicago: Ivan R. Dee, 2003.

_____. *Wilfred Owen: The Last Year.* London: Constable and Company, 1992.

Hill, Geoffrey. "Gurney's 'Hobby.'" *Essays in Criticism* 34(1984): 97–127.

Hoffpauir, Richard. *The Art of Restraint.* Newark: University of Delaware Press, 1991.

_____. "The War Poetry of Blunden and Gurney." *Poetry Nation Review* 12(1985): 46–50.

Hooker, Jeremy. "Honouring Ivor Gurney." *Poetry Nation Review* 17(1980): 16–18.

Hurd, Michael. *The Ordeal of Ivor Gurney.* New York: Oxford University Press, 1978.

Hynes, Samuel. "The Squaring of Human Sorrow." *Times Literary Supplement* 13 October 1978. 1137.

Johnston, John H. *English Poetry of the First World War: A Study in the Evolution of Lyric and Narrative Form.* Princeton: Princeton University Press, 1964.

Kardiner, Abram. *The Traumatic Neuroses of War.* New York: Paul B. Hoeber, Inc., 1941.

Kavanagh, P. J. "Being Just: Ivor Gurney and the 'Poetic Sensibility.'" *Grand Street* 9(1990): 235–49.

Keegan, John. *The Face of Battle.* New York: Vintage, 1977.

Kern, Stephen. *The Culture of Time and Space: 1880–1918.* Cambridge: Harvard University Press, 1983.

Kerr, Douglas. "Brothers in Arms: Family Language in Wilfred Owen." *Review of English Studies* 43(1992): 518–34.

_____. "The Disciplines of the Wars: Army Training and the Language of Wilfred Owen." *Modern Language Review* 87(1992): 286–99.

_____. *Wilfred Owen's Voices: Language and Community.* Oxford: Clarendon Press, 1993.

King, P. Joy. "'Honour,' 'Heroics' and 'Bullshit': Ivor Gurney's Private Vision." *Critical Survey* 2(1990): 144–50.

Lane, Arthur E. *An Adequate Response: The War Poetry of Wilfred Owen and Siegfried Sassoon.* Detroit: Wayne State University Press, 1972.

Lane, Christopher. "In Defense of the Realm: Sassoon's Memoirs." *Raritan* 14(1994): 89–108.

Larkin, Philip. "The Real Wilfred: Owen's Life and Legends." *Encounter* (1975): 73–81.

Leed, Eric. *No Man's Land: Combat and Identity in World War I.* London: Cambridge University Press, 1979.

Lehmann, John. *The English Poetry of the First World War.* New York: Thames and Hudson, 1982.

Lucas, John. *Ivor Gurney.* London: Northcote House, 2001.

MacCurdy, John T. *War Neuroses.* London: Cambridge University Press, 1918.

Mallon, Thomas. "The Great War and Sassoon's Memory." *Modernism Reconsidered.* Cambridge: Harvard University Press, 1983. 81–99.

Marr, Hamilton. *Psychoses of the War, Including Neurasthenia and Shell Shock.* London: Oxford University Press, 1919.

McKenzie, M. L. "Memories of the Great War: Graves, Sassoon, and Findley." *University of Toronto Quarterly* 55(1986): 395–411.

Moeyes, Paul. *Siegfried Sassoon: Scorched Glory.* London: Macmillan, 1997.

Myers, Charles S. *Shell Shock in France: 1914–1918.* London: Cambridge, 1940.

Najarian, James. "'Greater Love': Wilfred Owen, Keats, and a Tradition of Desire." *Twentieth-Century Literature* 47(2001): 20–37.

Norgate, Paul. "Shell-shock and Poetry: Wilfred Owen at Craiglockhart Hospital." *English* 36(1987): 1–33.

_____. "Soldiers' Dreams: Popular Rhetoric and the War Poetry of Wilfred Owen." *Critical Survey* 2(1990): 208–15.

_____. "Wilfred Owen and the Soldier Poets." *Review of English Studies* 40(1989): 516–30.

Orrmont, Arthur. *Requiem for a War: The Life of Wilfred Owen.* New York: Four Winds Press, 1972.

Owen, Wilfred. *Collected Letters.* Eds. Harold Owen and John Bell. London: Oxford University Press, 1967.

_____. *The Poems of Wilfred Owen.* Ed. Jon Stallworthy. New York: Norton, 1986.

_____. *The Collected Poems of Wilfred Owen.* Ed. C. Day Lewis. New York: Chatto and Windus, 1963.

Parfitt, George. *English Poetry of the First World War.* New York: Harvester Wheatsheaf, 1990.

Peschmann, Hermann. "Yeats and the Poetry of War." *English* 15(1965): 181–84.

Posey, Horace G. Jr. "Muted Satire in 'Anthem for Doomed Youth.'" *Essays in Criticism* 21(1971): 377–81.

Quinn, Patrick. *The Great War and the Missing Muse: The Early Writings of Robert Graves and Siegfried Sassoon.* Selinsgrove: Susquehanna University Press, 1994.

Ramazani, Jahim. *Yeats and the Poetry of Death.* New Haven: Yale University Press, 1990.

Rattenbury, Arthur. "The Sanity of Ivor Gurney." *The Ivor Gurney Society Journal* 6(2000): 5–22.

Read, Herbert. *Collected Poems.* New York: Horizon Press, 1966.

Richman, Robert. "In Search of Edward Thomas." *The New Criterion* 1(1982): 1–16.

Rivers, William Halse Rivers. *Conflict and Dream.* New York: Harcourt Brace and Company, 1923.

_____. "Freud's Psychology of the Unconscious." *The Lancet* 1(1917): 912–14.

_____. *Instinct and the Unconscious.* London: Cambridge University Press, 1922.

Rosenburg, Isaac. *The Collected Poems of Isaac Rosenburg.* Eds. Gordon Bottomley and Denys Harding. New York: Schocken Books, 1949.

Salmon, Thomas. *The Care and Treatment of Mental Diseases and War Neuroses ("Shell Shock") in the British Army.* New York: National Committee for Mental Hygiene, 1917.

Sassoon, Siegfried. *Collected Poems.* London: Faber and Faber, 1984.

_____. *Complete Memoirs of George Sherston.* London: Faber and Faber, 1964.

_____. *Siegfried Sassoon's Diaries: 1915–1918.* Ed. Rupert Hart-Davis. London: Faber and Faber, 1983.

_____. *Siegfried Sassoon's Diaries: 1920–1922.* Ed. Rupert Hart-Davis. London: Faber and Faber, 1981.

_____. *Siegfried Sassoon's Diaries: 1923–1925.* Ed. Rupert Hart-Davis. London: Faber and Faber, 1985.

_____. *Siegfried's Journey.* New York: Viking, 1946.

Shelton, Carole. "War Protest, Heroism, and Shellshock: Siegfried Sassoon: A Case Study." *Focus on Robert Graves and His Contemporaries* 1(1992): 43–50.

Showalter, Elaine. "Male Hysteria: W. H. R. Rivers and the Lessons of Shell Shock." *The Female Malady: Women, Madness, and English Culture 1930–1980.* New York: Pantheon, 1985. 167–194.

_____. "Rivers and Sassoon: The Inscription of Male Gender Anxieties." *Behind the Lines: Gender and the Two World Wars.* Ed. Margaret Randolph Higonnet, et al. New Haven: Yale University Press, 1987. 61–69.

Silkin, Jon. *Out of Battle: The Poetry of the Great War.* Oxford: Oxford University Press, 1972.

_____, ed. *The Penguin Book of First World War Poetry.* New York: Penguin, 1979.

Sillars, Stuart. *Structure and Dissolution in English Writing, 1910–1920.* New York: St. Martin's, 1999.

Simcox, Kenneth. *Wilfred Owen: Anthem for a Doomed Youth.* London: Woburn, 1987.

Sinfield, Mark. "Wilfred Owen's 'Mental Cases': Source and Structure." *Notes and Queries* 227(1982): 338–41.

Slobodin, Richard. *W. H. R. Rivers.* New York: Columbia University Press, 1978.

Sorley, Charles Hamilton. *The Collected Poems of Charles Hamilton Sorley.* Ed. Jean Moorcroft Wilson. London: Cecil Woolf, 1985.

Southard, E. E. *Shell Shock and Other Neuro-Psychiatric Problems, Presented in Five Hundred and Eight Nine Case Histories.* Boston: W. M. Leonard, 1919.

Sparrow, John. "Mr. Yeats Selects the Modern Poets." *Times Literary Supplement* 21 November, 1936.

Spear, Hilda D. "'I Too Saw God': The Religious Allusions in Wilfred Owen's Poetry." *English* 24(1975): 35–40.

Stallworthy, Jon. "Owen and Sassoon: The Craiglockhart Episode." *New-Review* 1(1974): 5–17.

_____. *Wilfred Owen.* Oxford: Oxford University Press, 1974.

Stephen, Martin. *The Price of Pity: Poetry, History and Myth in the Great War.* London: Leo Cooper, 1996.

Stephens, John, and Ruth Waterhouse. "Authorial Revision and Constraints on the Role of the Reader: Some Examples from Wilfred Owen." *Poetics Today* 8(1987): 65–83.

Sternlicht, Stanford. *Siegfried Sassoon.* New York: Twayne, 1993.

Tennyson, Alfred, Lord. *The Poems and Plays of Alfred Lord Tennyson.* New York: Modern Library, 1938.

Thomas, Edward. *Collected Poems.* London: Faber and Faber, 1936.

Thorpe, Michael. *Siegfried Sassoon: A Critical Study.* London: Oxford University Press, 1966.

Tomlinson, Charles. "Ivor Gurney's Best Poems." *Times Literary Supplement* 3 January 1986. 12.

_____. *Jubilation.* New York: Oxford University Press, 1995.

Trethowan W. H. "Ivor Gurney's Mental Illness." *Music and Letters* 62(1982): 307–8.

Walsh, John Evangelist. *Into My Own: The English Years of Robert Frost.* New York: Grove, 1988.

Waterman, Andrew. "The Poetic Achievement of Ivor Gurney." *Critical Quarterly* 25(1983): 3–23.

Welland, Dennis. *Wilfred Owen: A Critical Study.* London: Chatto and Windus, 1978.

_____. "Sasoon on Owen." *Times Literary Supplement* 31 May 1974: 589–90.

Williams, Michael. "Wilfred Owen: A Poet Re-Institutionalised." *Critical Survey* 2(1990): 194–202.

Wilson, Jean Moorcroft. *Siegfried Sassoon: The Making of a War Poet.* New York: Rout-
    ledge, 1999.
_____. *Siegfried Sassoon: The Journey from the Trenches.* New York: Routledge, 2003.
Winter, Denis. *Death's Men: Soldiers of the Great War.* London: Penguin, 1982.
Wormleighton, Simon. "'Something in Sassoon's Style': A Note on Wilfred Owen's 'The
    Dead Beat' and Other Late 1917 Poems." *Notes and Queries* 235(1990): 65–67.
Yealland, Lewis R. *Hysterical Disorders of Warfare.* London: Macmillan, 1918.
Yeats, William Butler. *The Letters of W. B. Yeats.* Ed. Allan Wade. London: Rupert Hart-
    Davis, 1954.
_____, ed. *The Oxford Book of Modern Poetry.* New York: Oxford University Press, 1936.

Index